The
Bristol
Story

ISBN 1 898432 25 2

Companion Volumes

Bedford Part One – 1923-1950
Fodens – My Life with the Company
80 Years of Guy Cars Trucks and Buses

In course of preparation

Bedford Part Two – 1950-1996
Bristol – Part Two, Bus Bodybuilding Works
Bristol – Part Three, 1950-Closure

For full list of all bus, truck and rail titles from Venture Publications Ltd please send stamped addressed envelope to:

128 Pikes Lane, Glossop, Derbyshire SK13 8EH

Front Cover Illustration

The final variant of the K-type was the KSW, designed to suit the 27ft length and 8ft width which became permissible in 1950. This KSW6B, with Bristol AVW engine, has chassis number 82.105 (the last in that sanction), and dates from 1951, being fitted with the 55-seat lowbridge version of the standard ECW body for the model. Even so, the operator, Hants & Dorset Motor Services Ltd, applied its own styling detail in the form of the visor over the windscreen as can be seen in this view taken in Wimborne Minster during a Hants & Dorset 'running day' in 1994.

Photo: John A Senior

Produced for the Publishers
Venture Publications, Glossop, Derbyshire,
by Mopok Graphics, Glossop SK13 8EH
using computerised origination

The British Bus and Truck Heritage

The Bristol Story

Part One - 1908-1951

Alan Townsin

Venture *publications*

CONTENTS

BTCC's first buses supplied for use elsewhere went to the Imperial Tramways Ltd branch at Middlesbrough. This C65 with sloping-floor bus body on a chassis numbered 1021 had entered service with BTCC in 1913, registered AE 731. In February 1914, it was one of several passed to the Imperial fleet, being re-registered DC 438 – in May a new chassis was supplied directly to this concern.

CONTENTS

The 4-ton model was the standard full-sized type of bus added to BTCC's own fleet between 1920 and early 1927. Pneumatic tyres were standard from 1925 and earlier examples soon converted thereafter, the model in this form remaining a major part of the fleet until the early 1930s. Here one is making its way from Hotwells to Avonmouth, using the newly-built Portway road to pass through the Avon Gorge.

INTRODUCTION

The story of Bristol bus manufacture is unusually complex, with a remarkable series of changes in control and policy, yet with the link with the operational side of passenger transport running through it like a strong thread, binding the whole together. Its roots lay in the unique position held by the Bristol Tramways & Carriage Co Ltd in the early years of the century, providing not only the then new electric tramway serving the city but also cabs and horse-drawn and then motor vehicle facilities for hire on a large scale.

Diversifying into making chassis for motor buses from 1908, at first equally suitable for goods bodywork, doubtless seemed a natural step, especially as buses bought for BTCC's initial service had proved unsatisfactory. Sir George White, the Chairman, launched into aircraft manufacture with if anything even greater gusto, and the two businesses, though separate, remained intertwined for many years. The Motor Constructional Works was set up in premises purchased in 1912 and sited near the Brislington tram depot and works, where the initial venture into bus manufacture had begun. Early output was almost entirely for use by BTCC itself, ceasing for most of the 1914-18 war when aircraft work was dominant, but from 1921-2 a growing number of the 4-ton and from 1923 2-ton chassis were sold elsewhere, not infrequently to other tramway operators, both municipal and company. On the goods side, petrol companies were prominent among the users.

Output was modest, only once exceeding 200 per year in the period up to 1934. The exception, 1922, resulted in unsold chassis and production was cut back sharply for a year or two, yet steadily strong customer loyalty was being built up, repeat orders coming in from a high proportion of users. The Bristol B-type bus built up a good name from its introduction in 1926, again largely with municipalities and tramway-operating companies, as well as with BTCC itself. A major exception was the remarkable order placed late in 1928, by far the largest received by BTCC up to then, for 130 B-type chassis for United Automobile Services Ltd. That firm was then one of the largest independent bus operators in the country, but it joined the Tilling & BAT group before the last of this order entered service in 1929. Output was sharply down in 1931-32, when the depression was at its worst, even though the new G double-decker and J single-decker were of promising design.

Yet the seeds of revival were already in place. Railway investment in bus operators, including BTCC, led to the purchasing of a shareholding by Thomas Tilling Ltd in 1931. Sales to associated companies began on a modest scale in 1933, and it was in that year that a Gardner 5LW five-cylinder diesel engine was tried for the first time in place of the company's own-make petrol units. The switch to diesel (or oil engines, as they were usually called in those days) was at first very tentative, and experiments with various new petrol engines, including a revolutionary unit with cylinders placed axially, continued.

Then, in 1935, Bristol moved to a centre-stage position in terms of the supply of buses to companies under Tilling influence, when Frederick Heaton, Tilling's Chairman, also took that position on BTCC's board, and Major F. J. Chapple came from the general managership of West Yorkshire Road Car Co Ltd to take up the same role at BTCC; a new regime had begun. Bristol became the main supplier of bus chassis to operating companies where the Tilling influence was dominant, and within the following two years or so, Bristol buses were to be found in rapidly increasing numbers in many parts of England, from Northumberland to Cornwall. Over 400 chassis per year were being turned out and, to achieve that, new assembly shops were opened at Chatsworth Road, a little under a mile along the Bath Road towards the city centre. A parallel policy made Eastern Coach Works Ltd, running what had been the United bodybuilding factory at Lowestoft, the main body supplier to Tilling-managed companies, creating a strong link between the two firms.

New K & L models were built in even greater quantities, over 600 per year in 1938-39, and although some of the oldest-established customers, such as the Doncaster and Rotherham Corporation undertakings, still came back for small batches, the overwhelming bulk of the output was now for associated companies, augmented by the tram replacement fleet for BTCC itself.

INTRODUCTION

The outbreak of war in 1939 cut back output of buses, though the period when Bristol chassis production ceased entirely did not last as long as with most makers, in this case from the latter part of 1942 for about two years. Again, aircraft and other war work became dominant for a time. In mid-1944, K-type production resumed, using AEC 7.7-litre engines under the wartime allocation system, and in 1945 over 300 were built.

With the return of peace, demand for long-delayed replacement buses was huge but shortages of materials and proprietary items held output back at first. Gardner engines were again available, though in limited numbers and, as well as continuing to use the AEC unit, output of Bristol's own AVW diesel, developed just before the war, began, in small numbers at first. Despite the Tilling group's general favour for standardisation, all three makes of engine were used, enabling operator preferences to be met but, more crucially, to allow maximum output, apt to be governed by engine supply in that period.

Output reached nearly 800 chassis in 1947 and although it slipped back slightly in 1948 to just over 750, the 1,000 mark was exceeded in 1949, the high point for Bristol bus production. A major political change came in 1948 when the Tilling group sold its bus interests to the newly-formed British Transport Commission set up by the then Labour Government to administer road and rail transport under State ownership. Included in this were the manufacturing facilities of both BTCC and ECW, which thereupon became subject to a ban on sales to non-BTC concerns beyond the fulfilment of existing contracts, particularly galling as a promising export trade with South Africa and India had been built up since a modest beginning in 1946.

Yet, contrary to a widespread misconception, design initiative did not cease and indeed, two new models were among the most important ever to emerge from Bristol. The Lodekka double-decker, on which the decision to go ahead was made just after the transfer to BTC was confirmed, appeared in prototype form in the Autumn of 1949. Despite conventional internal layout, it gave low overall height previously only attainable with the unsatisfactory 'lowbridge' design having a sunken side gangway on the upper deck. This was achieved by a combination of an ingenious transmission layout and close co-operation with ECW in unifying the chassis and body design to minimise height.

Then, in 1950, the underfloor-engined Light Saloon, better known as the LS, showed that close co-operation between BTCC and ECW could also be used to reduce weight, giving a 42-seat bus weighing less than 6 tons in prototype form and, at a time when most new bus designs were heavier than their predecessors, pointing the way for others to follow.

While these new designs were being made ready for production, revised versions of the K and L were being built from 1950 to take advantage of relaxations in legal limits on overall dimensions. They received no publicity because general sales were not permitted, but they had many merits and deserve their place in history.

When I was asked to write this book, I at first demurred partly because of several people who have devoted much of their time to almost exclusive study of this make and its history, but I was persuaded on the basis that my more detached approach might help to give a sense of perspective in relation to the whole industry. My own attitude to Bristol buses began rather badly, for I have to confess I was not a fan of pre-war examples in the United fleet, familiar when I began taking a boyhood interest in buses in 1937-39, finding the models of that period noisy and rough-running, with their 5LW engines bolted directly into the frame. Yet later types showed better attributes, sometimes outstandingly so, and as I learnt more about their merits, my respect steadily grew, not least when I began to visit Brislington as a technical journalist and editor in the 1960s, a period I look forward to covering in the next volume.

– continued overleaf

By 1913, the Bristol Tramways & Carriage Co Ltd was firmly re-established as the maker of most of its own bus and charabanc fleet and was expanding its operations into surrounding areas. This C45 model with 'torpedo' 22-seat body also built by the company dated from then and was allocated to the Gloucester branch, being registered FH 629 accordingly – it was given the chassis number 1105 in the series which had been begun that year. It is seen in Lydney, complete with leather-coated driver, on an all-male outing, perhaps from some local firm. There are some minor signs of wear and tear on the vehicle, suggesting that the picture might date from the fateful Summer of 1914 – one wonders how many of the younger men visible were to perish amid the carnage of the Western Front during the following four years.

Introduction – continued from page 7

Invariably, I find writing a book a voyage of discovery as even already-known facts are brought together and fresh research done. In this case, with excellent support from Allan MacFarlane, Mike Tozer, Allen Janes and Martin Curtis, all fountains of knowledge and material on the subject, this had proved to be true to an even greater extent. I can only hope that I have been able to convey some of the fascination of the story to readers.

Alan Townsin
Steventon
1996

1 Origins of the company and its status in local transport

The origins of the Bristol Tramways & Carriage Co Ltd went back to 1874, when the Bristol Tramways Co Ltd was formed, an amalgamation with the Bristol Cab Co Ltd leading to the formation of BTCC in 1887.

This volume concentrates on the story of vehicle manufacture by the company, but the following summary is intended to convey something of the nature of the business and the background to the decision to manufacture its own motor vehicles. This combination of transport operating concern and manufacturer of almost all the buses it used had a strong influence on the product. It was to continue, but with broader horizons, when the Bristol company became a major constituent of the Tilling group and its products were to form the bulk of major fleets in most parts of England and Wales, as explained in later chapters.

The main business of BTCC in 1905 continued to be the operation of a tramway system serving the city and its surroundings, the network then being recently converted to electric traction. The fleet of 232 open-top double-deck trams mainly dated from 1900-01 and had been ordered from the well-known tram-building concern of G. F. Milnes & Co of Birkenhead, and built to its design though sub-contracted to other concerns. BTCC itself had not constructed any trams at that date, though some were built or given new bodies at its Brislington works from 1920. As was almost universal, the trucks (equivalent to the chassis of motor vehicles) were of proprietary makes, mainly Peckham or Brill.

As the title of the company implied, there were other activities, including the operation of horse-drawn cabs and carriages of various types, including a number of horse buses. In late Victorian times this side of the business had been very substantial, and there was a saying that the Tramways Company looked after the Bristolian from the cradle to the grave – there were baby carriages drawn by dogs as well as hearses – but an advertisement of the 1890s described its activities as "private carriage proprietors, horse and job masters, livery stable owners and general horsing contractors". A readable account of the horse era was contributed to the commemorative volume called *The People's Carriage* (published by the Bristol Omnibus Co Ltd to celebrate the centenary in 1974) by T. W. H. Gailey, who at that date had recently completed his spell as Chief Executive of the National Bus Company but earlier had been Traffic Manager of BTCC and later its Chairman.

The background to the move into the manufacture of motor vehicles reveals tensions which may help to account

Sir George White, the Chairman of Bristol Tramways & Carriage Co Ltd. He was knighted in 1904.

for what was quite a bold step for a concern which, although substantial, had not engaged in any comparable type of engineering-based activity. Under the Tramways Act, 1870, Bristol Corporation had the right to purchase the tramway undertaking in 1915 and thereafter at seven-yearly intervals. For a complex succession of reasons, this was not exercised until 1936, discouraging development or modernisation of the tramway.

At least part of the initial cause lay in the relationship between an ill-briefed council and a dominant personality in the form of BTCC's Chairman, Sir George White, followed by something quite close to paralysis by succeeding councils. At times the council showed more interest in putting pressure on BTCC to keep fares down than getting on with a plan for purchase, as happened in most other major cities, and this produced an atmosphere of continuing mutual antagonism.

The company's refusal, despite high standards of maintenance, to carry out even the most basic improvements to the Victorian design of the trams may have been understandable but it played its part in producing a situation unlike all parallel cases elsewhere in Britain. It may well account for the fact that, even by 1915, under half the company's gross receipts came from the trams.

Looked back upon from 1996, at first thought it may seem charming to have had a 'preserved' Victorian tramway still in use in the late 'thirties, but the modern fascination with old forms of transport was shared by very few people at that time, an age when what was seen as 'modern' was fashionable, with a tendency to favour so-called streamlining even for vehicles where it had no practical significance. At a more practical level, open-topped trams with no weather protection for upper-deck passengers or the drivers can hardly have seemed appealing in wintry weather.

The end result of the 1936 agreement was for the Corporation to take a half interest in that part of the bus undertaking that replaced the trams but it was to continue to be run and managed by BTCC. So Bristol remained out of line with all other British cities of comparable size in continuing to rely on a company rather than municipal transport system through the entire period when the latter was the accepted practice elsewhere in Britain.

Thus at first the entry into bus manufacture could be regarded as largely a venture in diversification, even though also clearly related to the expansion of the company's main business in providing the public transport system for the Bristol area beyond the tram network. Yet the recurring doubt under which the latter's future remained must have influenced policy and encouraged the search for wider markets for BTCC's products.

One of the initial fleet of twelve motor buses, of Thornycroft make, placed in service by Bristol Tramways & Carriage Co Ltd in 1906, seen in Clifton near the terminus of the first route. After a few weeks, it was decided to remove the seats from the upper deck and operate them as single-deckers, due to dangers from overhanging trees and the excessive swaying experienced. Double-decker buses remained out of favour within BTCC for a quarter of a century. Some unreliability was experienced with these buses and, even more so, seven of FIAT make purchased later in the year, leading to the decision that BTCC should begin manufacture of its own chassis, though there were indications of Thornycroft influence in the early designs. Note the style of the uniforms, typical of the period, the driver having a longer greatcoat, doubtless essential with virtually no weather protection.

2 Beginnings of buses

Regular operation of motor buses by BTCC began in January 1906, replacing horse-drawn vehicles on a route to Clifton Suspension Bridge. Twelve Thornycroft type 80 chassis were chosen for this, with double-deck open-top bodies by United Electric Car Co, of Preston, but before long they were found to be unreliable when running over Bristol's hilly routes.

The upper-deck seats were soon removed because of excessive swaying and problems with overhanging branches. Although the company had used open-topped horse buses, this experience seems to have discouraged further use of double-decker motor buses until the 'thirties. The Thornycroft buses were run as single-deckers and several were rebodied, in some cases as charabancs, eight remaining in service until 1913-14, so it seems that the

The elegance of Edwardian Bristol is captured very effectively in this picture showing the Tramways Centre in 1909, with the styles of buildings, the vehicles on the streets and items such as tramway overhead and street lights all of harmonious design. Designers of modern tram systems could do well to study how a tram standard could add to, rather than detract from, the urban landscape.

Two of the first batch of six Bristol buses are seen, AE 772 facing the camera and setting out for Clifton Suspension Bridge with passenger wearing a straw boater seated alongside the driver. It is just about to pass what is evidently AE 774 returning to the centre. However, the translucent version of the number plate in the latter's rear window shows AE 773, possibly having been fitted into the wrong bus. The buses were in a short-lived 'Imperial Tramways' style of livery rather than the more usual blue and cream in which they were when new and to which they were restored later.

Two of the trams can be seen, looking much as they still did 30 years later. It is probable that some of the horse-drawn vehicles, and possibly the horses themselves, were hired from BTCC, even though the motor age was beginning – some of the cars and motor cabs parked by the bridge balustrade are likely also to have been BTCC vehicles.

This view of AE 772 taken at the Clifton terminus is thought to date from slightly later than that overleaf. The lamps are attached to the dash panel rather than being mounted in front of the radiator. The general design of this initial 1908 design of Bristol chassis, type C40, can be seen, though on these early vehicles individual variations were apt to be found. The frame design appears to be very similar to the Thornycroft, with similarly tapered front end though the spring attachment was evidently slightly bigger. There was a general similarity in the style of radiator, in both cases of neater outline than most commercial vehicles of the period and not unlike some contemporary private cars, with bonnet top aligned with the radiator top tank. The chain drive to the rear wheels is clearly visible, in this case being devoid of the cover fitted to the Thornycroft version. Road wheel design varied and in this case appears to be of cast manufacture.

The Bristol 16-seat body retains the rounded peak as used in the United Electric Car bodies on the Thornycrofts, but without the vertical stanchions which must have interfered with engine access. Detachable side window frames were a common feature at that date, though hardly ideal if a sudden shower developed, since they would have to have been left at the depot – this may account for the number error evident on the previous page. The number 98 visible on the side panels belonged to the early stock number system, no system of chassis numbering being used at first but in that used from 1913, this bus became 1030. The unladen weight of 2tons 19cwt 3qr is not out of line with modern vehicles of similar size.

early unreliability was reduced to acceptable levels, such a life being regarded as quite normal at that early period of motor vehicle development.

Seven double-deckers on chassis built by FIAT (Fabbrica Italiana Automobili Torino) were purchased later in 1906, the order being placed on a basis that they were to be free of the defects experienced with the Thornycrofts – the firm turned its initials into the marque name, Fiat, later that year. Despite encouraging demonstration runs with one of the vehicles, AE 773, including what was said to be a non-stop run from London to Edinburgh at an average speed of 14.7mph, they proved to be too lightly constructed for their duties in Bristol and were soon withdrawn. Successful court action was taken against Fiat Motors Ltd, London, the suppliers.

The decision that the company should make its own chassis was quite a bold step for a concern which had purchased its trams complete and had gone no further in vehicle manufacture than limited bodybuilding. Even so, the self-confident view that experience of trouble with

purchased vehicles provided a basis for doing better was by no means unique at the time. In addition to the buses, the company also operated a number of motor cars, taxi-cabs and goods vehicles of various makes, so was building up useful experience of their characteristics.

The first two buses with chassis made by the company itself entered service in May 1908 – six, all 16-seat single-deck buses, were built and added to the fleet that year, taking the registration numbers AE 770-775, thought to have been transferred from the Fiat buses. Designated type C40, they were of generally conventional design, with four-cylinder petrol engines made by the company and known as the X type. The frames were constructed from rolled channel-section steel, the wheelbase being 13ft.

The general appearance of early Bristol buses was not unlike that of the Thornycrofts, with a somewhat similar style of radiator, evidently having brass top and bottom tanks, at first with the bonnet top flush with the top, giving a neater effect than on most vehicles of the period. They were said to be notably quiet-running, though they had chain drive, as was common at that period.

Two further C40 buses, again 16-seat, AE 779-780, were built in 1909 and a further five, this time including a 22-seat charabanc in 1911, together with one example of another variant, type C45, also with 22-seat charabanc body. In 1912, BTCC built five C45 and twelve of a further type, the C60, with a variety of bus and charabanc bodies seating between 16 and 24. A C45 was fitted with a lorry body for the company's own use that year, marking the beginning of what was to be quite a substantial part of the output for the next two decades.

The C45 and C60 were similar to the C40 in general design, but minor details varied among the various buses, even between those of nominally the same type. Later examples had the bonnet top set slightly lower than that of the radiator, and the latter had separate slotted side standards. The design of wheels also varied somewhat. No specific information on the meaning of the various designations has come to light, but the evidence points to a weight-related system, probably based on the cwt as a unit.

Another matter on which there has been controversy is when the early chassis were built. The initial batch of 1908 was produced in the Brislingrton tramway works but no evidence has come to light to support the idea that chassis were built in the small works attached to a bus depot which was established at Filton, about five miles north of the city, which may have been more of a maintenance workshop. On the other hand, nothing has been found which refutes the idea that chassis were built there for a time which has appeared in earlier histories. I am grateful for the comments of Allan Macfarlane and Mike Tozer on this point – both have carried out extensive studies on early BTCC bus history.

At that early date no chassis numbers were issued for the Bristol-built vehicles though they received what were described as stock numbers among the vehicles of other makes then in the fleet. The initial individual numbers of these early Bristol vehicles are not known, although they are understood to have been included in a series running from 1 and reaching 131 by early 1913.

A BTCC 'heavy' chassis number series beginning at 1001 began to be used early in 1913, although at first this also included chassis of other makes within the fleet, including both buses and haulage vehicles. Numbers in this new series were issued retrospectively to the earlier vehicles. The first two numbers, 1001 and 1002, went to a pair of Berliet double-deckers dating from 1909 and which had registration numbers AE 776-777, but the allocation of numbers to existing vehicles was not in a clear-cut order, the first Bristol-built buses dating from 1908 (AE 771-775) becoming 1029-33.

This C45 of 1912, registered AE 2773, had shaft rather than chain drive, the differential casing of the worm drive rear axle being clearly visible – this was one of the features in an improved design produced by Mr B. A. Payne earlier that year. By that date, the bonnet top was set slightly lower than the radiator top tank, the latter's design also differing from the 1908 style, with a more rounded outline. The 22-seat charabanc body was of the 'torpedo' style, similar to an extended private car of the period, that had then recently come into favour. A BTCC stock number, 109, can be seen on the side panelling – under the system adopted by early 1913, this vehicle was allocated the chassis number 1038. In November 1914, this chassis was fitted with a brewer's lorry body but in April 1920 it became a 22-seat charabanc again before final withdrawal by the end of the following year.

A concept used for some of the BTCC buses in the 1912-13 period was the composite type of body, open-sided at the front but enclosed at the rear – it was designed by Mr Charles Challenger, BTCC's Manager of the day. The first example, dating from July 1912, was for use at Weston-super-Mare but that shown, AE 3183, dated from 1913, and was on a C45 chassis, running in Bristol on the service to the suspension bridge at Clifton. The number 100 is visible; under the new chassis numbering system the number 1109 was allocated to this chassis. It is recorded as being fitted with a new charabanc body in November 1914 and survived until 1923, when it was scrapped.

Two C45 models exhibited at the 1913 Royal Agricultural Show, held in July of that year at Durdham Downs, Bristol and attended by King George V, were the first Bristol vehicles exhibited at any public event and represented a new venture in being fitted with goods bodywork, this one designed for operation by a brewery.

Some chain-drive models were still entering service in 1913-14, including AE 3189, a C60 with open-sided 27-seat body of the style sometimes called 'slipper', with sloping floor designed to give rear-seat passengers a better view. This was an idea adopted in a number of early vehicles intended for excursion work but was going out of favour by then. There seems to be precious little clearance over the rear tyres to allow for spring deflection, though admittedly many of the passengers, on a W. D. & H. O. Wills staff outing, were standing for the benefit of the photographer, throwing more weight to this side. Note the driver's leather coat. In this case, a chain-guard was provided.

3 The Motor Constructional Works

Meanwhile, in February 1910, Sir George White had announced his plan to build aeroplanes, founding the Bristol Aeroplane Co Ltd and three other related companies with capital from his family, and thereby creating a parallel business to BTCC in the aviation field, of which he was also Chairman.

Thus were founded from a common origin the separate bus and aeroplane manufacturing businesses that were to make the Bristol name so widely respected, often far from the city of their origin.

Much later, the Bristol Aeroplane Co Ltd began manufacturing high-performance cars as a diversification of activities following the 1939-45 war, creating a subsidiary for this purpose called Bristol Cars Ltd, this later becoming an independent business. Its products from 1947, when production started, to the present are also highly regarded, even though built only in small numbers, but the family link with BTCC had gone long before this activity began. What is less well known is that a private car was designed and built by BTCC itself in 1924, as described in the next chapter, though not put into production.

Deciding that aircraft construction would be based at Filton by initially leasing the former bus sheds there from BTCC, he instructed that the buses were to go elsewhere. So premises at Brislington, about two miles from the city on the road leading south-east to Bath, where there was already a nearby tram depot and works, were acquired from C. Bartlett & Sons Ltd, scale and weighbridge makers in February 1912 and bus manufacture was transferred there.

Chassis manufacture at what became known as the Motor Constructional Works restarted on a small scale in the autumn of 1912, at first continuing with various types in the C-series. Re-equipment of the works was then still in hand, not being completed until June 1913, and that year two further models were added, the C50 and C65.

During 1913, two C40, 29 C45, four C60 and four C65 were added to the fleet, together with five Dennises and two Lacres. Seating capacities of the variety of bodywork built by the company for the Bristol chassis was in the 16- to 24-seat range, the other makes being used for smaller vehicles, save for some Dennis with charabanc bodies.

The Motor Constructional Works at Brislington, originally built in 1902 for Charles Bartlett & Sons, scale makers, but acquired by BTCC in 1912. The sheds visible in the top right of the picture were part of Brislington Tram Depot, the location of the Body Building Works and where the first Bristol bus chassis had been built.

This scene within the Motor Constructional Works during its early days shows how chassis were assembled, on trestles until the axles and wheels had been fitted, a system which remained largely unchanged in later years. Seven chassis in course of construction can be seen, that nearing completion in the left foreground showing the main characteristics as by then being produced, with worm-drive rear axle. The engine, of type X, had four cylinders and side-valve layout, typical of the period; this was to remain true of engines made at Brislington until six-cylinder models began to go into production in 1930.

Appointed as designer was Mr B. A. Payne, who had served his apprenticeship with John I. Thornycroft & Co Ltd, Basingstoke; he was promoted to Chief Designer in 1912, remaining in that post until 1938. Despite the problems with the Thornycroft buses with which BTCC began operation in 1906, this may account for some similarities in methods between the two concerns.

An improved version of the C45, designed early in 1912 by Mr Payne, had a worm-drive rear axle in place of the previous chain drive, a system originally applied to bus chassis by Dennis Bros. A worm-drive rear axle was virtually silent, save perhaps for a tendency to a low-pitched hum when worn, and was to be standard on subsequent Bristol bus and lorry chassis.

Chassis number issue was somewhat complicated by the switch to the new system described above, some 33 chassis having received old-style stock numbers 99-131 before being given chassis numbers in the 1001-up system, and the sequence was not maintained in this process. As a result the Bristol vehicles built that year received new style numbers which ran as high as 1131 but were intermingled with those of older vehicles, as explained.

The 1914 input to the fleet was entirely on Bristol chassis and with Bristol bodywork, comprising 34 C50, one C60 and three C65, again with a variety of body types and seating capacities ranging from 22 to 28. The chassis numbers were becoming more logical, most being between 1130 and 1171, though the vehicle with the earliest Bristol registration number issued that year to a BTCC bus, AE 3189, had chassis number 1003.

It is in reference to this point in the story that the first information on a characteristic feature of Bristol production methods has become available. As was common practice in engineering work, authorisation for the construction was issued at intervals for specific numbers of chassis. BTCC referred to these batches as sanctions, the quantities involved varying considerably according to circumstances. At first they were often quite small, though there were some exceptions in the early 'twenties, but in later years quite commonly round number quantities of 50, 100 or

more were specified. Chassis in a sanction could vary in specification but, being authorised at a given date, tended to have common features while the issue of a fresh sanction provided a convenient opportunity for a change to be brought in.

In later years, from the beginning of the K and L types in 1937, each sanction had a fresh set of chassis numbers prefixed by the sanction number. Information on early sanctions is sometimes sketchy and none on the first has come to light, but sanction number 2 covered 24 chassis numbered 1135-1158 and sanction 3 included 30, numbers 1159-1188. The vehicles entering service in 1914 were largely drawn from both of these.

Bodybuilding was also concentrated at Brislington, the part of the premises so engaged being described as the Body Building Works, often abbreviated to BBW. The use of these initials and MCW for Motor Constructional Works became common practice internally and was occasionally mentioned in external publicity, though in later years MCW was liable to be confused by outside observers with the same initials more generally applied to the Metropolitan-Cammell Weymann concern set up in 1932, with which there was no connection.

In the early years, building of chassis and bodywork was entirely related to the company's own needs for buses on routes being developed to various Bristol outskirts not served by tram, and increasingly to and in surrounding districts. At that stage, when vehicles were based in Bath, Cheltenham, Gloucester or Weston-super-Mare, they were registered or re-registered appropriately, so some buses received registration numbers in the Bath, Gloucestershire or Somerset series, though Bristol registrations, either previous or new, were taken up again if they returned to operate in the city area, thus making identity not always easy to trace.

The first Bristol bus built new for use elsewhere was supplied in May 1914 for the Imperial Tramways Ltd branch at Middlesbrough, BTCC then being a member of the Imperial Tramways group. It had chassis 1145, being registered DC 495 and had a Sankey 28-seat charabanc body, entering service in May of that year. Imperial's Middlesbrough branch also acquired some further vehicles, almost new and nominally drawn from BTCC's fleet, and some of these were re-registered. Another associated concern using early Bristol vehicles was the Corris Railway, of Machynlleth, but these early examples were operated on hire from BTCC's own fleet.

Despite BTCC's membership of the once-substantial Imperial Tramways Company group formed in 1878, only a very small proportion of the subsequent large output of bus or lorry chassis went to other companies in that group. The Corris Railway in north Wales proved to be one of the last remnants of the Imperial group, and latterly was owned directly by BTCC. It ran an almost exclusively Bristol fleet of buses and charabancs from 1911 until sold to the Great Western Railway on 3rd August 1930 – a total of eighteen Bristol vehicles, from C40 models to 4-ton and 2-ton types was supplied, the last in 1926.

Early bus chassis differed little if at all from those of similar size and weight capacity used for goods-carrying purposes and it is known that one C45 was fitted with a goods body for use by BTCC in 1912 and two were exhibited at the 1913 Royal Show, one with brewer's body and the other for dairy use. Another, chassis number 1136, reported as being of MWS type, was built as a mobile workshop later that year, intended to provide facilities for repairing aeroplanes, and exhibited on the stand of the British Colonial Aeroplane Co at the Paris Air Show that year. It was broadly similar to the C45 but used a different frame. The engine in the 1913 lorries was of a new Y-type of 4¼in bore, 5in stroke and 4.648-litre capacity, the Royal Show vehicles quoted as of 28.9hp and hence evidently standard. The MWS was described as of 35hp, possibly because of the extra weight of the equipment carried. The Y-type engine was adopted as standard on buses delivered to BTCC's operating department after being fitted to some vehicles from early 1913, all chassis numbered from 1134 to 1158 are recorded as having been so fitted.

The outbreak of the first world war on 4th August 1914 put a brake on bus manufacturing activities, and the Bristol Aeroplane Co Ltd assumed a new level of importance. In addition, nineteen chassis, numbered 1159-61/74-89, were supplied to the War Department, these then being allocated to the Royal Naval Air Service. It seems probable that they were under construction but diverted for military use, delivery continuing until mid-January 1915 – many vehicles were compulsorily acquired for military use from whatever sources could be found soon after the outbreak of war. This also applied to a number of BTCC's operational fleet, although normal services largely continued and, to overcome restrictions on petrol availability, some buses were converted to run on town gas, using a large gas-bag carried on the roof.

A new 4-ton model appeared in prototype form designated type W (although also known as a type C50), in February 1915. Its general appearance suggested that the chassis, numbered 1190 immediately after the WD vehicles, may have been intended to conform to the War

The solitary W-type built in 1915 was the prototype for the 4-ton model that was to be the main product of the Motor Constructional Works in the period from 1920. This view shows it with spoked wheels of the type used on production 4-tonners but another photograph indicates that it ran on pierced disc wheels at one stage. Although the vehicle was fitted with a bus body, it seems probable that production as a military vehicle was in mind, though in the event the works was fully occupied making aircraft sub-contracted from the Bristol Aeroplane Co Ltd. The cast radiator, which had horizontal bars across the core, not visible in this view, but much as used on later 4-ton models, may have been designed to meet the War Department subsidy vehicle specification. It was registered AE 4973 and entered service in March 1915. In 1920, the vehicle lost the body shown, transferred to a production 4-ton chassis, but continued in use as a breakdown vehicle until 1937 but even then survived until 1941 as a hack vehicle for use internally within the company's repair works at Lawrence Hill.

Vehicle production by BTCC ceased for almost the whole period of the 1914-18 war because most of its production capacity was enlisted to expand the output of the Bristol Aeroplane Co Ltd, of great importance in that first major conflict involving aerial warfare. The best-known type was the Bristol Fighter, of which 1,045 were built by BTCC - this view was taken in the Body Building Works at Brislington. Here much of the structure is complete and the massive engine installed, almost ready for attachment of the wings. The large-scale use of women workers was also a new development, and although related to the vast numbers of men in military service it was an example of changes in society that were to leave their mark more permanently.

Department subsidy specification that had been laid down shortly before the outbreak of the war in 1914, to which many vehicles were being built at the time. For a time, it had wheels of a pierced disc type, similar to those found on the Thornycroft J type built in large numbers for military use.

However it received a 29-seat bus body and entered service on the Centre-Suspension Bridge route on 10th March 1915. It had a gearbox with the lever centrally-mounted, instead of to the right of the driver as was usual at that time, and a worm-drive rear axle, a feature by then standardised because of its silent running. The engine was described as an AW-type 30hp unit, rather suggesting that the bore size was slightly more than the 4¼in of the Y-type engine, using the RAC formula, widely used as a means of classifying engine size at that date.

It did not go into production then because assembly of Bristol military aircraft, sub-contracted from Filton, intervened. A total of 1,236 aeroplanes were built at Brislington between January 1915 and September 1919. They comprised Bristol 'Boxkites', Bristol Scout C, Coanda T.B.8 trainers and Bristol Fighters, the last-mentioned

representing the biggest share of Brislington's aircraft output, amounting to 1,045, which was 22% of the total of this famous type that were built.

It must also be recorded that the redoubtable Sir George White died in November 1916 and was succeeded as Chairman by his brother, Mr Samuel White. Normal chassis production did not resume until 1920, though it is understood that the 4th sanction, to which the prototype chassis 1190 belonged, extended as far as 1208.

4 The era of the 4-ton and 2-ton models

The production 4-ton model, again of normal-control layout, had the simple but rugged BW four-cylinder side-valve engine, now of 5.99-litre capacity, with 4½in bore and 5¾in stroke, a size that was to remain characteristic of several successive models right up to the mid 'thirties. The 4-tonner was the Motor Constructional Works's standard type from 1920, remaining in production through that decade, although later joined by other models and largely phased out as a bus after 1926. It had a single-plate clutch, giving a smoother action than the cone type still favoured quite widely at that date, a four-speed gearbox and the worm-drive rear axle.

The radiator had a deep top tank, on which the script form of the Bristol name was cast, and three horizontal bars protected the core from damage. The wheels reverted to the cast spoked type favoured on many of the C-type buses, though of a heavier-duty pattern with the spokes well rounded into the rim.

It is appropriate here to explain Bristol's system of designating engines and other major units, beginning with the 4-ton model. There was a two-letter system, the first being an alphabetical sequence, a principle to which the Motor Constructional Works was to become rather addicted, while the second was a letter allocated to each type of unit.

Many of the early 4-ton models were fitted with charabanc bodies, five being in this scene dated 28th June 1922 on the occasion of a master bakers' outing. There could hardly be any doubt as to the identity of the make, with the Bristol name emblazoned on the radiator top tank casting in the script form so long associated with both the tramways and aeroplane companies. The two charabancs on the right of this picture, HT 1042 and 1046, were very early examples, dating from May and June 1920 with chassis numbers 1214 and 1215 in the post-war continuous run of chassis numbers for the 4-tonner which began in April of that year at 1209. They were among a number of early chassis having what the records describe as an 'old-type' dash. Nearest the camera on the left, HT 3590, on chassis 1367, dated from April 1921, and a month later had been noteworthy in being put on special Michelin wheels and tyres, the first 4-ton model to receive pneumatics. Next in line was HT 2655 (1330), new in February 1921, while HT 1514 (1224), third in line, dated from June 1920, though having the style of dash common to the later vehicles. Note that one front-seat passenger was carried to the right of the driver, as well as two to the left.

The BW engine was of very simple design, with four cylinders, cast in pairs and with non-detachable heads. One is seen here complete with the cross-members which supported it in the frame – note the clutch lining material, attached to the flywheel rather than the clutch plate, yet to be fitted.

Thus, the frame of the 4-ton model was type AA, and frames for succeeding models were BA, CA, DA etc, and similarly for other units, though the sequence seems not always to have been followed in strict alphabetical order, and some combinations did not appear on production chassis.

After the early days, engines were in a series with the second letter W, and hence the AW engine of the prototype and then the BW engine was later followed by EW, FW, GW etc. In certain cases, a single letter was used at first, thus the 4-ton radiator was type V, followed by AV, BV etc. The 4-ton gearbox was quoted as S C50, and then later gearboxes were AS, BS, CS etc.

Normal production resumed in 1920 at chassis number 1209, and from that point this straightforward numerical series consisted only of Bristol 4-ton chassis. The first post-war sanction, Number 4, ran to chassis number 1308, thus covering 100 chassis, the last one dating from 30th December 1920, though a few did not enter service until 1921. Sanction 5 ran to 1533, covering 225 chassis and running until February 1922. It seems that output had been expanded, perhaps on the basis of favourable comment when examples were exhibited at the 1920 Commercial Motor Show, but despite orders being obtained from several new customers, some of the above were not sold until 1923 or 1924, and output virtually ceased for a time, the market being severely depressed.

An increase in wheelbase length from 14ft 6in to 16ft became standard at chassis 1534, the first in Sanction 7 though there were exceptions where the shorter version continued to be specified. This first longer-wheelbase vehicle, with a two-door Bristol bus body, was displayed at the 1923 Commercial Motor Show, and then sold to N. Hall & Co, of Broughton Astley, Leicestershire.

At first, most 4-ton models were used for the company's expanding bus services, mainly with Bristol bus bodies seating 29 to 31, but others had charabanc bodies. Quite a large proportion of the bodybuilding work in 1920, and indeed the majority in 1922-24, was subcontracted to the Bristol Aeroplane Co, which was looking for work after the wartime demand for aircraft largely vanished. There were also a few BTCC lorries on the 4-ton chassis in that period, and one for the Bristol Aeroplane Co. A few chassis went to other users in 1920-21, including five tankers for BP and a furniture van for a Birmingham operator, Fletcher, exhibited at the 1920 Show, along with a Show chassis.

Among other buses, there was a demonstrator and a few others were sold, such as four for the Devon Motor Transport Co and two for the Bath Tramways Motor Co, the latter not then associated with BTCC. The Imperial Tramways undertaking based in Middlesbrough was taken over by local municipalities in April 1921, but Middlesbrough Corporation took delivery of two 4-ton

One of the first examples of the 4-ton model to receive a bus body, No.190 in the BTCC fleet, based on chassis 1222, registered HT 1506 and seating 29 passengers. There was clear resemblance to the 1915 prototype but the driver now had a windscreen and the outline was less rounded at the upper part of the rear.

An idea far ahead of its time

A design project that might have put Bristol into the forefront of bus design technology but was not pursued was the underfloor-engined 41-seat type sketched out in 1920. Its existence was revealed in a paper 'The development of transport and commercial vehicles in Bristol' by A. W. Hallpike, then General Manager of the Motor Constructional Works, read at a meeting of the Institution of Mechanical Engineers on 18th June 1952. He did not go into any detail, simply saying that "a design of this type was considered in 1920, but did not materialise as a production job because conditions did not then seem to warrant it".

However, examination of the sketches indicates that the basis for the design was a chassis and body having features in common with the then new 4-ton model, but with the engine mounted under the floor and a little way behind the front axle. It was also of forward-control layout, a feature not entirely novel at that date, having been used on the Lothian bus introduced for its own use by the Scottish Motor Traction Co Ltd in 1913, and also adopted, in half-cab form, on the AEC K-type double-decker built for the London General Omnibus Co Ltd from 1919.

The drawings make it clear that the engine, evidently shrouded from below by an undershield of the type then quite common, was not to protrude above floor level, the seating layout being in uniterrrupted rows, save that a pair of seats immediately behind the driver was to face rearwards. The dimensions of the vehicle are not given, but seem likely not to have exceeded 26ft, which implies closer seat spacing than would have been allowable in later years, as indeed was found in some vehicles of other makes built in the earlier part of the 1920s.

What the form of the engine was intended to be is not clear, but a horizontal version of the BW engine seems very likely – the fact

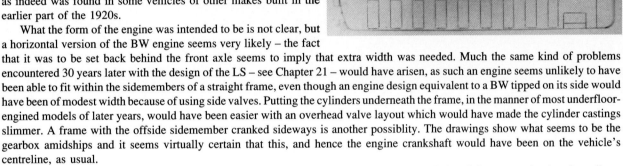

that it was to be set back behind the front axle seems to imply that extra width was needed. Much the same kind of problems encountered 30 years later with the design of the LS – see Chapter 21 – would have arisen, as such an engine seems unlikely to have been able to fit within the sidemembers of a straight frame, even though an engine design equivalent to a BW tipped on its side would have been of modest width because of using side valves. Putting the cylinders underneath the frame, in the manner of most underfloor-engined models of later years, would have been easier with an overhead valve layout which would have made the cylinder castings slimmer. A frame with the offside sidemember cranked sideways is another possiblity. The drawings show what seems to be the gearbox amidships and it seems virtually certain that this, and hence the engine crankshaft would have been on the vehicle's centreline, as usual.

There seems no reason to doubt that such a bus could have been built and run successfully – it is noteworthy that the radiator was left in its normal place, which suggested that cooling would have been satisfactory (as later generations of Bristol engineers were to show with models such as the RE and VR).

Had the project gone ahead and been protected by suitable patents, Bristol would have been in a very powerful position to build up sales. Even though bus design was generally cautious at the time, there was growing interest in bigger seating capacites and yet the use of double-deckers was still quite limited outside the special conditions of London. As it was, the idea seems not to have been pursued anywhere for over a decade, the German Bussing concern seeming to be the first to exploit it effectively, and although there were British ventures later in the 1930s, most notably the London Transport and Leyland TF-type, it was not until a quarter century after this Bristol project that the underfloor-engined bus was taken seriously, again primarily by an operator, Midland Red, standardising on such vehicles for its post-war fleet from 1946.

buses later that year. Another bus went to Powell and Gough of Ludlow, and one for the Romilly Motor Co, Cardiff, had bodywork by Bence, a small Bristol concern which was to build a number of bodies on Bristol chassis over the years as well as being an operator.

In 1922-23, there was a higher proportion of vehicles for other operators, and some names which were to become regular Bristol customers appeared among the users for the first time. Notable among them was West Riding Automobile Co Ltd, in whose fleet 22 4-ton buses were in service by the end of 1922, with a further sixteen in 1923, and Lancashire United, which took six in 1923. Half of the

West Riding total and all the Lancashire United buses had bodywork by Strachan & Brown, in those days one of the leading bodybuilders based in London.

Doncaster Corporation also became a 4-ton user with its first nine buses, these having Bristol bodywork, as applied to most other examples, including five for Jersey Motor Transport, three more for Devon Motor Transport, two for the Corris Railway and one for Rhondda Tramways.

However three chassis for the Hull municipal fleet delivered in January 1923 had Dick, Kerr open-top double-deck bodies seating 53 and a further six similar chassis were delivered in September 1923. These nine vehicles

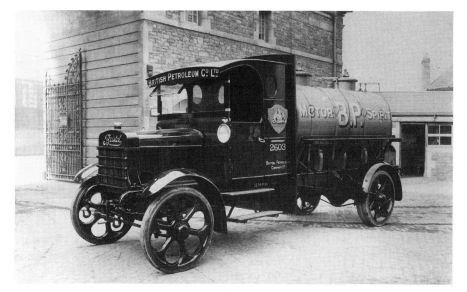

One of the first three of a total over 100 tankers on the 4-ton model for well-known oil companies was chassis 1306, No.2603 in the British Petroleum fleet, seen standing ready for delivery just inside the arched entrance to Brislington tram depot, where the body had been built, in 1921. It was registered CY 4264, suggesting allocation to the Swansea area, though most such vehicles in national fleets with headquarters in London were registered there. Note the embossed coat of arms on a shield with the lettering 'By appointment to His Majesty the King' on the cab side and, in similar vein, the elaborate wrought-iron gate with BTCC lettering at the depot entrance, which itself would not have looked out of keeping on a royal palace.

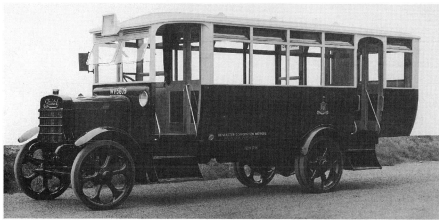

Doncaster Corporation's first buses were Bristol 4-ton models, No 2, on chassis 1479 being seen here when new in 1922. The 30-seat body, of BTCC's standard pattern of the time, was one of a high proportion at that period constructed by the Bristol Aeroplane Co Ltd, short of aircraft orders at the time. Doncaster was to remain a regular customer for Bristol buses until 1947, even though the quantities involved were not large and other makes were purchased.

were the first Bristol double-deckers and the only ones on the 4-ton chassis, having 14ft 6in wheelbase and heavy-duty rear springs. There were two more tankers, this time for Shell-Mex, and BP was again a customer, though this time for a lorry.

The 2-ton model

An additional chassis type appeared in 1923, this being the 2-ton model, unusual at that period in being of forward-control layout, especially for so relatively small a model. Fully-fronted cabs were standard, a feature that at that date was more usual for forward-control passenger models than applied two or three years later, and remained usual for goods versions. Mechanically, and in regard to details of appearance apart from the driving position, it could be regarded as largely a scaled-down version of the 4-ton model, with a 3.6-litre four-cylinder engine, type EW, of 3¾in bore and 5in stroke. A choice of solid or pneumatic tyres was offered. Most passenger examples seated 20, although a few accommodated 24, and, as with the 4-ton model, quite a number were sold as goods vehicles, including several batches of tankers. Most had an 11ft 6in wheelbase but three early chassis and six dating from 1925 were 12ft 6in.

Sanction No. 6 provided for the construction of the first batch, and a new chassis number series was begun with numbers 0100-127, built in 1923-24, except that 0109 and 0110 were not built, making this initial batch amount to 26 chassis. It was quite a common idea for chassis number series not to begin at 1, to avoid alarming nervous customers, and for some years Bristol types tended to begin at 101. Of these early 2-tonners, only four were added to BTCC's own fleet from new, the largest batch being six for Devon Motor Transport, though West Riding had four and there were three demonstrators (including the first two chassis 0100 and 0101), plus one bus for St Helens Corporation, all the foregoing having Bristol bodywork. Two of the BTCC buses and the St. Helens bus were at the 1923 Commercial Motor Show. Rotherham Corporation had three of these early vehicles, with Roe bodywork, beginning an association with this operator which was to continue to 1950.

From that point, for several years the 4-ton and 2-ton models were both produced, several operators having batches of both types to cater for appropriate variations of passenger demand on different routes. Sanction No. 7 is understood to have run from 1534 to 1654, being placed in service in various fleets between the end of 1923 and 1925. It included batches for Bristol's own fleet, West Riding,

The 3.6-litre EW engine fitted to the 2-ton model had a detachable cylinder head and duralumin connecting rods. The carburetter was of the updraught type, as usual at the time, but its unusually low mounting seems unlikely to have been helpful for cold starting. It developed 45bhp at 1,880rpm, almost as much as the BW.

The 2-ton chassis, seen as exhibited in solid-tyred form at the 1923 Show, was Bristol's first forward-control model. The foot-brake acted on the transmission and the handbrake on the rear wheels.

Devon Motor Transport, Doncaster and other existing users but also introduced new names – Manchester Corporation, with six; Chesterfield Corporation, three, and Sunderland District Transport Co Ltd, an initial two followed by 24 in 1925, these latter having Ransomes bodywork Another name appearing in the list of buyers for the first time was A. & R. Graham, of Kirkintilloch, a rare case of an independent operator in Scotland which was to purchase examples of most Bristol models until 1938 – its first 4-ton model, delivered in 1924, had Martin bodywork, also specified for some later vehicles for this fleet.

Over much the same period, Sanction No.8 covered 2-ton models, beginning at 0127 and thought to run to 0253.

This time the batches of this smaller model ran to greater numbers, beginning with an unbroken run of 50 for BTCC, all but four of which were 20-seat charabancs – there were seven more, all buses, in 1925. West Riding had 46, all buses, delivered in 1924. A petrol company, Anglo-American, trading in those days as Pratt's, had ten with lorry bodies, there were a pair of buses for Lancashire

Chassis number 0101, fitted with a 20-seat Bristol charabanc body and registered HT 6520 as first completed in 1923, is seen making a restart on the 1 in 4 gradient of Porlock Hill in Somerset, the driver just releasing the handbrake. The photographer has slightly exaggerated the gradient, as indicated by the post and standing figure, but even so the report that it pulled away smoothly and without fuss is impressive. Note the large-diameter pneumatic tyres fitted. This vehicle was rebuilt with a bus body and the smaller pneumatics standardised for the type. It was then delivered to the West Riding concern in December of that year, numbered 153 in that fleet and registered HL 1778, remaining in service until 1932. The charabanc body was stored and then fitted to chassis 0263 in 1926.

United, plus four for West Hartlepool Corporation, and Rotherham had a further five, these last with Roe bodywork. Bristol bodywork, mostly made by the aeroplane company, was otherwise universal.

Pneumatic tyres were fitted to 4-ton passenger models as standard from 1925 – conversions of earlier deliveries to pneumatics followed rapidly. Sanction 9 of 4-ton models began at 1655 and is thought to have ended at 1714, entering service with operators in 1925-26, the users being mainly established names, though it is noteworthy that Doncaster switched to Roe bodywork for its four vehicles.

By that period, a new generation of passenger models was appearing, as described in the next chapter. The 4-ton model in particular was rapidly becoming obsolete in terms of bus design trends. Smaller numbers of bus versions continued to enter BTCC service in the period up to 1927, although by then having been largely superseded by later types. The next sanction of 4-ton models was No. 12, beginning at chassis number 1715 and running to

1829, it is thought. The bulk dated from 1926-27, with a few into 1928. Of this series, 1719-49 were buses delivered in 1926, almost all with Bristol bodywork, of which BTCC took fourteen and Chesterfield Corporation eleven, Aberdare Urban District Council two (delivered in 1925) and West Riding two. West Hartlepool Corporation also took two, but bodied by Roe. After that, 1762-63 (dating from 1926-27) and 1795-99 (new in 1927) were BBW-bodied 29-seat buses for BTCC, all the remainder from 1715 being goods, with a high proportion of tankers for both BP and Shell Mex.

The final 4-ton sanction, No. 17, which continued the series to the final chassis number in this series, 1857, was all goods, and nearly all tankers. Most, including a batch of 20 tankers for BP which had registrations in the London GJ series familiar on LGOC ST-type buses of the period, were new in 1930. However, the final two chassis dated from 1931, of which 1856 was a demonstration chassis, sold to W. D. & H. O. Wills, the tobacco firm, whose

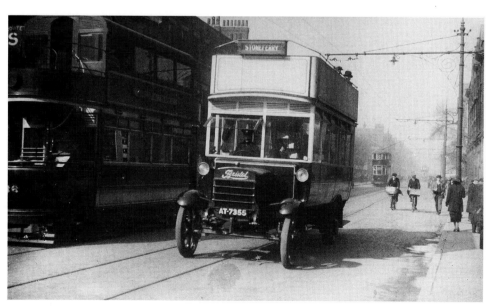

The one and only Bristol car was made in 1924 to the design of C. G. Nevatt, Works Manager, being registered HU 416. It was described as purely experimental, though there was considerable public interest in ultra-light low-powered cars at the time. It was very advanced in concept, with front-wheel drive and independent suspension all round as built, though at the rear a modification introduced a dead axle with springs using a cam system, the latter feature similar in principle to that used on Bristol production models for many years. The engine was a Douglas 6hp horizontally-opposed air-cooled twin-cylinder, much as used in motorcycles of that make, with three-speed gearbox and differential beneath it. The petrol tank acted as a cover for the engine, giving a rounded nose as commonly used much later, though the engine was exposed beneath it, and even the windscreen was of the wrap-around form fashionable in more recent times, though it seems almost certain to have been made of celluloid. It weighed 10 cwt and is said to have been capable of 50 mph.

headquarters are in Bristol, but it was never bodied and was scrapped in 1934. The last 4-ton model of all, 1857, was a lorry for Rickett & Son of Hull, with a body by Barnaby, well known as a bus bodybuilder.

Meanwhile, the 2-ton went through a rather similar pattern of an increased proportion of goods models, though in this case the final batches were passenger. Sanction 10 is believed to have run from 0254 to 0335, entirely bodied by Bristol (goods and passenger) and largely dating from 1926-27, though a van (0259) went to the Stroud Piano Co and nine tankers (0264-73) to Shell Mex in 1925. The

1926 deliveries were largely goods, and mainly for oil companies, though there was a van for Carson's Chocolates, of Bristol, but there were thirteen buses for BTCC and a pair for Llandudno Blue.

Chassis 0297, the first 2-ton model delivered in 1927, marked a turning point, being the first of this type with half-cab layout, by then firmly established on the larger B-type as described in the next chapter, the 2-tonner thereby taking on something of the look of a shortened version of that model. It was the first of eleven 20-seat buses for BTCC that year, the half-cab layout being standardised for

In October 1924, The Sunderland District Electric Tramways Co Ltd decided to abandon its trams and buy more buses. Two Bristol 4-ton buses were already in use, in a largely AEC fleet, and 24 more were ordered, this time with 26-seat two-door bodywork by Ransomes, Sims & Jefferies Ltd, of Ipswich. The company's name was changed to The Sunderland District Transport Co Ltd from February 1925, and No.12 (PT 4711) on chassis 1649 is seen ready for delivery with the then new title. Pneumatic tyres were coming into favour and these vehicles were converted to them during the next year or so. For financial reasons the name changed again to The Sunderland District Omnibus Co Ltd in June 1927 and when some new Leyland Lion 32-seat buses were purchased, fourteen of the 4-ton buses, including this one, were sold in 1928 via a London dealer. They were all acquired by Manchester Corporation, already a substantial Bristol user, to replace some troublesome buses of other makes and PT 4711 was among the last two to remain in service, surviving until 1931, then becoming a lorry in Sheffield.

Pneumatic tyres were of obvious benefit in the safe delivery of the Stroud Piano Co's products and this neat-looking van on 2-ton chassis 0259 dated from 1925. The bodywork was built by Bristol and no doubt the slogan painted on the side was applied with approval, in the sense that it was also apt for the vehicle.

passenger versions. A similar model with coach body was exhibited at the 1927 Show, entering service with BTCC in 1928. Remaining deliveries made in 1927, taking the chassis numbers up to 0335, were mainly lorries for the Pratt's fleet, though a van was also built for Scott of Edinburgh.

A smaller 2-ton sanction was No. 19, covering the 20 chassis 0336-55 built in 1928-29, of which twelve were passenger, all for BTCC itself, and split equally between bus and coach versions. The remainder comprised four BP tankers, a tower wagon and a lorry for BTCC's own use, a lorry for Bristol Aeroplane, and a demonstrator van, not sold until 1932, to a local firm.

When a need for some new 20-seat buses for BTCC arose in 1932, a final eleven 2-ton chassis were built, forming Sanction 21, on chassis 0355-66. By that date tastes in appearance had moved on and these were noteworthy for having a new style of radiator, listed as 'AV, Special Shroud' more in keeping with the times, having some resemblance to the JV type then being fitted to larger models. However, its proportions rather suggest that it might have been partly inspired by contemporary small Guy models, a few of which came into BTCC's fleet around that time, and the casing, less slim than the JV, gave a hint of the KV type used on early K and L models five years later. The concave front wheels hitherto fitted to 2-ton models with pneumatic tyres gave way to a more up-to-date convex shape which would also have given space for front-wheel brakes, another respect in which accepted design practice had moved on. The Bristol 2-tonner was a remarkable survivor in an era of very rapid development, virtually unique in originating in 1923 yet being still in production nearly a decade later.

This view of chassis in the final stages of manufacture evidently dates from about 1928, B-types being predominant by then, as described in the next chapter, though a 2-ton chassis has a wooden bench fitted for test or delivery and a finished 4ton lorry on pneumatic tyres can be seen in the background. The B chassis with test weights was B370, retained as an experimental chassis until being bodied for BTCC's own use, registered HW 7097, in 1930 - it had a Ricardo-head engine and the records show indications of work on brakes, balanced clutch and propeller shaft, while alternative carburetters were still being tested in 1933.

The half-cab layout had become usual for full-sized buses and from 1927 it was decided that the 2-ton model should follow suit. This example was one of six with 20-seat coach bodywork built in 1929 on chassis numbered in the 0344-55 range, the photograph dating from June that year.

The final batch of 2-ton 20-seat buses was built on chassis 0355-66 in 1932 and were of modernised appearance. The radiator, though internally based on the standard AV unit for the model, was given an appearance remarkably close to that of the KV type adopted five years later for the K and L, except for being less tall. An angled window allowed the driver to collect the fares.

5   Low-loaders and Superbuses

A new alphabetical series of type letters was initiated at the same time as specialised chassis intended purely for bus use took over from the dual-purpose chassis hitherto used. As indicated in the previous chapter, the 2- and 4-ton models continued for a few more years but no further goods models were made until the circumstances of the 'fifties opened up an opportunity for Bristol to build vehicles for British Road Services.

The A type was announced in October 1925 and offered for both single- and double-deck bodywork. It was an up-to-date design, comparing well with what was available at the time from other makers, yet only 23, all but the first three, listed as 'experimental', covered by Sanction 13, were produced in a period extending to 1928. It was of the layout then described as low-loading and coming into general favour, the main part of the frame being lower than the straight type used previously and was upswept over the front and rear axles in the manner then becoming accepted practice for passenger chassis. The wheelbase was 16ft, allowing for an overall length of 25ft as a double-decker, or up to 26ft as a single-decker.

The four-cylinder side-valve engine, type FW, had an unusually large capacity for such a unit of 6.97 litres, being of 4¾in bore and 6in stroke, giving 85bhp at 2,200rpm. The drive was taken through a double-plate clutch, four-speed gearbox and worm-drive rear axle, this last being of the underslung type, with the wormshaft below the wormwheel rather than above as used previously, this allowing the transmission line to be lowered to suit the frame height.

Until the mid 'thirties, each type was given a new series of chassis numbers prefixed by the type letter and beginning at 101. Only the first A-type chassis, A101, joined the BTCC fleet after acting as a demonstrator, this vehicle

Bristol's first 'low-loading' bus and also its first full-sized forward-control model was the initial A-type, A101, which was displayed at the 1925 Commercial Motor Show, being seen here after being added to BTCC's fleet. It had full-fronted bodywork, built by Bristol, and the radiator was designed to suit, though later examples were all of the half-cab layout. Pneumatic tyres suitable for a vehicle of this size had only recently become available. This vehicle, registered HU 4325, was used as a demonstrator before being added to the BTCC operational fleet.

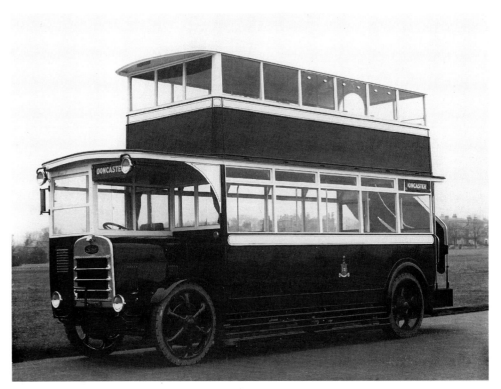

The first Bristol covered-top double-decker was A103. The chassis had begun life as a 'test wagon' in January 1926 but in April was sent to the Rochester works of Short Bros, already well established as builders of double-deck bodywork, to receive the 52-seat body shown. The unladen weight was 5tons 17cwt 1qr. It was registered HU 7326 and used at first as a demonstrator and development vehicle, receiving front wheel brakes in September, just before being painted in Doncaster Corporation livery and sent on demonstration to that undertaking; it was purchased almost immediately, in October 1926. It became No. 55 and was joined by similar buses A104 and A106 in December that year, followed by another, A108, in 1928.

having a full-fronted 32-seat two-door BBW body. It had an unusual style of radiator, with polished shell having an outline not unlike that of the 4-ton model when viewed from the front, though broader and with slightly sloping sides, but very slim when viewed from the side, and with filler cap inclined forward. This was clearly intended to suit full-fronted bodywork but was also used on the half-cab versions – as it turned out, all the other A-types were of the latter layout. Both A101 and A102 were at the 1925 Commercial Motor Show, the latter then in chassis form. At that date, pneumatic tyres suitable for a large single-decker had been developed and were fitted to these two, but were not yet available for the double-deck version.

Most of the A-types were double-deckers, though it took a little time for even the limited sales the model achieved to gain momentum, and it seems that some chassis built speculatively may have been left unused for a year or two. This could have been largely because of the interest then being shown by potential users in six-wheeled (three-axle) buses, an example of which had been exhibited in chassis form by Karrier at the 1925 Show. The initial attention to this layout was partly related to it being seen as a means of applying pneumatic tyres to double-deckers, the first six-wheel double-deck motor bus in Britain being a Guy, on pneumatics, which entered service with Wolverhampton Corporation in July 1926. For a time, six-wheelers attracted much attention, both Guy and Karrier receiving quite lively demand, largely for double-deckers, all with pneumatic tyres.

Meanwhile, at Bristol, chassis A103 was completed as a double-deck demonstrator despite having to be on solids, the 52-seat covered-top open-staircase body being by Short Bros. This vehicle was added to the Doncaster

Corporation fleet in October 1926, being joined by two similar buses, A104 and 106, purchased new that year, while A105 and 107 with Short 48-seat bodies of similar pattern were supplied to Hull Corporation in 1927.

The nearest to a breakthrough for the A-type was an order for six vehicles from Manchester Corporation. They had 52-seat bodies built by Bristol, again to the accepted outline of the time, entering service in April 1927. They too were on solid tyres, but pneumatics suitable for two-axle double-deckers had just become available. Among the first examples was an AEC NS-type operated in Bristol by Greyhound Motors on pneumatic tyres well before any of the large fleet of the type run by the London General Omnibus Co did. At that date Greyhound was a competitor to BTCC.

When Hull Corporation placed a repeat order for six further double-deck A-types for delivery in 1928, the early ex-Show chassis A102 was used together with A117-121, and these had pneumatic tyres together with enclosed-staircase 50-seat Roe bodywork.

The Bath Tramways Motor Co Ltd, in those days also unconnected with BTCC, had three single-decker A-types with Bristol 36-seat rear-entrance bodies, A115 in 1927 being followed by the last two chassis of the type (A122-3) placed in service in May 1928, these having pneumatic tyres, as did A116, sold with Curtis Bros horsebox body to Mrs V. Thomas of Okehampton, Devon in 1927.

By 1928, the A-type was no longer competitive in the double-deck market, even with pneumatic tyres. Not only were the six-wheel models from Guy, Karrier and others at about the height of their success, but there was a new and vastly stronger contender in the form of the two-axle Leyland Titan TD1, introduced in time for the Commercial

Manchester Corporation's order for six A-type 52-seat double-deckers, all delivered in April 1927, was the nearest that model got to gaining business from major operators. In this case the body order also went to Bristol, the official records showing them as "built by the Tram depot" in the manner usual at the time. The Short Bros influence is not hard to find, especially in the outline of the upper deck, though the sloping windscreen gives a touch of similarity to the B-type single-deckers being built by then. Seen here is A111, which became Manchester No. 61 (NF 4079), which remained in service until December 1935, the last of the class to be withdrawn from passenger use though A112 survived as a breakdown crane until 1954.

The six Manchester A-types, A109-115, were delivered on solid tyres as seen in this line-up but were later converted with pneumatics, as applied to others of the type. Among differences in specification these buses had Zenith carburettors, also found on A101 and the Bath single-deckers, whereas the other A-types had Solex.

By the time Hull placed a repeat order for six A-types, pneumatic tyres suitable for a two-axle double-decker had become available. This picture of A117, Hull No. 42 (KH 6239), was taken for the bodybuilder, Charles H. Roe Ltd, of Leeds, the enclosed-staircase 50-seat body being typical of that concern's products of the period in its appearance, with the patented waistrail and Roevac ventilators over the side windows on both decks. Also included with A117-121 in this order was the erstwhile 1925 polished Show chassis, A102, all delivered in January-February 1928. With A105 and A107 already in service, Hull thus became the largest user of the type.

The prototype B-type chassis, B101, after initial test running, began life as a demonstrator in chassis form in September 1926. An experimental 30-seat two-door body for it was built at the Motor Constructional Works in December 1926, the complete vehicle being recorded in the chassis register as the demonstration Superbus. Its weight at that stage was the very modest figure of 4tons 4cwt 1qr. The body, of wooden construction, was left in natural finish for a time. It bore a London registration, XW 5904, in a photograph taken at the time, but this belonged to a 1925 2-ton lorry, 0231, built for Anglo-American, so was evidently 'borrowed' merely for cosmetic purposes.

It was registered HU 9991 when first licensed for service in July 1927 but it seems to have continued to be treated as a test vehicle to some degree. In September 1928 a Ricardo-designed cylinder head and pistons were fitted, and the vehicle was used as a demonstrator from October 1928 to March 1929 before returning to service. It was weighed again in November 1929 when it was 4tons 14cwt 2qr, just over half a ton more than when new. It received a new 31-seat body in July 1930 and it was probably at that stage that it was fitted with a later DV-style radiator. It remained in service until the late 1930s and was scrapped by BTCC in 1942.

Motor Show held in November 1927 and entering service with a wide variety of operators in large numbers by mid-1928. Bristol, not itself interested in double-deck bus operation at that stage, by then had a far more successful single-deck model on the market in the form of the B-type and hence the A-type was dropped, with no direct replacement at that stage.

The B-type

The next model, the B-type, also called the Superbus, was announced in October 1926, immediately proving considerably more popular. Indeed, it was one of the more successful bus models of its period, a time of intense competition. It was aimed at the growing market for forward-control single-deckers, both for bus and coach duties, and was thus up against such models as the ADC 416, Albion 30/30hp types, Dennis E, Leyland Lion PLSC, Maudslay ML3 and Tilling-Stevens Express.

It is significant that, although the speed limit in force at the time for buses of this size was 12mph, the description in *The Commercial Motor* at the time of the B-type's introduction referred to it being tested at up to 50mph. It was typical of its period in having a four-cylinder side-valve petrol engine, and indeed this, of type GW, was

derived from the 4-ton model's BW engine. It had the same 4½in by 5¾in bore and stroke and 5.99-litre capacity, rather greater than the more typical size of about 5 litres of most competitive models, but in addition, development took the power output up from the earlier model's maximum of 55bhp at 1,700rpm to 77bhp at 2,000rpm, the latter speed corresponding to 40mph with the 5¼ to 1 axle ratio offered. This output made it among the most powerful of the comparable models available at that date, appealing to operators who, despite the unrealistic official speed limit, wished to attract custom by running tightly-timed services. It is known that Bristol was among the concerns which turned to Harry Ricardo for advice during this period and on most later examples his skill in getting side-valve engines to perform as well as, or sometimes even better than, typical overhead-valve engines of the day was called into play, from about the end of 1928.

The chassis design was largely conventional for the period, with similar 'low-loader' frame profile to that of the A-type, but despite the rugged construction always typical of Bristol models, total chassis weight of the prototype, B101, was kept down to 2tons 16cwt, again helping to ensure lively performance. The drive line was inclined slightly and offset in the manner becoming usual to allow the gangway level to be low. The clutch was of

The first operator to put B-type buses into service was Chesterfield Corporation, which had been a user of 4-ton models since 1924, taking delivery of its first sixteen B-type chassis between August and December 1926. The first to arrive was B103, delivered on 23rd August and hence probably the first to be completed by the bodybuilder, Reeve & Kenning, before being the subject of this official photograph – it was No. 67 and registered RA 427. A noteworthy feature is the use of a bonnet which extends forward to the slim casing of the CV-type radiator – most other B-types with this radiator had the style seen in other photographs, with a strip behind the casing. Reeve & Kenning was a predecessor of the Reeve Burgess concern familiar in more recent times as a builder of minibus bodies.

single-plate type and the four-speed gearbox, originally of type DS, had single-shaft control by a lever to the left of the driver, an advanced feature at the time that had been introduced on the 2-tonner and was the subject of a Bristol patent. Most forward-control models of other makes were still using right hand gear-changes with heavy and complex linkage. The four-wheel brakes had Dewandre vacuum servo, but at first the handbrake operated on the transmission, in a manner not uncommon at the time. The wheelbase was 15ft 7in at first and overall length usually just under 26ft.

Overall, it was a thoroughly sound and practical vehicle. The Bristol company's direct experience of operation meant that much emphasis was put on durability and ease of maintenance, with generous lining areas on the clutch and brake shoes, for example. This was to remain a

characteristic feature of Bristol vehicles of successive types over the years.

Chassis B101 had been illustrated in press descriptions in October 1926 but was not licensed by BTCC until July 1927, evidently being used for development work meanwhile. However, Chesterfield Corporation took delivery of its first sixteen chassis (B102-109,111-114,116-119) before the end of 1926 all bodied by the local concern Reeve & Kenning, and over 100 had been built in the first year of production. The prototype and other early examples had a radiator, type CV, which, when viewed from the front, was almost identical to the A-type, with broad outline, slightly narrower at the top than the bottom and three bars across the core. However, on the prototype and most others of this style the thickness of the casing when viewed from the side was increased by the addition of a

Doncaster Corporation was another early B-type user, taking four in the early months of 1927, numbered 23-26 and receiving the registration numbers DT 1-4. The example seen here is thought to be B120, which became No. 23 (DT 2), of which the chassis was one of two delivered to Roe for bodying in January, the other two following in March. The 31-seat body had the entrance set back slightly from the front bulkhead.

As early as the Spring of 1927, Chesterfield Corporation was taking delivery of a second batch of eight B-types, again with Reeve & Kenning bodywork, but with some detail differences in body design. A rounded cowl had been added to the cab dash panel and the arch over the centre entrance was omitted. Caught by G. H. F. Atkins's camera in Vicar Lane, Chesterfield in March 1934 is B140, No.40 in the fleet, registered RA 1809, of which the chassis had been delivered in April 1927, with another of the same batch behind. The CV-type radiator shown here was about to be dropped and B143, of the same batch of Chesterfield buses, was the last chassis so fitted. At almost seven years old, these would have been regarded as old buses at that time.

polished strip ahead of the opening portion of the bonnet.

By the Spring of 1927, a new design of radiator had been introduced, not quite so broad and having a one-piece straight-sided polished aluminium surround to the rectangular grille opening, which had horizontal slats (though in later years these were generally removed). A smaller oval badge displayed the Bristol name and a round Calorimeter temperature gauge of the type used on contemporary Morris cars was fitted to the radiator cap, the latter being another feature often removed in later years. This time the surround was unusually 'thick' when viewed from the side, and it was this style of radiator that was to be most associated with the model. A unit of this DV type was fitted to B125, which began life as an experimental chassis, and was adopted as standard from B144, the first of a pair of coaches for Lewis Omnibus Co Ltd, of Watford.

Sanction 14 ran from B101 to B125 followed by Sanction 15, which covered B126-175. Sanction 16 (B176-215), and Sanction 17, which was subdivided, the first covering B216-276, which 17/1 ran from B226-276 and 17/2 covered B277-326. At that point a second means of grouping chassis began to appear in the records. The sheets from B277 onwards are inscribed '14th series' this also applying to B327-416, in Sanction 18.

The B-type was developed over the years, even though its basic design, and in particular the GW-type engine, continued to the end. The handbrake acting on the transmission, though quite common on commercial vehicles and cars of various types of the mid-'twenties, quite soon went out of favour because of the damage it could cause to rear axle gears and even propeller shafts. It was replaced by a more conventional system acting on the

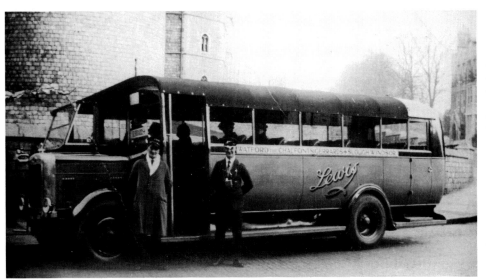

The first pair of production vehicles to have the new DV-type radiator were B144 and 145, supplied in May 1927 as chassis to Lewis Omnibus Co Ltd of Watford. They were fitted with folding-hood coach bodies by Strachan & Brown, and B145, the operator's B2, registered RO 7065, is seen at the Windsor Castle terminus of this concern's route from Watford, running via the Chalfonts, Gerrards Cross and Slough, as displayed on the route board on the waistline. They passed with the undertaking to London Transport on 1st October 1933, but were withdrawn the following year and sold to a dealer in October 1934.

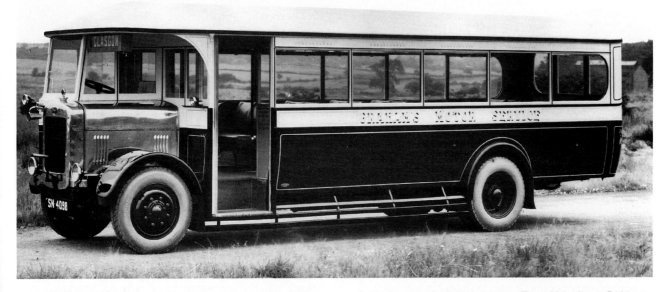

A. & R. Graham of Kirkintilloch, on the north-eastern outskirts of Glasgow, was becoming a regular Bristol customer. The vehicle shown, B163, was the firm's first B-type, the chassis being delivered to Roe for bodying as a 32-seat bus in June 1927. It became No. 3 in the fleet, registered SN 4098. The aluminium radiator shell had been buffed up to shine almost like chromium plate, this also applying to the unpainted bonnet, a feature quite often found on Bristol vehicles over the next decade. Like quite a number of early B-types, this vehicle was modified in later years. The gearbox and rear axle were changed in January 1928, the latter changing from the original DM to an EM unit, and on October 1929 the engine was modified to full-pressure lubrication.

rear wheels, evidently from B277, the first of the chassis quoted as '14th series'. The design of various other units, such as the axles, also changed and, in conjunction with the revised appearance in 1927, and again towards the end of the model's life as described later in this chapter, in effect the model could be sub-divided into three main generations, with several sub-variations.

Although many early buyers were already Bristol users, by 1927-28, the B-type was finding a wider spread of customers, sales extending to quite a number of municipal and company operators in the north of England as well as

Wales and smaller concerns in almost all parts of the country. The Bristol company's own fleet received fairly modest numbers in that period, quite a high proportion being coaches. It is noteworthy in view of later events that Bristol vehicles built up quite a sizeable market in this period almost entirely with operators having no financial link with their manufacturer.

Among the most noteworthy individual Bristol users was the West Riding company, putting 159 Bristol buses in service between 1922 and 1931, including 47 B-types, but there were also such instances as Lancashire United,

Only modest numbers of B-type buses were supplied to BTCC's own fleet in the first year or two of production. Among them was B224, one of twelve with Bristol two-door 31-seat bodywork of the style then current, placed in service in the winter of 1927-28. This was one of several which were modified before hand-over to the operating department, receiving an EM rear axle in place of a DM unit in December 1927 and being delivered in January 1928. It is seen in Clifton in July 1928, with destination display reading 'Tramways Centre' for the journey into Bristol.

The B-type attracted orders from independent operators in various parts of the country, but notably from the Midlands. Williamson's Garage Ltd, of Heanor, Derbyshire ran a service into Nottingham via Ilkeston, and four B-types were the first full-sized buses purchased. The chassis were delivered in October 1927, three, B227-9, going direct to Roe for bodying as 32-seat buses, though the fourth, B232, went initially to Williamson's premises before being bodied similarly and entering service the following year. By then the firm had become associated with Midland General, by which it was later absorbed. Seen here is the first, B227, registered as RA 4517.

Norwich Electric Tramways, Rhondda Tramways and the Musselburgh and District Electric Light and Traction Co Ltd, this last-mentioned based a few miles from Edinburgh and operating under the fleetname Coast Line. In addition, the municipalities of Aberdare, Bradford, Chesterfield, Doncaster, Exeter, Manchester, Merthyr Tydfil, Pontypridd, Rotherham, Stockton, West Hartlepool and Wigan were also all B-type users. Although this municipal trade diminished in the 'thirties as Bristol became more involved in the supply of buses to the companies with which it became associated, the municipalities of Aberdare, Doncaster, Pontypridd and Rotherham were to remain regular customers for many years.

Quite a number of Bristol users in that period continued to be tramway undertakings which had moved into bus operation, both municipal and company, suggesting that there was still some feeling that there would be a special understanding of their needs. The B also built up quite a significant trade with independent concerns in various parts of the country; there was quite a following among various concerns running bus services around Stoke-on-Trent and other parts of the north Midlands, for example. Some orders from small firms were for examples with coach bodywork, the model's lively performance doubtless accounting for the attraction, despite the very severe official speed limits then in force. Manchester Corporation was another case where lively performance was valued, setting up a series of fast services linking surrounding areas on which the undertaking's 23 B-types dating from 1927-28 were prominent.

A new subsidiary also came into the picture when a controlling interest in Greyhound Motors Ltd was acquired by BTCC on 31st March 1928. This concern was an enterprising independent company established in Bristol in 1921 and which had the distinction of running what was then the longest all-year-round express service in Britain when its route to London was established with Dennis coaches in February 1925. The fleet was largely of AEC,

A dozen municipal fleets in various parts of England and Wales favoured the B-type, among them Wigan Corporation. The vehicle shown, B242, was the first supplied, with two-door Bristol body "built by the tram depot" and delivered in March 1928, becoming No. 31 and registered EK 6282. Two more, B252 and 253, followed the next month, but these were supplied in primer to be painted on the operator's premises. Note the '12mph' lettering on the lifeguard rail, still the official speed limit for a vehicle of this type at the time, despite being well able to run at three times that, even with the 6 to 1 axle ratio as fitted in this case.

There was no lack of self-confidence in the advertising for the B-type. This one dated from March 1928, the model being described as the "Bristol" Low-loading Light Passenger Chassis. The view shows the frame profile, with side-members shaped to rise over both axles but low enough to allow a two-step entry from ground level. A noteworthy feature in this case was the provision of outrigger brackets to support the bodywork, a concept which did not become common practice until much later. The fuel tank was behind the rear axle, a position not uncommon at that time but which gave way to a side-mounted position on later models. A feature of the B-type which continued on later Bristol chassis was the graduated suspension system in which the normal spring shackle was replaced by a cam device which shortened the effective length of the leaf springs, thus allowing a 'softer' ride with a light passenger load while avoiding excessive deflection as the load increased.

The best chassis for carrying 30-34 passengers!

Semi-plan view of the "BRISTOL" Low-loading LIGHT PASSENGER CHASSIS.

ADC and Dennis make, and included AEC NS-type covered-top double-deckers as already mentioned – at that date BTCC had no double-deck buses. After the change in control, Bristol vehicles, at first largely B-type, were supplied, with occasional exceptions. A somewhat similar pattern applied to the smaller Bence concern run as a subsidiary from 1930.

Quite significant by their absence at that date were orders for Bristol buses from member companies of the Tilling or British Electric Traction empires. This included those in the Tilling & British Automobile Traction group newly set up in 1928 to deal with the many cases where

West Riding Automobile Co Ltd had been a consistent Bristol user since 1922. Although Leyland buses began to be purchased from 1926, batches of B-types were added to the fleet in 1927, 1929, 1930 and 1931, with bodywork by Davidson in 1927-8 or, thereafter, Bristol. Most were buses but in 1929, just after twelve of these were supplied, there were also two 26-seat coaches – or to use the contemporary description, "'parlour' type buses' – added to the fleet, B333 being shown here after completion by "the Tram depot" – it was West Riding No. 268 (HL 4218). The two chassis, the other being B344, may have been stock items, official records showing that the engines were fitted with Ricardo heads in January 1929, the vehicles being delivered in March. It had become common practice to pick out the figures on the small cast chassis number plate in white, visible above the HL letters on the registration plate, and on the original print this is clearly readable – the B-type was one of the few models on which one could read the chassis number as an example passed by, if not going too fast and the plate was reasonably clean.

United Automobile Services Ltd made a dramatic start to its use of Bristol vehicles by placing 130 B-types in service in 1929. Over the years, this company was to prove perhaps Bristol's most important individual 'outside' customer, largely due to the subsequent common link to the Tilling organisation, yet neither concern was connected to it or to each other when this initial order was placed. The chassis were to the latest specification, with Ricardo-head version of the GW engine and 16ft wheelbase.

The 32-seat bodywork was built by United to its characteristic style of that period at its coachbuilding works in Lowestoft, later itself to have strong links to Bristol when it passed to Eastern Counties and, from 1936, Eastern Coach Works.

This view of B449 was taken when ready to enter service as L35 in the United fleet in May 1929, the last two digits of the registration number VF 5135 matching the fleet number in the manner already usual for this concern. The livery at that date was a shade of beige and brown, with a cream waistband, much as retained until the 1950s by East Midland, which had been a United offshoot, though the latter's own buses became red from 1930. This bus became B35 in the 1935 renumbering and remained in service until 1949, being sold to a West Hartlepool contractor, and reported as still in use in 1956.

both Tilling and BET held interests – in practice one or the other of those concerns held a controlling interest which inclined policy in one direction or the other. However, a few of the previously-mentioned tramway-based companies that had become Bristol users were acquired by these groups in later years.

Tilling, naturally enough, tended to favour the Tilling-Stevens make which had been set up largely to supply its needs and this was then also true of quite a number of TBAT companies. The BET group, in the early post-1914-18 war years, had quite often left individual companies to favour local makes. By the late 'twenties, Leyland was emerging as a widely favoured choice, though several of its subsidiaries were taking the SOS vehicles made by its largest bus-operating subsidiary, Midland Red.

A surprising order for 130 Bristol B-type buses came in 1928 from United Automobile Services Ltd, then one of the largest independent operators in the country and hitherto favouring AEC buses – they were bodied by the operator's own coachbuilding premises at its then headquarters in Lowestoft. This was the biggest single order Bristol had received and was even more remarkable in that United had no previous experience of Bristol vehicles, although a visit from one of the demonstrator B-types seems likely. A factor in the switch of allegiance may have been uncertainty as to the future of AEC, following

the break-up of the association with Daimler in the ADC link. Bristol's specification for the B was being improved and B101's engine was fitted with a cylinder head and pistons to Ricardo design in September 1928, being sent out on demonstration the following month.

The United buses incorporated this feature and were also the first to have a slightly increased wheelbase of 16ft 0in, both these items being adopted as standard. It seems possible that the initiative for the increase in wheelbase may have come from United, for a similar change had been a feature of that concern's previous orders for AEC and ADC single-deckers.

So large an order justified fresh production arrangements and a new sanction number, 19/1, and series number, 15, began at the first United chassis, B417, delivered to Lowestoft on 19th December 1928. Most unusually in that period, there was an almost unbroken run of chassis numbers, the United vehicles being B417-59, 462-526 and 528-549. Sanction 19/1 ran to B450, followed by 19 to B526, and 20 then covered 100 vehicles, B527-626, which included buses for other operators as well as the last 22 for United, for whom chassis delivery was completed by May 1929. Entry into service of the United batch spread from March to August. Most of them survived until 1948-9 and the author has vivid memories of them running in the Northumberland area – though still quite

The B-type was quite often chosen for coach duty, and Harrison and Ives Ltd, of Norwich, trading as Eastern Motorways had four in an otherwise largely AEC and Daimler fleet. The first two, B371 and B372 were on 15ft 7in wheelbase chassis and had Eaton bodywork, entering service early in 1929. The second pair, B460 and B461, with 16ft wheelbase and Ricardo-head engines, were on chassis which may well have been drawn from United's allocation, having numbers which fall amidst its big order for 130 chassis though the specification was slightly different. They were sold through United, as agents, the firm then acting in that role for several makes, and were bodied by United to the rather stylish design shown. All four passed to United ownership when Eastern Motorways was taken over in October 1930, being numbered L131-134, immediately after the big bus batch, and then were transferred to Eastern Counties in 1931.

Bristol was also adding B-type coaches to its own fleet, there being a total of seventeen with London Lorries 26-seat two-door bodywork, placed in service in the summer of 1929. Three were based on former experimental or stock chassis, including B125, the first to have the DV radiator and dating from October 1927, though that had been brought to current standard in November 1928, while B259 and 261 dated from 1928. Others were on new chassis B345-51/3-8/81/6, built to the 15ft 7in wheelbase specification and drawn from Sanction 18. Among these was B357, seen here, which was delivered in July 1929. These vehicles were painted in a slightly lighter shade of blue than BTCC's standard below the waistrail, the latter having a speckled finish which seems to have been a speciality of this bodybuilder. The fixed part of the roof was fabric-covered, and a noteworthy detail was the small hinged vent over the cab, of a type often fitted to cars of the day and quite effective in providing draught-free ventilation. It was registered HW 6282 and after conversion to a bus was rebodied to wartime utility specification by Bence, remaining in service until 1947.

lively, they were prone to quite severe vibration at speed, setting the backs of any unoccupied seats into a continual tremor – worn propeller-shaft joints was probably the cause. By the time delivery of these buses was completed, United had been acquired jointly by the TBAT group and the London & North Eastern Railway. Although no further orders for Bristol buses from that quarter ensued until 1933, the possible significance of this large batch of vehicles in a prominent Tilling-managed fleet in relation to later events is a matter for speculation.

Still demand for the model continued, and Sanction 21 covered B627-726, followed by Sanction 22/2 covering B727-776, these latter being series 15, which had began at B417, the first bus of the United batch, ended at B726. Changes in specification appeared from time to time, sometimes in step with the above although not always. A new gearbox, type ES, to be standard on various other models until the early 1930s, was standard from B550, at which point a Dewandre brake system, type EQ, appeared. This gave way to SQ, using a vertical Bristol servo, from B727, the beginning of the Series 20 chassis, and the rear axle changed from EJ to JM at the same point. Marles steering was used on B627-726, in conjunction with slightly larger-section tyres.

The above buses mainly entered service in 1930-31, with a few in 1932. By this stage a higher proportion of B production was for BTCC itself, by then replacing many of the 4-ton buses. Most of these had Bristol bodywork, but Northern Counties and Beadle produced part of BTCC's needs, Northern Counties also supplying Greyhound.

Orders continued to come in from regular customers, such as Doncaster and Rotherham, both continuing to prefer Roe bodywork, though Rotherham continued to favour the centre-entrance layout and gave part of its order to Cravens, a Sheffield firm and thus more local – it was to be a preferred choice for this fleet in later orders on subsequent Bristol chassis types. Independent operators continued to buy examples and, although often only in ones and twos for concerns such as Graham of Kirkintilloch or Milton Bus Service, Hanley, they added up to form a substantial minority in the overall output. The Merseyside Touring Co was another repeat customer, putting four with coach bodywork into service in 1930, two each with bodies by Burlingham and Massey.

Further changes in design continued to occur, this being an increasingly active time for new projects generally. From B727, there was also a revised frame, 2JA. Steering generally reverted to a Bristol-made design, type JG, again also used on other models for some years, though there were a number of cases of changes, with modified steering ratio and other modifications suggesting that the action with the larger tyres, of size 36 x 8.25 had proved unduly heavy.

More fundamentally, in late 1929, a six-cylinder engine was introduced, and contemporary advertising makes it clear that this was at first simply regarded as an option for what was still being called the Superbus or Light Passenger model. This type is described in the next chapter but it should be mentioned here that two prototype six-cylinder D-type chassis were replaced, the originals being rebuilt with four-cylinder engines, D101 and D103 thus becoming B777 and B778 respectively, in July 1930. B777 (ex D101) was a 15ft 7in wheelbase chassis and the body was that originally carried by B101 – it received engine number BW101 the original engine fitted to B101 when new in 1926. The resulting vehicle was registered HY 1969 when it entered service in 1931. B778 (the former D103) with standard 16ft wheelbase, had received a 24-seat Northern Counties coach body transferred from B561, which had been supplied to the bodybuilder to act as a basis for an exhibit at the 1929 Commercial Motor Show and had been returned to BTCC in May 1930. Mounted on B778 the resulting vehicle was registered HY 4. A new Bristol bus body was built for B561 which was supplied to the operating fleet in April 1931, registered HY 1961, its chassis by then being nearly two years old.

Rotherham Corporation had been a regular B-type customer from its introduction, and this scene near the railway station captured by Geoff Atkins's camera in September 1929 sums up a northern town landscape of those days, complete with tramway overhead wiring and track, as well as a typical bus in that fleet, with centre-entrance body by Roe, thought to be one of those delivered that year.

West Riding took a further fifteen B-type buses with the well-proportioned Bristol bodywork of that period in January-February 1930, No.306 (HL 4549), on chassis B593, being seen here parked in Marine Drive, Scarborough, while on excursion duty in June of that year. Although nominally buses, such vehicles were sufficiently comfortable – these seated 30 – to lend themselves to a trip of about 60 miles from, say, Wakefield, the West Riding concern's headquarters.

Seen here thundering up the hill out of Ilfracombe when operating for the Merseyside Touring Co Ltd in June 1931, B662 had been built for Greyhound Motors Ltd, its Northern Counties 26-seat coach body having been completed in June 1930 – it was registered HW 6506, and was evidently on hire, still being in the Greyhound fleet when absorbed by BTCC in January 1936 – it remained in service until 1946. Greyhound had been a BTCC subsidiary since 1928, and use of its vehicles as demonstrators was not unknown. However Merseyside already had nine B-types, three buses and six coaches, in its fleet, purchased in 1929 and 1930, and had become a Ribble subsidiary in January 1930 – the chassis for the four last coaches were delivered in March of that year, but were probably already on order at the date of transfer.

The final batches of B-types for West Riding and Rotherham were among the Sanction 22/2 buses numbered B727-776 but also noteworthy was a batch of ten for Pontypridd having bodywork by Eastwood and Kenning. The two rebuilds from D-type chassis were quoted as Sanction 22X in the chassis register. A final ten chassis, B779-788 brought the Series 20 chassis to a close, though their Sanction, 23, continued on to the new design of vehicle described below.

A revised design for the B appeared almost at the end of production. As described in the next chapter, a new model of similar dimensions to the B but with a six-cylinder engine, the D-type, appeared towards the end of 1929. Rationalisation resulted in a revised version of the B having the same JA frame instead of the DA frame used on early B-types, and having similar appearance with a new style of radiator, much deeper in conformity with changing tastes and with a slender surround. The actual unit numbers for this item and the bonnet differed between

The later deliveries of B-type chassis with the traditional-style DV radiator current since 1927 are represented by B730, one of ten examples supplied to Pontypridd Urban District Council in 1931. They were noteworthy in having bodywork by Eastwood & Kenning, successor to Reeve & Kenning and by then based in Manchester. Number 9 in the fleet, registered TG 1951, it is seen in July 1952, shortly before withdrawal – two others ran until 1953 and one until 1954, and may have been the last such buses in passenger service.

The appearance of the B-type chassis was transformed by the adoption of a new type of radiator, with associated details such as the bonnet design, producing a general style which was to remain current on subsequent Bristol chassis of various types until 1937. The unpainted engine-turned finish to the aluminium bonnet was also to be found on many Bristol chassis in this period, though this was a matter for customer choice. The chassis shown, B789, was the first production example of this style on a B-type, though six slightly earlier chassis for the Greyhound Motors fleet, B764 and B767-771, had been fitted with it, doubtless in response to a desire for up-to-date appearance for coach duties.

The effect on a completed vehicle is conveyed by the view below of B811, of BTCC's 1932 batch, seen in green livery after the war - it had a BTCC body and was registered as HY 6893, being renumbered 498 in 1937. It appears that the EV radiator may have been slightly less tall that the JV unit introduced for other models of that period, aside from the effect on appearance of an elderly vehicle clearly sitting rather low on its springs. It was withdrawn in 1949, though retained as an instruction vehicle for a further year.

the two models for functional reasons, the D-type bonnet being slightly longer and having more louvres to suit the six-cylinder engine. The B radiator became EV instead of the previous DV, but externally it looked like the JV used on the D-type, which was to be standard on most Bristol models until 1937.

However, another common unit with the D-type was the new front axle, FE instead of the B-type's previous DE; other units already established were also carried over and used not only on the D but also other models of the early 1930s, including the JM rear axle, and ES gearbox, though the steering temporarily went back to DG, using a Marles steering box.

From B789, the Sanction number became 23 and the Series number was 22. The chassis was chosen for official chassis photographs along with D140. Almost all were for BTCC's own use, and with Bristol bodywork – by that date, the two-door body was favoured to a degree then rare in Britain, generally seating 30. The exceptions were B790-793 for Doncaster, three of which had Roe bodywork and were placed in service late in 1931; B815 and B866-7 for Aberdare in 1932-3, and B816-7 for Musselburgh & District, also in 1933.

The BTCC batches among these late vehicles comprised B789 and 794-813 which entered service in 1932; B818-865, all but one of which dated from 1933 and B868-878, new in 1934. The 1933-34 vehicles were noteworthy as including examples with three-letter registrations, an unusual event for a model which had first appeared as early as 1926, these being in the AAE and AHU series. The highest numbered chassis, B878, had actually appeared

earlier, in 1933, being registered HY 8880 in a registration batch in which the others went to buses around B840.

Last of all to appear was B226, which had first seen the light of day exhibited as a chassis at the 1927 Show, then being used as an instructional chassis in the company's driver training school, but updated and with a 1935 body, finally entered service in 1935 as BHU 635, in a series of registrations that otherwise consisted of J-type coaches. Many buses of 1927 had gone for scrap by then, but clearly 'waste not, want not' was part of the BTCC philosophy.

So ended the B era, with 778 examples built since production began in 1926, a total not exceeded by any other model until the era of the K and L, post-1937. No comparable model from any other manufacturer survived so long in a period when bus design was changing rapidly, and even if the final manifestation was almost a new model and largely dependent on the needs of BTCC itself, what had been still clearly a mid-'twenties design had still sold well to a variety of operators up to 1931.

6 Six-wheelers and six cylinders

Slightly earlier, at the end of the 'twenties, the Motor Constructional Works seems to have been aiming its efforts in new directions.

The six-wheeled double-deck bus had become very fashionable among municipal operators in the late 'twenties, users including several which also had Bristol buses, and the Bristol C-type six-wheeled chassis with a six-cylinder engine, type HW, of 8.6-litre capacity, with 4½in bore and 5½in stroke, developing 110bhp at 2,000rpm, was one of three new models introduced in time for the Commercial Motor Show of October 1929. At least one chassis had air-pressure brakes, as used on several six-wheel designs of that period, and the first chassis had a 19ft wheelbase and overall length of 29ft.

Photographs of the first chassis, C101, show an impressive-looking machine, with a radiator similar to that of the contemporary B in appearance, though actually a different unit, type HV. The engine was evidently an overhead-valve unit, unusually among Bristol petrol engines, and an interesting detail was that the polished aluminium rocker cover had a shape curving gently from end to end, in a manner found much later on Bristol's first production diesel engine, the AVW. The sparking plugs were on the driver's side, and would have required a removable cover in the cab side, as on the Leyland Titan TD1.

The gearbox, type FS, was of unit construction type, bolted directly behind the engine, a feature not found on other Bristol models until the K and L types of 1937. The frame, type HA, was of the 'spectacle' type, in which the two driven axles of the rear bogie protruded through apertures in the sidemembers, a feature favoured in Karrier six-wheelers. Another noteworthy detail was the instrument binnacle attached to the steering column.

Two such chassis were built, evidently on a speculative basis, but found no buyers – the six-wheel motor bus era

Bristol's first six-wheel chassis makes an impressive sight as it is posed for a photograph when nearing completion in 1929 – a fuel tank had yet to be fitted and wiring seems to be absent. It was designed for bodywork, either double- or single-deck, of up to the maximum length of 30ft and weighed 5tons 1cwt 3qr according to the chassis register. The 8.6-litre six-cylinder petrol engine had a cylinder head of Ricardo design, Solex carburettor and Simms magneto. The radiator is quoted in the chassis register as type DV, the same as used on the B, but a separate unit chart quotes HV; certainly more cooling capacity than suitable for the B would have been needed. Also noteworthy in this view is the instrument binnacle attached to the steering column. An entry in the chassis register reads 'Test Chassis 2/11/29', this probably being the date when it was handed over to the test department.

This three-quarter rear view of chassis C101 shows the 'spectacle' type of frame design. The rear section, high enough to carry a spare wheel beneath it, seems to imply a two-step entry from ground level, even though rather lower than the main section. The mounting of the gearbox directly behind the engine is noteworthy, as is the shape of the engine rocker cover, giving an outline not unlike the AVW oil engine of later years. The two rear axles, both quoted as of type HM, rather suggesting that there was no third differential, had a worm-drive ratio of 7.5 to 1 and the wheels had 36x8 high-pressure tyres. It seems remarkable that no operator could be found to purchase what appears to have been quite a promising model, especially given Bristol's first-class reputation for sound design, when some very unsatisfactory six-wheelers were bought in sizeable numbers. Note the tram track and the sheet being held up in an attempt to give an uncluttered background.

Thought to be the only picture of a Bristol C-type six-wheeler on the road, this photograph shows what seems certain to be C101, loaded with test weights and in company with a B-type (or just possibly one of the prototype D-types), stopped for refreshment of the crew while on test. The location is Chippenham, which was a regular port of call for Bristol chassis on test runs.

was beginning to fade, with the notable exception of the large AEC fleet then beginning to enter service in London. The first C-type chassis, C101, was rebuilt as a trolleybus, E121, as described below. C102 was exhibited at the 1929 Commercial Motor Show, together with the first trolleybus, E101.

Examination of the chassis records reveals some clues to the story of the two C-type chassis. Although no specific dates of build are given, it seems that the two chassis were built at about the same time in the latter part of 1929. In general, the unit numbers are 101 for most components on C101, as would be expected on an all-new design, but front axle HE101 was fitted to C102, while C101 had HE102. Financial records show that £1,893 14s 3d was spent on C101 in the period to December 1929, the figure for C102 being slightly less at £1,825 8s 11d. The model was offered at a list price of £1,500, but the excess cost is not surprising on prototypes of an entirely new model.

The record for C102 shows quite a number of alterations. The engine and gearbox, originally HW102 and FS102, were both switched to the HW101 and FS101 units that had been in C101, perhaps because they had been modified after road testing, or possibly suggesting the original units in C102 were incomplete, as was not unknown on Show vehicles. However, the C102 gearbox entry alone includes a reference to a Westinghouse compressor, which would have supplied the air-pressure brake system, and indicates where it was mounted. A struck-out entry "decambered" for both front and rear axles suggests that there was a plan to lower the chassis slightly by flattening the springs, not followed through.

Particularly significant is an alteration of C102's wheelbase from 19ft to 17ft, though whether this was actually altered, implying new frame side-members, or changed before construction is not clear. This would have suited an overall length of about 27ft 6in, as standard on the London General LT-class double-deckers for example. A reference to C102 as a 1929 Show exhibit refers to a potential seating capacity of 60, which would have been quite possible on that length.

The record indicates that neither a radiator nor a petrol

An idea of what the C-type might have looked as a bodied vehicle is given by these drawings prepared by BTCC to show the effects of the Conditions of Fitness Regulations introduced in the aftermath of the Road Traffic Act 1930, and summarised in 'Bus & Coach' for June 1931. The JV-style radiator outline and the architecture of the single-deck body is recognisably to Bristol standards and so it seems probable that the proportions are quite accurate. The bonnet length is a little longer than shown on similar drawings of two-axle models, not surprising in view of the larger-capacity engine, giving a side elevation not unlike an AEC of about that period when fitted with the 8.8-litre oil engine, though Bristol evidently intended also to make the cab longer, eliminating any need for a projecting radiator. The drawing is interesting as an indication of the double-deck body style favoured at that date, with upper deck not projecting over the cab, an idea going out of favour generally by then and not pursued in the body built on the first G-type two-axle chassis a few months later.

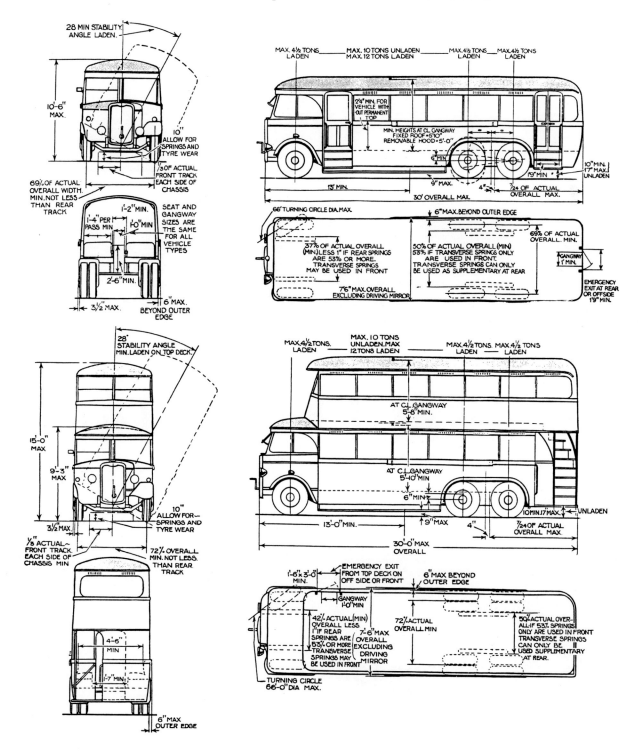

tank were fitted to C102 originally, possibly on the grounds that their absence made examination of a Show chassis easier, though perhaps alternatively suggesting that there was beginning to be doubt as to whether the radiator style as fitted to C101 was becoming outdated by the standards of current taste.

Financial records show that £19 1s 10d was spent on a radiator for C102 in the October-December 1931 period, and the chassis record shows that a JV radiator, as used on four-wheel six-cylinder models, was fitted to this chassis, as well as an HU petrol tank. The sheet for this chassis has a pencilled note 'Reconstructed and sent to the Tram Depot 8th December 1931', giving rise to the question of whether this was intended to be for bodying, even though this did not occur, or simply storage. There is a note that it was weighed in October 1931 and again in July 1933, but an entry of unspecified costs for 1933 may imply simply the final dismantling.

The D-type

Also new at that time was a two-axle single-decker, the D-type, with dimensions similar to the B-type chassis with 16ft 0in wheelbase but with a side-valve six-cylinder engine, type JW and, as originally announced for this model, of 4in bore, 5in stroke and 6.179-litre capacity developing 80bhp at 2,000rpm. It was clearly intended to give Bristol an answer to competitors' six-cylinder single-deckers, fast growing in popularity. However, it was publicised as a lightweight model, the body weight being intended not to exceed 30cwt.

The brake system included a single servo mounted vertically near the driver's seat and with mechanical linkage to all four wheels. The handbrake operated conventionally on the rear wheel brake drums, the lever being mounted to the left of the steering column, as also found on the C-type, a Bristol characteristic that was to remain until the K and L were introduced, and a feature echoed on the much later London Routemaster design.

The early story of the D-type was quite complex, the sequence of action suggesting that the motive may have been to provide demonstration vehicles at short notice. The first example, D101, was exhibited as a chassis at the 1929 Show, without radiator, in the same manner as C102, and the engine, JW103, is understood not to have had pistons at that stage. In April 1930, it received a DV radiator as used on most B-types, and was reassembled on a 15ft 7in wheelbase frame, this latter to enable it to receive the body, dating from 1926, from B101. It is understood to have been demonstrated to Glasgow Corporation in this

The initial D-type prototypes retained the DV radiator as fitted to most of the B-types. Seen here is the original D103, soon after being fitted with the Northern Counties 24-seat coach body which had been that concern's exhibit at the Commercial Motor Show in November 1929 when mounted on a B-type chassis, B561, which had been supplied to that firm for the purpose – that complete vehicle had been returned to BTCC on 30th June 1930. The additional louvres in the bonnet, and even the cowl immediately behind it, may have been provided to increase cooling for the six-cylinder engine. The vehicle remained only briefly in this form, receiving a standard GW four-cylinder engine and being renumbered B778 on 11th July 1930, then being transferred to the operating department on the 24th of that month, registered HY 4. Meanwhile B561 received a Bristol bus body, as HY 1961, and a new D103 with Bristol coach body became HY 1952, both of these in April 1931.

Almost twins. These two views seem at first glance to be of virtually identical chassis. The upper one shows one of the late B-types, almost certainly B789, of which a three-quarter view is shown at the end of the previous chapter. The lower one shows D140, and although the general appearance is very similar, the slightly longer bonnet accommodating the D-type's six-cylinder engine causes the rear dash to be set two or three inches behind the rear edge of the front mudguard, whereas that of the B-type is in line with it. In addition practically the whole side panel of the D's bonnet is covered by louvres to give extra cooling.

form. This vehicle was converted to four-cylinder with a GW engine, and thus becoming to B-type specification, was renumbered B777 on 11th July 1930, going into service registered HY 1969. A new D101 was then built and fitted with a new Bristol 31-seat two-door bus body, completed in October 1930 and run as a demonstrator until added to the BTCC operating fleet in May 1931, this being registered HY 747, remaining in service until 1948.

The chassis for D102 was delivered to the tram depot for bodying in April 1930 where a double-entrance 31-seat body was completed in May, when it became a demonstrator, registered HY 20, and then joining the operating fleet in May 1932. D103 had as complex a story as D101, having two identities, the first very brief when it received the Northern Counties coach body as shown on the opposite

page, that chassis then being converted to four-cylinder and being renumbered B778 in July 1930. The original D101, 102 and 103 all had DV radiators, but the longer JV type with slim surround was fitted to the replacement D101 with new Bristol bus body completed in October 1930 and registered HY 747; the replacement D103 of April 1931 with Bristol coach body, registered HY 1952, plus D104, built new as another demonstrator with Bristol bus body in October 1930 and registered HY 1284, and all subsequent examples.

The JW engine design was also being revised quite extensively, it being thought that the 6.179-litre version may have been fitted to the first few D-type prototypes only – the chassis records of D101 and D102 give the engine type as X-JW, suggesting 'experimental'. The bore and

The only production D-type to have non-Bristol bodywork was D135, bodied by Eaton (H. E. Taylor & Son) as an exhibit on that firm's stand at the 1931 Commercial Motor Show. It was described as a 32-seat coach, although perhaps a more appropriate name might be the word 'saloon' once widely favoured for a rather superior bus body. It was subsequently repurchased by BTCC and added to the fleet. Although it remained unique, somewhat similar frontal styling, eliminating the peak up to then normal over the windscreen, was adopted for various later bodies on Bristol chassis.

stroke were increased to $4\frac{1}{8}$th by $5\frac{1}{2}$in, raising the swept volume to 7.258 litres – in this form, the power output was quoted at 115.5bhp at 2,600rpm. Effectively, this was a new engine, even though still designated JW and of similar side-valve six-cylinder form to the original – it is described more fully in Chapter 8.

Production of the model ran to 50 examples, generally covered by Sanction 22/1 and Series 18, save for the prototypes. Most entered service in 1931-32, mainly with BTCC and all but one having Bristol bus or coach bodywork. The exception was D135, sold to H. E. Taylor & Son, of Cringleford, Norwich, which traded as Eaton Coachwork, as a basis for its 1931 Show exhibit, though sold back to BTCC and added to the fleet in July 1932. There was also D136, with Bristol front-entrance bus body, which was taken into BTCC's own stock, although not until December 1932.

The D-type, like the B, faded from production as a consequence of new length regulations permitting the use of longer single-deckers than could be accommodated on its chassis.

The E-type trolleybus

The third new type was a six-wheel trolleybus, type E, another type of vehicle attracting growing interest among quite a number of municipalities. This was a line of business in which BTCC's experience of electric traction was clearly of value, and one which was being seen as a likely means of replacement for tramways. It seems that a possible expansion of business of this type was largely in mind and indeed the golden age for the trolleybus in Britain was just about to start, though in the event the E type got no further than the C type, neither progressing into production models.

The first chassis, E101, was built for display at the 1929 Commercial Motor Show. Chassis records show the entry for the wheelbase having been altered from 19ft 0in to 17ft 0in, in the same manner as applied to C102, though whether the chassis itself was altered or began as 17ft 0in is not clear. The axle units, of the same types as on the C-type motor bus, had serial numbers 103, following on from those in the petrol chassis. The motor, mounted near the front of the chassis, was a BTH 80hp, type 508. Westinghouse air-pressure brakes were provided, the compressor being driven by a Metrovick motor.

The chassis was sent to the works of Charles H. Roe Ltd in Leeds in April 1930 for bodying, where it received a double-deck body seating 32 on the top deck and 28 downstairs. Development of the vehicle had been encouraged by Doncaster Corporation, which standardised very largely on Roe bodywork. In addition Charles H. Roe himself was very knowledgeable on trolleybus work. He had worked for the pioneer firm Railless and, incidentally, had spent some time in his early career working in Bristol for a Railless director, Mr Munroe of Munroe, Brecknell and Willis, makers of trolley gear – one wonders whether the quite frequent appearance of the Roe name as bodybuilder on early Bristol buses may have any connection with this.

In August of that year, E101 was sent as a demonstrator to Doncaster, already running a fleet of six-wheel 60-seat trolleybuses bodied by Roe to the same style, mainly on Karrier chassis – the adoption of the 'spectacle' frame for Bristol six-wheelers in general may have been influenced by this. It was registered locally as DT 2620, weighed while on test at 8tons 8cwt 3qr and was purchased by Doncaster, becoming No.31 in that fleet, in April 1932.

Meanwhile a second trolleybus chassis, E102, was built, using the axles from C101, dismantled to provide parts for the purpose, though the wheelbase is recorded in this case as 17ft 0in from the beginning, implying the use of new sidemembers. In this case a Bull motor was used and, being bulkier than the BTH unit, had to be mounted

This photograph of Bristol's first trolleybus chassis, E101, shows what at first sight appears to be a tramway-style hand controller – some early trolleybuses were so equipped, despite the obvious difficulties of steering, which on such a vehicle would have been very much a two-handed job. However, chassis records show that this vehicle did have a foot controller, probably housed in the box alongside the steering column, and it may be that the hand control was used merely for reversing.

The second Bristol trolleybus, E102, used the axles from C101; this view shows the chassis in Brislington depot yard. The bulkier Bull motor is evident, with a smaller but still quite substantial motor driving the compressor and mounted on a platform to the left of the driver. The registration number HW 7092 rather crudely painted on the rear of the frame was that of the towing vehicle doubtless about to haul it to Dartford, a Bristol 4-ton model, chassis number 1823, which had begun as a 1927 Show exhibit and added to the BTCC fleet as a lorry in 1930.

slightly higher, though this would have caused no problem with saloon floor level as it was mounted sufficiently far forward to be within the cab. The bulky tram-style controller had vanished but the Westinghouse brake compressor and its substantial Metrovick motor was mounted on a platform which would also fit within the full-width cab. In this case the chassis was sent to J. C. Beadle, of Dartford, Kent, for

bodying, being towed back to Bristol in January 1931.

Some test running was done within the confines of Brislington tram depot using modified tramway overhead and the vehicle was registered HY 2391, but in March 1931 it was sent to Pontypridd UDC, already running a small trolleybus fleet, and was purchased by that undertaking in April 1932, becoming No. 9.

Trolleybus E102 was bodied by Beadle to a traditional style, rather more angular than usual for that bodybuilder; the rows of small louvres in the panel just above the lower deck window suggest that the general appearance might have been specified by Bristol. It was completed by December 1930, when it was weighed in Dartford at 7tons 17cwt 1qr, though photographs taken on its return to Bristol suggest it might not have had the trolley poles fitted at that stage. It is seen here outside Pontypridd UDC depot during the 1939-45 war – note the Bristol-bodied buses to the left.

7 The railway connection as a route to the Tilling group

The four main-line railway companies, after a brief period around 1928-30 when their direct operation of buses had expanded, were following a policy of acquiring interests in existing bus-operating companies in their respective areas. The Great Western Railway, acting under the powers of the Great Western (Road Transport) Act 1928, included BTCC among the companies in which it would have wished to acquire an interest but was inhibited by the fact that it had no statutory powers to operate tramways or taxi-cabs, or to manufacture motor vehicles. It was thus not in a position to pursue the taking up of a 50% share of the company, it being in mind that this would be a joint venture with the London, Midland & Scottish Railway, which also operated into Bristol.

However, the GWR Board was approached by the executors of the late Sir George White offering his shares, which gave over 50% of the voting capital. It was decided that these shares would be purchased as a simple commercial venture, the GWR's status being simply that of a shareholder, with no representation on the Board. This offer was accepted and the purchase agreed in 1929.

That this was seen as a temporary situation is indicated by agreement with the LMS that the question of any proportionate share of a railway holding in BTCC that railway might take be left in abeyance. The GWR shareholding was reduced to 50% from 1st May 1930, still without representation on the Board.

When BTCC became linked to the Tilling group as the result of an agreement reached in December 1931, Bristol was an almost completely unfamiliar vehicle make to the other operating companies with which it henceforth became associated. Here a Southern National Leyland Titan with Strachans body is seen at Ilfracombe. It was one of the last of the TD1 type, dating from early 1932.

Then events took an unexpected turn. It was agreed on 24th December 1931 that this interest would be transferred to the Western National Omnibus Co Ltd, also associated with the GWR since its formation in January 1929. Western National was a subsidiary of the National Omnibus & Transport Co Ltd, and WNOC was one of the parts into which the former direct operation of buses by NOTC had been split after amalgamation with local railway bus operations in different areas, in this case in the south-west of England and with headquarters in Exeter. A controlling interest in NOTC had been acquired by Thomas Tilling Ltd in February 1931, and thus BTCC became an associate company of Tilling.

This very unusual device, in which BTCC became a subsidiary of WNOC, a smaller concern, was not completed until March 1932. It overcame the railway's problems of direct association with some of BTCC's activities. The Chairman of BTCC continued to be Mr W. G. Verdon Smith, who had taken over after the death of Mr Samuel White on 29th November 1928, and thus the general character of the company and its policy did not greatly alter.

At first there was no direct indication on the manufacturing side of the effects of the new association with Tilling. The venture into six-wheelers and trolleybuses having found insufficient customer interest, the development of new models followed more orthodox lines, and the new possibilities of supplying vehicles to associated companies must have been obvious from the start.

The break of the Tilling link to Tilling-Stevens Motors Ltd was marked by a change of the latter's title to T. S. Motors Ltd in August 1930, the company's products subsequently becoming known as TSM for a time. In practical terms, several operating companies within the Tilling or TBAT groups continued to purchase the TSM concern's products for two or three further years, notably the Express B10 single-decker and derivatives thereof. The parent company, Thomas Tilling Ltd, switched to AEC Regent double-deckers for its direct operations in London and Brighton from 1930. Some Tilling-managed companies purchased Dennis buses, notably the Lancet single-decker, for some years in the early 'thirties and many had already standardised on the Leyland Titan TD1 for routes where double-deck buses were needed, some also using the equivalent Tiger single-decker, particularly for coach duties. How Bristol could play a larger part in providing bus chassis for associated companies took some years to evolve.

Bristol's first G-type chassis, G101, was completed by 5th May 1931, when its weight was found to be 4tons 5cwt. The second chassis, G102, was sent to Roe for bodying as seen here, being completed and weighed at 6tons 13cwt 2qr (a little on the high side for that date) on 28th October 1931. The JV radiator gave an up-to-date appearance though the piano-front bodies built by different builders on all three of these initial vehicles were of rather conservative style, G101 being bodied by Bristol and G103 by Brush – this one, registered HY 3628, was broadly to Roe's standard pattern as adopted the previous year. This photograph dated May 1932 shows the vehicle in Doncaster livery though without the coat-of-arms or lettering – it was purchased by that undertaking in December of that year.

8   A new range – G, H and J – and new customers

In the autumn of 1931, a new two-axle double-decker, the six-cylinder G type (with 16ft wheelbase), and two new single-deckers, the four-cylinder H and six-cylinder J (with 17ft 6in wheelbase), were announced, taking advantage of new maximum lengths applicable to two-axle buses of 26ft for double-deckers and 27ft 6in for single-deckers. There was no Bristol production model F. As indicated in previous chapters, the older B four-cylinder and D six-cylinder single-deckers with 16ft wheelbase continued in production for another year or two, largely for the company's own fleet.

In general chassis design, the G, H and J, having many resemblances to the D and the B in final form, were broadly in line with most other maker's chassis of the period, with petrol engines, the ES sliding-mesh four-speed gearbox,

underslung worm-drive rear axle and vacuum-servo brakes. There had been major changes in bus design over the previous few years but the new Bristol models looked up to date as well as having many practical merits. They differed from the C-type six-wheeler in continuing with the separate mounting of the gearbox which had been abandoned by Leyland in its Titan and Tiger range at the end of 1927 and was beginning to fall out of favour more generally, though ease of clutch lining replacement was a virtue the older layout offered.

The Bristol chassis height was also not quite as low as most makes of the period and while this was not a problem for single-deckers, it did mean that the G tended to be slightly taller than other makes, a matter that was to cause difficulties in certain cases. The new H and J models were,

Ready to roll out of the Brislington workshops is the chassis of G104. Alongside, to the left, another G-type chassis can be seen upside down on trestles for attachment of the springs before being turned over for assembly to continue – Bristol did not use an assembly line, and fitters worked from the benches in the background – note the padlocked drawers for their personal sets of tools. The JW side-valve six-cylinder petrol engine was of lower height than the overhead-valve and, especially, overhead-camshaft engines favoured by other bus makers, an effect emphasised by the tall JV radiator. Like several other early G-type chassis, this one was not bodied until some time after higher-numbered chassis, eventually emerging with a Bristol body as a 1933 Show exhibit. This view shows the original dynamo position on the side of the engine – later Bristol adopted a location under the floor for this item.

in effect, extended versions of the previous models, and the whole range now had the new deeper style of radiator, type JV, with slim surround, first introduced on the D.

The G and J, as introduced, and also now the D, as in production by about July 1931, had an engine capacity of 7.26 litres, with $4\frac{1}{8}$in bore and $5\frac{1}{2}$in stroke (both these figures having been increased from the 4in by 5in dimensions of the engine as introduced for the D), still of side-valve layout and designated JW. It was quoted as developing 115.5bhp at 2,600rpm, this latter being quite a high maximum-output speed for a commercial vehicle engine of this size and character – from all accounts it was a refined and lively engine.

Contemporary descriptions refer to it having 'a one-piece Whatmough-Hewitt cylinder head', and the performance figure suggests that this was notably efficient. The engine had seven main bearings and pressure lubrication with an external oil cooler, and the relatively tall radiator was said to eliminate the need for a water pump. Later examples of the G and J, to similar specification but dating from after 1935, were designated G.JW and J.JW as a means of distinguishing the six-cylinder petrol version when various alternative engines were also being offered in the same chassis.

The H had a basically similar four-cylinder side-valve engine to that of the B, with $4\frac{1}{2}$in bore and $5\frac{3}{4}$in stroke, but improved in detail design and designated LW. It first went into production in 1933 and that designation was

In Britain, side-valve engines were apt to be regarded as less glamorous than the overhead-valve type, but a well-designed unit could be surprisingly efficient, and in the United States was chosen for some very high-quality cars, most notably the Packard. The emphasis on torque rather than maximum horse-power was well-suited to bus work, not that the JW seen here was inferior in this respect, its output of 115.5bhp from 7.26 litres being rather more than Leyland claimed from its 7.67-litre overhead-camshaft engine. This is an example of one of the later units, as built from 1933, without dynamo and with an improved type of ribbed oil-cooler beneath the front of the crankcase – early engines had something more akin to a miniature radiator, vulnerable to damage from stones.

A good deal of effort was put into demonstrating the G-type to potential buyers, but with very limited success at first. Perhaps the most ambitious effort was that of G114, fitted with a Cowieson body to Glasgow Corporation specification as fitted to existing Leyland, AEC and Vulcan buses, complete with the remarkable offside-front upper-deck emergency exit, and painted in that undertaking's orange, green and cream livery. Registered HY 6605 in August 1932, it was sent for trial by that undertaking but no order ensued and in fact Glasgow took delivery of no buses from 1932 until 1935, when orders went to Leyland and the locally-based Albion concern for oil-engined models. It returned to Bristol and was added to the operational fleet in May 1934. It remained in service until 1957, having been rebodied twice and receiving a Gardner 5LW engine in 1946. Latterly it looked like a post-war bus, having received a PV2 radiator.

Somewhat nearer home, two G-types received Beadle bodywork for demonstration to the Eastern National and Southern National companies, by then 'related' companies to BTCC, though less directly so than Western National. Eastern National received G116 seen here, registered as HY 6896 in September 1932. It returned to BTCC and was added to the operational fleet a year later. It had a somewhat similar history to the Glasgow demonstrator, being re-engined and rebodied twice.

doubtless chosen simply as the next available in the engine series (KW, curiously enough, had been allocated for the trolleybus 'engine', presumably being used as Bristol's designation for the motor). There was a certain irony in that another engine already in existence at that date and destined to be fitted to very large numbers of Bristol buses also had 'LW' as its basic designation, this being the Gardner, but clearly this possibility and the chance of confusion had not influenced the Bristol engineers' choice.

Sanction 24 covered 28 G-type chassis originally numbered G101-128, though only those up to G121 entered service in that form. Sanction 25 included 26 J-types, J101-126. Sanction 26, evidently issued slightly later, covered 100 H-type and 48 J-type, though here again, the actual outcome was more complex.

The G and J were sold in very small numbers at first, some being nominally added to the BTCC fleet but used as demonstrators. Competition from other manufacturers was intense, aggravated by the depression which made many operators limit their purchases. It appears that, at first, Bristol built more of these chassis than could be sold

The first batch of J-types was supplied to Rotherham Corporation, J102, seen here, being numerically the first of seven with Roe centre-entrance 32-seat bodywork delivered in 1932. With the modest weight of typical single-deck bodywork of those days, they would have been lively buses. It had evidently returned to Bristol, probably for rectification of some defect, and hardly looked its best on a wet day and having collected the odd dent.

immediately and held a number in stock for a time, some being modified before bodying.

In BTCC's own operational fleet, there were no double-deck buses until 1933, which was very unusual for a large operator serving an area based on a major city in Britain. However, Greyhound Motors Ltd had operated double-deckers since the mid-'twenties and took G103, with Brush body, in December 1931; G101, with Bristol body, and G119, with Beadle body, followed in June 1932, though the first two of these were also used as demonstrators. Doncaster received and then purchased G102, with Roe body. The first 'outside' order for a batch of G-types came from Norwich Electric Tramways Co, which took delivery of G110-3/5/8/20-1, with Weymann bodywork, in 1933, though this concern became a subsidiary of the Eastern Counties Omnibus Co Ltd in December of that year.

G114, 116 and 117 all licensed in the summer or autumn of 1932, were further demonstrators, G114 being intended to appeal to Glasgow Corporation and having that undertaking's standard type of 51-seat body, built by Cowieson, though it was unsuccessful in attracting an order, joining the BTCC operational fleet in 1933. G116 and 117 had Beadle 52-seat bodywork, demonstrating to Eastern National and Southern National respectively, and were also added to BTCC's fleet in 1933. All the foregoing G-type buses had bodywork of conventional full-height layout with rear entrance and enclosed stairs. The remainder of the initial G sanction, G122-128, were all converted with various types of oil (diesel) engine before entering service, as described later.

The first J-type, J101, though licensed to BTCC in July 1932 and having a rear-entrance Bristol body, was used as

Greyhound Motors Ltd, a BTCC subsidiary since 1928, was an obvious user for the J-type, and J111, registered HY 9378, seen here was one of six with Bristol 26-seat coach bodywork placed in service in May 1933. They were taken into BTCC's own stock when Greyhound was absorbed in January 1936 and this vehicle received a second-hand bus body in 1941, a Gardner 5LW engine in 1946 and then a new body to post-war Tilling bus style, believed to be by Longwell Green, in 1947, also acquiring a PV2 radiator – it remained in service until 1957.

The first significant 'outside' customer for the G-type was the Norwich Electric Tramways Co, which placed eight with Weymann 56-seat bodywork in service during 1933, No.47 (VG 5545) seen here being G121. The standard Weymann composite body seemed to suit this chassis quite well. The Norwich company, with 44 trams, ten Leyland Titan, eight Bristol B and two AEC Regent buses as well as the new G-types, passed into the control of the Eastern Counties Omnibus Co Ltd in December of that year, being retitled the Norwich Omnibus Co as tram replacement was in hand; it was absorbed into ECOC in 1948. The Bristol G buses received Gardner 5LW engines in 1937-8, running until 1952-3, though two then became open-toppers.

a demonstrator to Southern National Omnibus Co Ltd, the sister company to Western National, but with Southern Railway shareholding. The first operator to receive a batch of J-types was Rotherham Corporation, receiving J102-3/5-9 with Roe 32-seat centre-entrance bodywork in 1932. A. & R. Graham of Kirkintilloch received J104, with Martin coach body, in May 1932. Deliveries in 1933, all having Bristol bodywork included J110-1/23-6 for Greyhound, with 26-seat coach bodies, J112-22 all being buses and going to BTCC, mostly with 34-seat two-door bodies though J122 was of 36-seat rear-entrance layout and a demonstrator at first.

Further instances of chassis diverted from their original classification were J127 and J128, rebuilt as H101 and H102, the first two of the four-cylinder version of the 17ft 6in wheelbase single-deck model. Of these, H101, bodied as a demonstrator, was destined to move on again, becoming

JO5G.1, as described later, while H102 was sent as a demonstrator to the Western National fleet from February 1932 for two years.

It was the four-cylinder H-type that in 1933-34 established the pattern, at first on quite a small scale, of Bristol as supplier to companies under Tilling influence, almost the whole production output being divided between the Western National Omnibus Co Ltd, with 63 vehicles, and United Automobile Services Ltd, with 35. BTCC added two further vehicles (H162-3) to its own fleet. The chassis numbers ran up to H207, but H201-204 were renumbered on conversion to other types or, in the case of H202, not built, United receiving the final three chassis H205-7 as part of its total.

The Western National concern was by then technically BTCC's parent company, so its choice as recipient for Bristol chassis was logical. It is significant that, in the

Appropriately, Western National Omnibus Co, as BTCC's nominal parent company, was one of the first two companies under Tilling control to purchase Bristol chassis in quantity. The model chosen was the H-type, the four-cylinder equivalent to the J. The first two, H101 and 102, had been converted from J chassis (J127-8), and thus the first WNOC batch, H103-122, were the first built from new. The vehicle shown was H158, WNOC's No. 135 (FJ 8965), with Brush 32-seat bodywork, part of a series which followed on from that first order and shared the same registration series. As often the case with petrol Bristol chassis of this era, Gardner 5LW engines were fitted in later years, in this case in 1942, when a Bristol body replaced the original.

United Automobile Services Ltd was the other main user of the H model, and these vehicles established the link of Bristol chassis with bodywork built in the Eastern Counties coachbuilding works at Lowestoft (later set up as a separate concern, Eastern Coach Works) for companies under Tilling control. The vehicle shown, United LH132 (HN 9032) on chassis H124, was one of the initial 20 such vehicles, delivered to the operator in May-June 1933 – the well-appointed bodywork seated 36. Note that the 'all-louvre' bonnet side had become standard for all models.

By that date, United's headquarters had moved to Darlington, the East Anglian section of the fleet, and the coachworks, having passed to Eastern Counties. These vehicles were numbered in a series which followed on from the 130 Bristol B buses of 1929, though with LH prefix instead of L. From 1935 they were renumbered BH1 upwards, though from around 1938 most were fitted with Gardner 5LW engines, the fleet numbers then being prefixed BHO – as such, they became almost indistinguishable from the JO5G models described in the next chapter.

same 1933-34 period, the standard single-decker for the Southern National Omnibus Co Ltd, the sister company sharing the same headquarters in Exeter but with Southern Railway shareholding and hence not so directly linked to Bristol, was the TSM B39A7 model.

The H-type buses for United were particularly significant in carrying this pattern a stage further, gradually to become almost universal for Tilling fleets, of combining Bristol chassis with bodies built at the Lowestoft coachworks which was to hold a position of parallel importance to that of Bristol as chassis supplier. In 1931, the Lowestoft works had been transferred, together with United's East Anglian services, to the Eastern Counties Omnibus Co Ltd and most of its output was already being supplied to associated companies. In one sense they could be regarded as a repeat order following on from the 130 B-types bodied there by United in 1929 for its own use, and no doubt satisfaction with the operation of those vehicles had its influence, but United had no connection to Tilling when that B-type order had been placed.

The early H-type buses for Western National were bodied by Bristol or Brush, but the last 24 were also by Eastern Counties and this gradually became usual on Bristol chassis for most companies under Tilling influence, though BTCC continued to build almost all its own body requirements and those for closely-associated fleets.

Western National's final delivery of H-type buses also had Eastern Counties bodywork, seating 32 but not unlike that on the United vehicles in general concept though, as was often the case in those days, differing in many details, not least the oval rear window. The vehicle shown, on chassis H194, was the last of WNOC's examples of this type, delivered in 1934, though the fleet number, 139, and registration number OD 7824, were at the beginning of the batch of which delivery had begun in 1933.

9   Bristol's first diesel buses and a final petrol surprise

Not untypically during that period, Bristol was decidedly conservative in pursuing the idea of using the diesel engine as an alternative to the hitherto universal petrol engine for its bus chassis. In those days such units were almost always called oil engines in Britain, and experimental installations by other makers or operators had been made public from 1929, some chassis manufacturers having production models on offer by the end of 1930.

Some of these early ventures were far from trouble-free, but by 1933 regular production of oil-engined bus chassis was well established by AEC, Crossley and Leyland, while L. Gardner & Sons Ltd, of Patricroft, Manchester was becoming recognised as the leading British maker of engines sold on a proprietary basis for installation in commercial vehicles. Gardner had begun its activities in this field by offering a slightly-modified marine unit but its new LW range of road transport engines introduced in the autumn of 1931 in four-, five- or six-cylinder form was to prove highly successful, though it took a little time for their merits to be fully recognised.

Whilst BTCC may have been cautious, sound judgement was shown in the choice of oil engine for the first Bristol chassis so powered, for display at the Commercial Motor Show held from the 2nd to the 11th November 1933. This was the Gardner 5LW five-cylinder unit, with 4¼in bore and 6in stroke, giving a 7.0-litre capacity and developing 85bhp – although several other types were to be the subject of experiment, the 5LW was to become the standard engine in Bristol bus chassis from about two years later.

The chassis that had begun as J127, briefly becoming H101, was re-engined again with a Gardner 5LW unit and became JO5G.1 (the chassis numbering system was altering, the more complex designations, in this case signifying '*J* chassis with *O*il 5-cylinder *G*ardner engine' resulting in the use of series beginning at 1). An official photograph dated October 1933 shows it fitted with a Bristol 36-seat body and at that stage with the chassis plate H101 still carried on the frame. This may indicate that it was still petrol at that date or, perhaps more likely (since the decision to display such a vehicle, particularly with a proprietary engine, implies that there was confidence in its

A bus which set Bristol on a course that was to dominate its future output was this one, the first to be fitted with a Gardner oil engine. It was still displaying the chassis plate H101 in this view dated October 1933, but by 2nd November it was on the Bristol stand at the Commercial Motor Show at Olympia in London with a Gardner 5LW engine, causing it to become JO5G.1. The chassis had begun as J127, underlining the close relationship between the various Bristol single-deckers of that period, rationalised when it was decided to designate them all as variations of the J-type. The 36-seat body, dating from earlier in 1933, was by Bristol and of type AM3/36, one of a series of metal-framed body designs produced during the early 1930s. The bus was registered as AHW 393, and although Bristol had tended to use chassis numbers as fleet numbers within its own fleet, this one became JOG1 when it joined the operational fleet in 1934 until it was renumbered 2000 in the new system which began in 1937. It received a new Bristol body to wartime utility specification in 1943 and remained in service until 1954.

merits), that the decision on how to designate oil-engined models had not then been taken. It was used as a demonstrator until joining BTCC's fleet in 1934.

However, in terms of BTCC's engine development at Brislington, the design staff were still preoccupied with petrol engines of contrasting types. Two, announced in the autumn of 1933, types MW and NW, were further developments of the four-cylinder type, the MW being an unusually large unit of this form, with a bore of 4¾in reminiscent of the A-type but an even longer 6¼in stroke. The capacity of 7.26 litres was thus similar to that of the JW six-cylinder engine and the MW developed a healthy 105bhp. Only two were fitted in chassis, numbered J.MW.1 (supplied to Doncaster Corporation) in 1934, and J.MW.2, which was rebuilt from an unsold H-type chassis, H203, treated as an experimental vehicle.

Bristol produced a bewildering variety of side-valve four-cylinder petrol engines in the 1930s. This was the MW, one of a pair introduced in October 1933, and remarkable because of its size, the 7.26-litre swept volume making it possibly the largest four-cylinder engine offered in a British bus chassis during that period. It found little favour, only one J.MW bus so powered entering service, with Doncaster Corporation.

The NW was rather more successful, this being in what had been Bristol's tradition of engines of 4½in bore and 5¾in stroke that went back to the 4-ton model. It had dry cylinder liners unlike the wet type, in direct contact with the cooling water, found on the JW and MW. The fan was belt-driven. The J.NW chassis series using this engine ran to 100, though only 96 entered passenger service.

The Eastern Counties Omnibus Co Ltd was both operator and bodybuilder of ten of the J.NW buses, having taken over what had been United's East Anglian services and the coach factory, whose main doors are seen in the background, on its formation in 1931. These vehicles dating from 1935 had 36-seat bodywork of a general style almost identical to that on United's J.NW-type buses, classified BJ in that fleet's new numbering system. Later in the 1930s the two firms diverged in their preferred single-deck styles, even though built in the same Lowestoft works. Eastern Counties favoured the 'tin bible' destination display, so nicknamed because of its resemblance to a large book with sheet metal leaves, rather than the roller blind conventional by then – the 'Private' display showed when the 'bible' was removed. The Eastern Counties numbering system was also as inherited from United, 'L' continued to signify Bristol as it had since 1929, though LN was a new class created for these buses – LN1 (NG 9911) was based on chassis J.NW.73.

The final batch of J,NW buses to enter service consisted of twelve vehicles for Bristol's own fleet, fitted with Bristol 34-seat bodies with the two-door layout so characteristic of the company's buses. They entered service in 1936 and J.NW.86 briefly operated as N86 before becoming C628 in the 1937 renumbering. They received Gardner 5LW engines, in this case in 1938.

The NW engine could be regarded as the final development of the familiar 5.99-litre unit most widely known in GW form as used in the B-type, with further minor changes from the LW unit as used in the H model chassis. At this point the sanction system had become somewhat confused, because of the various changes of engine type before chassis were completed or delivered. The later vehicles in both Sanctions 24 (G-type) and 26 (H and J) had received a variety of oil and petrol engines. Sanction 27 covered 52 J-series chassis, including the first eight J.JW for Royal Blue plus five for BTCC, 26 of the J.NW (3-26 and 52-3) type and JO5G.3-15.

The J.NW chassis replaced the H, which it closely resembled, as the standard four-cylinder Bristol single-deck model for 1935, the chassis numbers beginning at J.NW.1 and running up to J.NW.100 when deliveries ceased in 1936 – United was the major user, with 50, most of the rest going to BTCC, though Eastern Counties took ten and the municipalities of Doncaster and West Hartlepool a couple each. Two chassis in this series, JNW.98 and 99,

were not built, and JNW.100 was converted with a later four-cylinder engine, type PW, as described later in this chapter. The author recalls the United J.NW buses as fairly typical four-cylinder petrol-engined buses of their period – the Eastern Counties 36-seat bodies they carried were quite well appointed, and when fully laden performance over the undulating terrain of the southern part of County Durham was hardly sparkling. The later J.NW chassis were distributed between Sanctions 29, 30 and 32, though the chassis which became J.PW.1 was included in Sanction 30.

More significantly in terms of later history, small numbers of oil-engined Bristol buses followed the initial example. Graham of Kirkintilloch took JO5G.2, with Bristol 32-seat coach body in May 1934, and Doncaster Corporation received the following three JO5G chassis, with that operator's usual Roe bodywork, later that year, Here again, the Sanction pattern became quite fragmented, JO5G.2 being in Sanction 26 while JO5G.3-15 were in Sanction 27.

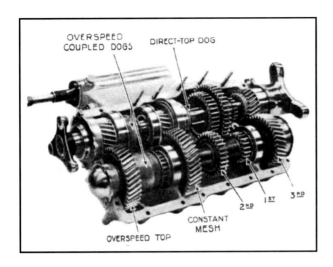

Bristol's introduction of a five-speed gearbox, type KS, in October 1933 was an important development, almost ideally suited to the Gardner engine because of its ability to exploit the latter's characteristics to maximum effect, allowing excellent economy and also quite a high road speed despite the limitations of the Gardner unit's tightly governed 1,700rpm maximum speed. The KS had a geared-up or 'overspeed' fifth gear – the word 'overdrive' came into general use a little later – while fourth was direct, and the illustration of the unit with the cover removed shows that it had constant-mesh helical gears for both third and fifth ratios, giving very quiet running, though this benefit was apt to be lost amid the general noise level from the 5LW engine. However, when used with the JW six-cylinder petrol engine, the effect must have been very refined.

The external view shows the dynamo drive from the gearbox also introduced with this unit – Bristol shared with London Transport the view that an underfloor position for the dynamo was beneficial as well as overcoming problems of space among engine auxiliaries. A four-speed gearbox with the dynamo drive feature was also introduced for the G-type chassis, this being type JS.

From October 1933 a five-speed overdrive gearbox was being offered as an option for the J-type, possibly the first such unit available on a bus chassis from by a major British maker, though the Gloucester Carriage & Wagon Co Ltd had introduced the idea on its Gloster-Gardner model, using the 6LW engine, of which the first example was placed in service by Red & White Services Ltd of Chepstow evidently a little earlier in 1933, an event of which BTCC was doubtless soon aware. The initial Bristol five-speed unit was type KS.

The resulting high fifth gear offered particular advantage when used with the Gardner engine, overcoming the problem of limited road speed due to the 1,700rpm governed engine speed – for many years, Gardner-engined Bristol single-deckers with overdrive and standard gearing would give a consistent 48mph at this engine speed, on level ground. More important to the operator, it improved the already good Gardner fuel economy, a matter of particular importance on the numerous rural routes served by many of the Tilling-controlled companies. Fuel consumption figures of 15 miles per gallon or better were to become quite normal for JO5G or the equivalent later L5G model, and even North Western Road Car Co returned an average of 13.9mpg for its vehicles of these types on mainly hilly terrain over a period of eight months in 1939.

It is of interest in view of later developments that early installations of Gardner engines in Bristol chassis used rubber engine mountings to reduce the degree of vibration experienced within the passenger saloon – they were reasonably effective when running at speed but, like some other early such designs, suffered from quite a pronounced 'shivering' effect at idling speed. This was because the natural frequency of the relatively stiff rubber mountings tended if anything to magnify the vibration transmitted at

very slow engine speeds, and this may have been the reason for adopting solid mounting by late 1936. Idling was indeed steadier but noise and vibration within the vehicle was significantly increased at speed, the effect being very noticeable with the 5LW engine by then standard and, overall, the passenger lost out quite markedly, especially on country routes with infrequent stops.

Further important development work on oil-engined Bristol buses concerned the G-type double-deck model. What were evidently stock chassis G122-128 from Sanction 24 were all used for experimental work of this kind in 1934-35. The most significant in relation to later history were GO5G.1 and 2, rebuilt from G123 and 124, using Gardner 5LW engines. They were bodied by Brush to a design using the side-gangway lowbridge layout – the first Bristol buses of this configuration, established by the Leyland Titan TD1 model which first appeared in 1927 and which had become the standard double-decker in numerous company fleets, including many under Tilling management. They were supplied in April 1934 to Keighley-West Yorkshire Services Ltd, an offshoot of the West Yorkshire Road Car Co Ltd which operated former municipal services in Keighley. They were also the first Bristol vehicles in the West Yorkshire or related fleets.

Two new Leyland Titan buses were also supplied to the Keighley-West Yorkshire fleet at the same time, based on the TD2 chassis which had superseded the TD1 from 1932, although generally it in turn had given way to the following TD3 from mid-1933. The obsolete Titan chassis may have been chosen because they also had Gardner 5LW engines, and are believed to have been the only Leyland buses of that era so fitted from new, though numerous TD1 and later Titan models had their petrol engines replaced by Gardner units in due course, especially in Tilling fleets.

For the 1933 Commercial Motor Show, the Bristol double-decker on display was this vehicle, based on chassis number G104, evidently held in stock from earlier construction but now fitted with the 48-seat Bristol body shown, type AM6/48. Even with the benefit of what was quite a stylish body, no 'outside' business resulted from its spell as a demonstration bus, probably because interest in oil-engined models was growing fast, especially among municipalities. It was added to BTCC's own fleet by May 1934, registered AHW 74, the chassis number being used as the stock number in the usual fashion, becoming C3006 in 1937. It received a 5LW engine in December 1938 and was rebuilt with PV2 radiator and new ECW body in 1949, the chassis being withdrawn in 1955.

Far more influencial were the first two GO5G models, with Gardner 5LW engines, supplied to a subsidiary of the West Yorkshire company in April 1934, which not only began a long spell of standardisation on Bristol buses within that concern and its offshoots but signalled widespread use of the GO5G and subsequent double-deck models thoughout companies under Tilling influence. They were also noteworthy in being the first Bristol buses to have lowbridge bodywork, also soon to become a combination produced in large numbers, though the use of bodywork by Brush, a concern more usually favoured by the BET group, was less common. Seen here is GO5G.2, registered YG 5734, which was Keighley-West Yorkshire K112 when new though soon renumbered K302, the series 301-399 being used by West Yorkshire entirely for Bristol double-deckers.

The West Yorkshire company and its satellite fleets switched to Bristol chassis with 5LW engines, both double- and single-deck, for its main fleet requirements from the following year and, indeed, from that time a similar pattern spread increasingly across the Tilling empire.

The 8.4-litre six-cylinder Gardner 6LW unit was chosen for two double-deckers based on chassis, originally numbered G126 and G127, supplied to municipal fleets based in the hilly valleys of south Wales in 1934, GO6G.1 going to Pontypridd and GO6G.2 to Aberdare, both having

Bristol 48-seat bodywork. A third chassis, originally G128, was at first fitted with a 5LW, briefly becoming GO5G.3, but was then altered to 6LW, becoming GO6G.3, bodied by Bristol to normal-height style like the previous two but seating 54 and retained by BTCC, initially as a demonstrator, from September 1934, going to the operational fleet in June 1935. Chassis G122 became GO5G.4, bodied by Bristol and supplied to Doncaster Corporation in 1934.

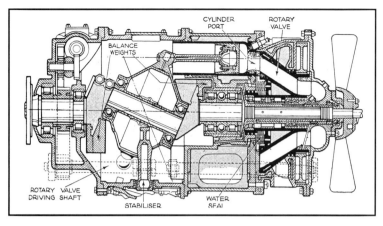

The Bristol axial or 'wobble-plate' engine was based on the work of C. B. Redrup, who operated as a free-lance inventor, but with the active participation of Major C. G. Nevatt, BTCC's Chief Mechanical Engineer and Works Manager, in regard to this project. The nine cylinders surrounded the crankshaft, with pistons moving parallel to it; the wobble-plate conveyed their movement to the special form of crankshaft. This version had a large fan on the front of the crankshft but it was mounted higher and beltdriven on the version installed in a test chassis. The single large rotary valve was geared to rotate at one-eighth of engine speed, uncovering ports allowing air in and exhaust out of each cylinder in the required sequence. This was simple in theory but very troublesome in practice.

The wobble-plate engine

While this work was going on, effort was also being directed in a quite different direction in a three-year programme beginning in 1933. Easily the boldest engine design ever to emerge from Brislington was the nine-cylinder wobble-plate engine designed by Mr C. B. Redrup, and developed under the supervision of BTCC's Works Manager, Major C. G. Nevatt, in this period. The basic idea was that the cylinders were arranged rather like the chambers in a revolver, turning the crankshaft at its centre-line via a rather complex mechanism which could be likened to a disc set at an angle which 'wobbled' and thus turned the crank.

It was more compact than a conventional engine and was claimed to be more efficient but the loadings on some parts seem likely to have been considerable. Providing adequate lubrication and careful balancing emerged as matters needing care in development. Five engines were made before the bus version, and one of these was a seven-cylinder unit fitted to a de Havilland Moth light aeroplane, replacing the original Cirrus in-line engine. It was test flown, seeming to be successful, but when stripped down afterwards proved to have identical cracks in all seven

conrods, this leading to the use of ball joints to connect the conrods to the wobble-plate. It was also decided that for the second nine-cylinder bus engine the conventional poppet valves were to be replaced by a single rotary plate revolving at one-eighth of crankshaft speed.

The prototype bus engine made by Bristol to the Redrup design was designated RR. It was of 7.2-litre capacity, and thus directly comparable with the JW six-cylinder unit in this respect though claimed to develop up to 150bhp at 3,000rpm – indeed 120bhp, a figure still a little above the JW's output, was available at a modest 2,000rpm. It fitted easily within the standard bonnet of the J-type chassis but extended only a little above frame level – in later years it was suggested that it would have made an almost ideal unit for underfloor installation. It also weighed 7cwt as compared to the 12cwt of a JW unit.

The second engine built was fitted in place of the MW engine in chassis J.MW.2 (which had begun life as H203) for road testing. In this form it was allocated the further new number J.AX.1, though there seems some doubt as to whether it was carried – a contemporary picture shows the chassis with a load of test weights and Mr Redrup seated in a passenger seat just behind the bonnet. The plan was that full power would not be used. It is understood that it

The first version of the bus engine, type RR1, installed in a chassis. This one had conventional poppet valves and is said to have worked quite satisfactorily. Auxiliaries such as the dynamo were mounted on top but could have been fitted elsewhere in a production version.

The axial engine test chassis J.AX.1, the former J.MW.2, carrying test weights and with the inventor, C. B. Redrup, seated behind the bonnet. For trial purposes, the engine was fitted in the same place as the conventional vertical unit, and the open bonnet reveals a largely empty space, demonstrating the potential for underfloor mounting. It was fitted with a KS five-speed gearbox.

was demonstrated to the press in this form in May 1935.

A 32-seat front-entrance body was fitted at BBW and the vehicle was registered BHW 429, a number implying a date in the summer of 1935. It then started on what was intended to be a rigorous test programme by the chassis works, though the speed was supposed to be limited so as to avoid any need to alter gear ratios from the standard model. Testing of J.AX.1, once again as a chassis, resumed in September 1936 and reports indicate that when running well, the results were quite encouraging. With test weights fuel consumption varied from 4 to 6.2 mpg, which was comparable to a conventional petrol engine and quite lively-seeming performance on hills was possible. However, providing enough oil to prevent seizure of the big rotary valve caused the emission of clouds of dense blue smoke, especially on accelerating after descending a hill. Sealing of the valve faces was also apt to be unsatisfactory and created cold starting problems – there are reports of this taking 10 minutes and of a tow being needed – on one occasion even when hot, the starter had to be operated for 30 seconds.

It is said that finally the clutch disintegrated in an alarming and disastrous way, which suggests that for whatever reason power or speed had been allowed to go well above normal limits – it does sound rather as if someone may have simply yielded to the temptation "Let's see what she'll do!". No more was heard of the idea in terms of a bus power unit. The chassis was dismantled and the engine, evidently not significantly damaged by the incident, together with the other unit of the type, sold to the Royal Navy – it seemed that the principle of the engine was of interest as a means of driving a torpedo, and the shape and dimensions suited this.

A Redrup engine had been displayed on the Bristol stand at the 1935 Commercial Motor Show and also at that Show was the final conventional Bristol petrol engine, yet another development of the series of 4¾in by 5½in bore and stroke four-cylinder 5.99-litre units that began with the 4-ton model, this one designated type PW.

The PW engine was offered with a choice of bore sizes of 4½in or 4¾in, both with 5¾in stroke, the larger version giving a capacity of 6.7 litres.

Contemporary descriptions referred to it as having an oil cooler and timing-gear drive to the fan, features common to the JW six-cylinder unit. Just one chassis was so powered, J.PW.1 being produced by converting chassis J.NW.100; fitted with a 34-seat two-door Bristol body, it entered service with BTCC in 1936. By that date, however, the petrol engine had come to the end of the road for use in Bristol chassis and the diesel, in particular the Gardner 5LW, had taken over as the standard power unit. This may also account for the decision not to proceed further with the Redrup engine, although in theory there was no reason why a diesel version could not have been built – indeed, a few years later C. B. Redrup designed a two-stroke diesel for aircraft work.

But in 1935 the down-to-earth world of bus development was working on different lines. In more ways than one, a new era was beginning for Bristol vehicles, and after being among the last major manufacturers of full-sized buses in Britain to take up the diesel engine, the Motor Constructional Works was among the first to abandon petrol-engined vehicles for all new production.

The identity of this Show chassis is not certain though the chassis-mounted dynamo and what appears to be a KS gearbox imply that it is either J.MW.2, as exhibited at the 1933 Show (and before conversion to J.AX.1), or J.PW.1, as exhibited in 1935. The four-cylinder petrol engine has the magneto mounted high at the front near-side as on the PW unit seen above but other minor details differ, but that type of variation seems to have been not unknown among Bristol petrol engines, especially on prototypes.

10   A new broom....

The year 1935 was to prove a turning point for the Bristol Tramways & Carriage Co Ltd. In October, John F. Heaton, Chairman and Managing Director of Thomas Tilling Ltd, took over as Chairman of the Bristol company from W. G. Verdon Smith, and the other members of the White and Smith families resigned, including the General Manager, Colonel S. E. Smith. Mr Verdon Smith thereupon concentrated his business activities as Chairman of the Bristol Aeroplane Co Ltd, which position he continued to hold, as did other members of the Smith and White families, but the link between the tramway and aeroplane companies had gone. The new BTCC Board included George Cardwell of Tilling (who had been appointed in 1932 as a consequence of the Western National takeover), F. C. Coventry of the Great Western Railway, A. R. Hoare, who was also Chairman of the Isle of Thanet Electric Supply Co Ltd, which ran buses in Kent, and of Norwich Omnibus Co Ltd (the latter being renamed in 1935 from Norwich Electric Tramways Co and having come under the control of Eastern Counties Omnibus Co Ltd in December 1933), and S. E. Baker, who was evidently a local man.

There were some changes in the financial structure around this time – *Motor Transport Year Book 1935-6* records that the authorised capital was increased in 1935 to £2 million, by creating 500,000 additional Ordinary shares, all of which were issued in January 1936. Western National is also recorded as having its capital reorganised in December 1935.

The new General Manager was Major Frank J. Chapple, who had been General Manager of the West Yorkshire Road Car Co Ltd since January 1928 and, between them, Heaton and Chapple were to transform BTCC, both as operators and manufacturers. Chapple had concluded that the motor bus had a more promising future than the tram since a much earlier period in his career when he had been General Manager of Yorkshire (Woollen District) Electric Tramways Ltd from July 1921, advocating the reinstatement of bus operation which had begun before the 1914-18 war but had been allowed to decline during it. He eventually persuaded the British Electric Traction Co Ltd, which was Y(WD)'s parent company, and re-established a bus fleet which grew rapidly.

The West Yorkshire company, however, was one of the brightest stars in the Tilling firmament and Heaton took a special interest in it, having been associated with its predecessor, Harrogate Road Car Co Ltd, before joining Tilling's in London in 1915. Chapple was appointed General Manager of West Yorkshire Road Car Co Ltd on 1st January 1928, the change from BET to Tilling being quite uncommon and possibly reflecting a hope for greater scope in pursuing his belief in the future of the motor bus. Since Heaton, who was by then Joint Manager of Thomas Tilling Ltd, was WYRCC Chairman, the two men had built up eight years experience of working together before continuing the relationship in regard to Bristol Tramways & Carriage. During that time, West Yorkshire had formed special relationships with the municipalities of Keighley,

The old order at Bristol was changing, but at the Commercial Motor Show held in November 1935, it went out in style, at least so far as this exhibit was concerned. It was the last J.JW chassis to be built, J.JW.226, on which was mounted a 26-seat Bristol coach body of stylish design, somewhat similar to a 32-seat body on JO5G.2 for Graham of Kirkintilloch built earlier in the year though in this case with a sloping rear profile in the manner of that on contemporary private cars. Registered CHW 567, it was added to BTCC's coach fleet in 1936 as J226, renumbered 762 the following year. It was refurbished in 1949, receiving a 5LW engine and PV2 radiator and having the windscreen deepened slightly to suit, remaining in service until 1958.

A clear indication of the future path for the Bristol company as a whole as well as the Tilling influence on associated bus operating company fleets was given by events in Yorkshire. The new General Manager for BTCC was Major F. J. Chapple, who previously held the same post with the West Yorkshire Road Car Co Ltd. Even before he took up his new appointment, a fleet of Bristol buses with Gardner 5LW engines was entering service there, some of them on services run under joint operating agreements with municipalities of a type very similar to that soon to be found in Bristol. This scene opposite York railway station shows a GO5G with Eastern Counties highbridge body working on a service administered by the York-West Yorkshire Joint Committee. These buses were owned by the West Yorkshire company (unlike the generally similar situation in Keighley, where a jointly-owned company owned the buses) but had 'York-West Yorkshire' fleetnames. It was one of a batch which entered service in October-November 1935. The vehicle was GO5G.46, numbered Y327 and registered AWW 32, the photograph being taken in June 1937, by which date West Yorkshire had adopted a short-lived livery variation, as evident on the similar bus on the opposite side of the street and the 1929 Leyland Titan TD1 following – West Yorkshire was a typical example of Bristol buses being adopted where Leylands had been used previously.

in 1932, and York, in 1934, where relatively small municipal transport systems had been replaced by buses operated under joint names but managed by the company and following West Yorkshire standard practice in choice of vehicle types and livery, so there were strong clues as to the direction of future policy in Bristol. In addition, it will be recalled that Keighley-West Yorkshire had been the operator of the first two Bristol GO5G buses since April 1934, so Major Chapple was already familiar with the implications of recent developments at the Motor Constructional Works.

At the Commercial Motor Show held in November 1935, the Bristol stand gave no clue to what was afoot – doubtless the change of direction from the new Board was too recent to alter the exhibits. There was a J.JW, which turned out to be the last of that type to be built, this being J.JW.226, with stylish Bristol coach body seating only 26 which entered service with BTCC the following year registered CHW 567; a G.JW chassis, G.JW.139 (subsequently re-engined, becoming GO5G.115 before joining the BTCC fleet); a J chassis with the PW four-

cylinder petrol engine already mentioned and, as a separate exhibit, the Redrup wobble-plate petrol engine. There was only an oil-engined G-type with metal-framed body for Exeter Corporation as a pointer to future trends. All in all, it was a rather strange display when all other major manufacturers of heavy-duty bus chassis were putting strong emphasis on oil-engined vehicles.

Admittedly, most of the major operators in England were still tending to favour petrol engines for coach duty, and indeed the J.JW had found a niche in this regard. The 73 chassis with 'plain' J-prefix chassis numbers built since the model was introduced in late 1931 and continuing up to 1935 had been supplied to BTCC's own fleet or Greyhound, apart from the seven early examples for Rotherham and one for Graham already mentioned, plus four chassis fitted with other engines and hence renumbered out of the series.

The final 53, mostly entering service in 1935, were numbered as J.JW.174-226 though essentially the same model as the 'plain' J. They included 28 for the newly reconstituted Royal Blue fleet – this followed the take-over

When the Royal Blue coach services were acquired by Tilling, their operation was transferred to the Western National and Southern National companies, retaining the former fleetname. Clearly a good impression was sought, and a new fleet of coaches based on Bristol J.JW chassis was placed in service in 1935. The style of bodywork of the first batch of eight bodied by Eastern Counties established a pattern not only for this operation but formed the basis for several subsequent coach and bus designs from the Lowestoft factory, mostly on Bristol chassis. Here Western National 167 (BTA 457) on chassis J.JW.178 is seen when new – the 20 further examples bodied by Beadle or Weymann were very similar in appearance. They were converted to diesel in later years, half of the 28 receiving Gardner 5LW engines but the others were fitted with AEC 7.7-litre engines – bus bodies by Beadle replaced the originals in 1947-9.

at the beginning of 1935 by Tilling of the Bournemouth-based Elliott Bros business, which had used the Royal Blue fleetname, and the transfer of its long-distance activities to the Western and Southern National companies, each of which owned its share of the vehicles. A well-appointed and up-to-date 32-seat rear-entrance coach design was introduced for these vehicles, the first batch built by Eastern Counties though others to similar style came from Beadle and Weymann. Another ten similar vehicles were supplied to Eastern Counties Omnibus Co Ltd, bodied by that concern to much the same pattern as the Royal Blue examples. Some, at least, of these coaches had the five-speed gearbox, the combination with the smooth six-cylinder petrol engine giving exceptional refinement. The remaining J.JW models were bodied by BBW and placed in service by BTCC, including nine 34-seat two-door buses and six coaches, including the final example of this type, mentioned above.

Production of oil-engined Bristol chassis had, in fact, begun to develop quite strongly during 1935, even if a

contrary impression might have been given by the Bristol stand at the Show. The petrol G-type had followed a similar pattern to the J, but in smaller numbers – there had been 28 'plain' G-types laid down, of which only eight had gone to an 'outside' customer, the Norwich Electric Tramways batch of 1933, the remainder all going to BTCC or Greyhound, apart from the seven fitted with other engines and renumbered as such before bodying. The ten further chassis numbered G.JW.129-138, which were the last of the type to enter service with petrol engines, all received BBW 52-seat bodies and went to BTCC's own fleet in 1935-6. One further chassis was that at the 1935 Show already mentioned, becoming GO5G.115 for BTCC.

One of several cases of different makes of oil engine being tried in Bristol chassis was the Beardmore six-cylinder unit, which had the same 4¼in bore and 6in stroke as favoured by Gardner and thus was of 8.4-litre capacity. One was fitted into the chassis laid down as G125, becoming GO6B.1. It was fitted with a Weymann 48-seat metal-framed body and became a demonstrator to

Only 31 G-type models entered service in petrol-engined form over a production period of about five years. The last were ten added to BTCC's own fleet in 1935-6, having 52-seat Bristol bodywork of similar style to the 1933 Show exhibit. Seen here is G.JW.131, one of the four dating from 1935, which was fleet number G131 initially, registered BHY 694. It became 3014 in the 1937 renumbering, being a 'country' bus and hence not having the C prefix. It received a Gardner 5LW engine in April 1939, the others being converted at various dates between 1938 and 1947. It is seen here in Marlbrough during wartime, the original livery modified by the application of grey paint in place of white in a manner quite common in the south of England where vehicles were liable to be a daylight target for German aircraft.

Although the Gardner 5LW was rapidly becoming the standard engine for Bristol buses, there were some interesting exceptions. Beardmore also attempted an entry into the proprietary oil engine market, and its six-cylinder engine was used in this vehicle. The chassis had begun as G125 but became GO6B.1 in this form. It was fitted with a metal-framed Weymann 48-seat body, painted in Exeter Corporation livery and registered AHW 593 in 1934 for a period of demonstration to that undertaking. The Beardmore engine seems not to have been regarded as a success, and a 5LW was fitted, the chassis becoming GO5G.29 and the vehicle was exhibited at the 1935 Commercial Motor Show, being the only exhibit which could be regarded as a pointer to future trends. It was sold to Exeter together with four new GO5G models. This photograph is thought to show it with the Beardmore engine, the projecting starting-handle shaft not being a Gardner feature.

Only five Bristol double-deck chassis were fitted with the six-cylinder Gardner 6LW engine in the 1930s, yet in postwar years, and especially the 1950s, this was to become a much favoured power unit for Bristol double-deckers. Red & White Services Ltd took delivery of GO6G.4, seen when new in March 1935 – the 48-seat body was by Northern Counties. The 6LW was about 6in longer than the 5LW and thus, unlike that unit, would not fit into the standard Bristol bonnet as fitted to other models of the time. In this case, a separate extension was fitted at the rear end, the effect being emphasised by it being painted in body colours rather than being the typical engine-turned aluminium of the standard item. The vehicle came back to BTCC when the Stroud services were transferred in 1950 but it was scrapped later that year.

Exeter Corporation from August 1934. It was to be the only Bristol so powered, not surviving long in this form – in later years, the letter B was used to signify Bristol's own oil engine. Beardmore did not have much success as a bus engine maker, though Glasgow, supporting local industry, had 30 in Albion Venturer double-deckers in 1936.

Output of the GO5G had been much livelier, and it was more than a little significant that West Yorkshire and its satellite Keighley and York fleets had followed the initial two vehicles with orders for thirteen delivered early in 1935 and then 27 later in the year. Another sign of group interest was the batch of ten for United, delivered in January-February, all these being bodied by Eastern Counties. With four 1935 examples (GO5G.31-34) with BBW bodies (plus the former Beardmore-engined demonstrator GO6B.1, converted with a 5LW and becoming GO5G.29) purchased by Exeter Corporation, and the early vehicles already mentioned, the total delivered by the end of the year was 60, outnumbering the petrol G despite its much more recent introduction.

Only two more examples of the GO6G were produced in 1935-6 to add to the three dating from 1934. Red & White Services Ltd, in those days the main company in the Red & White group and quite unconnected with BTCC or Tilling, took GO6G.4, with Northern Counties body, quite a rare choice for Bristol chassis of any period, in 1935, and Pontypridd added GO6G.5 to the first vehicle of this type already in the fleet, again with Bristol body, this being the last of the type and the only one delivered in 1936. No further Gardner 6LW engines were fitted to Bristol double-deckers until after the war years, though by the mid-'fifties this unit was to be the most-favoured engine.

The JO5G also made quite strong progress in 1935, and again it was West Yorkshire that placed the largest early orders, taking 20 delivered in April-May which were noteworthy as the first Bristol single-deckers to receive Eastern Counties bodywork to this operator's distinctive pattern, having clear hints of BET practice and perhaps reflecting Major Chapple's earlier spell within that organisation, when managing the Yorkshire (Woollen

The West Yorkshire company had sprung from being a non-user of Bristol buses of any kind prior to the Spring of 1934 to having by the end of 1935 what was at that point easily the largest fleet of Bristol models with the Gardner 5LW engine to be found anywhere, most if not all ordered before Major Chapple left his post there as General Manager to move to BTCC. At that point, Bristol's own fleet had yet to move beyond the point of running more than isolated prototype or ex-demonstrator oil-engined buses. In addition to the 40 GO5G buses by then in use by WY or its offshoots, there was an initial batch of 20 of the JO5G model that had been delivered in April-May 1935, including JO5G.26 seen here in Bradford with destination board set for Baildon in September 1936. There were also a further 20 in course of delivery from the bodybuilders and 20 more were supplied in June-July 1936. All these JO5G buses had Eastern Counties bodywork to the style shown, with distinct touches of BET-group ideas that reflected Major Chapple's period with Yorkshire (Woollen District).

District) fleet. Rotherham Corporation took eight with Cravens centre-entrance bodywork early in 1935 and United took five, these having that operator's version of the Eastern Counties body and outwardly identical to the 50 on J.NW chassis also placed in service by the same operator that year. With a second coach for Graham to join its 1934 example and a demonstrator, the chassis numbers of examples delivered had reached JO5G.41 by the end of 1935, with a further 20 for West Yorkshire in course of delivery though not placed in service until 1936.

During this period the sanction system began to recover a little more of its normal orderly nature. Sanction 28 covered 25 G series double-deckers (GO5G.5-28 and GO6G.4); Sanction 29 and 30 were each for 50 J-series models (29 comprising J.NW.27-51 and JO5G.16-40, while 30 covered J.JW.187-216, J.NW.54-72 and JO5G.41). Sanction 31 was for 45 G-series (GO5G.30-61, G.JW.129-39 and GO5G.62-63).

Bristol continued its experiments with alternative oil engines, and JO4D.1 appeared in the BTCC fleet during 1935, with a Dennis four-cylinder engine in a Sanction 26 chassis originally J164 and having a Bristol coach body. Although not adopted on a large-scale, further examples of this type were made in 1937.

However, the emphasis was clearly on the GO5G and JO5G. Increasingly, Tilling policy, both for its own direct subsidiaries and for TBAT companies in which Tilling was the dominant influence, was to standardise on Bristol chassis, generally with Gardner engines, mostly in conjunction with bodywork built at Lowestoft by Eastern Counties.

The demand for such vehicles was thus becoming greater than the Motor Construction Works had experienced previously, a particular need being room for the larger-scale chassis assembly. Accordingly, it was decided that premises at Chatsworth Road, about a mile nearer the city centre from Brislington, be taken and used primarily for assembly. They were almost ideally suited to the purpose,

The Chatsworth Road premises allowed much greater room for assembly work, with space to allow chassis to be built in three rows in a workshop having other bays devoted to building up sub-assemblies, hence allowing construction to be carried out in a more orderly way and on a larger scale. Even so, assembly was still carried out in the traditional manner, the chassis frames being mounted on trestles initially, and Bristol chassis could truly be called 'craftsmen-built'.

having been used to assemble BAT chassis, this marque (the initials signifying 'British Associated Transport') being the name used by Harris & Hasell (1929) Ltd for models made up from proprietary components. This venture had begun in 1929, the firm's predecessor having been an agent for various American makes of commercial vehicle, including Reo. The most popular BAT model was the Cruiser which had a Continental six-cylinder petrol engine of 59bhp and was offered as a light goods vehicle or bus in the 20-seat class, but sales were insufficient to allow manufacture to continue after 1931. Latterly the firm operated from a Pentonville Road, London, address.

The premises' availability was a stroke of good fortune, for its internal layout was well suited to the intended purpose and played a major part in the ability to increase output as needed to meet the need arising from Tilling's new policy of placing greater emphasis on Bristol chassis for new buses throughout the group.

There was also plenty of activity in other directions. The negotiations with Bristol Corporation soon took on a more positive tone, clearly influenced by Heaton's mastery of such activities but also by a more realistic attitude on the part of the Corporation as the result of a change of chairmanship of its Tramways Option Committee. For over 20 years the Corporation had acted on the assumption that the option to buy the tramways was something that could be traded with the company for cash. Mr Heaton made it clear that this was not so, challenging the Corporation to exercise its option if it believed it had any value of this kind.

Serious consideration of the possibilities soon got under way and by July 1936 the Tramways Option Committee presented a report to the council which put forward two alternative schemes to replace the trams by buses as quickly as possible. Under scheme 1, the trams would have been replaced by company buses, the Corporation simply abandoning its option to purchase, with a modest cash settlement to cover the cost of removing the tram tracks. In scheme 2, the tram system was to be purchased by the Corporation and a scheme put in hand for them to be replaced by a 'City' bus system worked as a joint undertaking, in which Corporation and company would each have a half share in the net revenue. The undertaking would be managed by the company, working in conjunction with a joint committee composed of equal numbers of Corporation and company members. In effect, the tram system was to be purchased by the Corporation as a means of gaining a half interest in the City buses, the cost being spread over 30 years.

The resemblance of this to the scheme used in York is obvious and doubtless both Mr Heaton and Major Chapple consulted their files in the process of drawing up the scheme. The Corporation decided in favour of scheme 2. There was brief delay while the possibility of using trolleybuses rather than motor buses was considered – no doubt not one favoured by Heaton or Chapple though one could imagine that there would be electric traction enthusiasts among the council and perhaps in the tramway department of BTCC. However, and as might have been anticipated, the bus won the day and the Bristol Transport Act, 1937, provided the basis to go ahead.

There had also been activity by BTCC in other directions, some further widening the potential demand for Bristol vehicles. Greyhound Motors (1929) Ltd was absorbed on 1st January 1936, and Bence Motor Services Ltd followed on 29th June 1936. These were simply

This scene in Bristol's Tramways Centre at about the time in 1937 when agreement was reached on the replacement of the trams was much the same as it had been in Edwardian times, save for the discreet appearance in the background of a few of BTCC's much more recent buses. Cars 56 and 167 both belonged to the main fleet of trams ordered from Milnes, based on Peckham trucks and delivered in 1900-01. They had been sub-contracted to various concerns, but were all built to Milnes's standard pattern and had not been modified, as was common on those trams of similar age which survived in other British cities. Even so, they were smartly maintained and the blue and ivory livery, with red cornerposts, was striking.

'tidying up' acquisitions, Greyhound surviving as a trading name for express services, but more significant was the agreement with Gloucester Corporation, under which BTCC took over the municipal fleet of 38 buses, of Thornycroft and Vulcan make, in April 1936, local services being provided after that date under another joint committee arrangement. At Bath, the tramway was another instance of company ownership, and in 1936 BTCC gained control of both Bath Electric Tramways Co Ltd and its subsidiary, Bath Tramways Motor Co Ltd when most of the shareholders agreed to a purchase offer. The trams were withdrawn in 1939 but Bath Tramways Motor Co Ltd continued to be operated as a subsidiary, the 91 vehicles being given fleet numbers within BTCC's new fleet numbering system of January 1937. They were largely of AEC make, including 42 Regal models dating from 1929-34, though the Commer Invader had been favoured as a 20-seater in 1930-31, and the three Bristol A-type single-deckers survived, running until 1938-9.

AEC had not figured in the earlier BTCC experiments with oil engines, but two J-type chassis were fitted with AEC engines, being numbered JO6A.1 and 2, and joined the BTCC fleet with Bristol bus bodywork early in 1936. The second of these had been numbered JO5G.206 originally, though evidently renumbered before bodying. The engines were of 7.7-litre nominal capacity and at that date seem almost certain to have been of the A171 type with Ricardo Comet indirect injection system.

However, it is known from an AEC experimental department report dated 7th July 1936 that one of the earliest production direct-injection A173 engines, fitted in an AEC single-decker, had been sent to Bristol by its makers to take part in comparative tests with a Bristol single-decker with Gardner 5LW engine, presumably a JO5G, the latter with five-speed gearbox, though it was agreed that the overdrive would not be used during the tests. The results were reported as quite encouraging from

AEC's point of view, and it is clear that both makers must have shown some mutual interest, perhaps with the wider use of AEC engines in Bristol chassis in mind.

Another brief experiment was with a Leyland six-cylinder oil engine, presumably an 8.6-litre of the type then standard in the Titan TD4, fitted in a chassis numbered GO6L.1 which joined the BTCC fleet with Bristol 54-seat body in 1936 but was quite rapidly fitted with a Gardner 5LW engine in August 1936, though retaining its original chassis number. The early conversion to what had become standard suggests a firm decision not to proceed with any further Leyland-engined chassis, despite this unit's widespread success elsewhere, and noteworthy in view of what might be regarded as continuing 'dalliance' with AEC and Dennis.

The BTCC was beginning to add significant numbers of GO5G models to its fleet, 33 being placed in service during 1936, about a third of total deliveries of the model that year. Most of the remainder went to Tilling-controlled fleets, notable newcomers as Bristol customers being Brighton Hove & District, Eastern National and Westcliff, the latter two both taking batches with Brush lowbridge bodywork. However, a noteworthy new user was Maidstone & District Motor Services Ltd, a company with a Tilling minority shareholding but under BET control, which took twelve for its own fleet plus four for its subsidiary, Chatham & District, all having Weymann bodywork.

Progress within BTCC's fleet with the corresponding single-deck JO5G was still slow, only one being added to the earlier three in the fleet, in contrast to the total of about 277 which entered service, mainly in Tilling-controlled fleets, that year.

A new variant was the JO6G, of which eight were supplied in 1936 to Black & White Motorways Ltd. This concern, specialising in long-distance express services and using the word 'motorway' to convey this in a manner not uncommon in those days 30 years before the word took

Output of GO5G buses was expanding, about 90 reaching operators' fleets in 1936. Bodywork was quite varied and the newly set-up Eastern Coach Works Ltd delivered eight examples of this quite stylish design to what had just become its parent company, Eastern Counties, in July 1936. They, and two more GO5G with bodies transferred from Dennis Lance chassis on which they had operated briefly, were used on Norwich city services, the bodies being of the highbridge type seating 56. Seen here is LG12 (AVF 354), on chassis GO5G.95, which remained in service, latterly with fleet number modified to HLG12, until 1954. Eastern Counties, like a number of company operators, had its own radiator nameplate badge which replaced the maker's badge, in this case altering the appearance significantly.

The JO6G chassis, with Gardner 6LW engine, was chosen by only one operator, Black & White Motorways Ltd but the initial eight vehicles supplied in 1936 set a pattern for later deliveries to this fleet. The body order went to H. V. Burlingham Ltd of Blackpool, which concern produced a style partly based on its own standard designs of the time but with various features to the operator's specification. A distinctive overall appearance resulted, adopted as the basis for subsequent pre-war deliveries from other bodybuilders to this operator on JO6G and L6G chassis. The vehicle shown was the final coach of that batch, No.85 (BAD 638) on chassis JO6G.8 – it is seen in 1950, looking much as when new apart from the quick-action radiator filler cap often fitted in post-war years. It is seen at Bristol's 'coach station', in fact no more than a roadside departure point.

on a different meaning, was based at Cheltenham, a pioneer interchange centre for services linking London and the Midlands with the West and South of England and South Wales. Black & White, originally independent, had been taken over jointly by BTCC, Midland Red and City of Oxford Motor Services in 1930, but until 1936, no significant additions had been made to its fleet of full-sized coaches, largely Gilford 168OT and Leyland Tiger.

The Bristol JO6G, with Gardner 6LW engine, inherently smoother as well as more powerful than the 5LW, and the overdrive gearbox, made a very effective long-striding coach chassis, and Black & White was to standardise on the type and its successor the L6G until well into the post-war years. Although the numbers were modest, the entire output of JO6G being sixteen chassis, delivered to Black & White in batches of eight in 1936 and 1937, they were widely admired, the Burlingham bodywork of the 1936 batch setting the standard for later pre-war deliveries although actually bodied elsewhere.

Overall output, aided by the extra capacity resulting

from the activation of Chatsworth Road works, was rising quite sharply, reaching 409 chassis of all types in 1936, the emphasis now swinging strongly to Gardner 5LW-engined chassis, which represented about 90% of the total. The last deliveries of petrol-engined models were made that year, including the last six G.JW, ten J.JW and thirteen J.NW, all supplied to BTCC's own fleet.

BTCC's interest in AEC chassis and engines around 1936-8 may well have been related at least in part to the Bath take-over. It has been suggested that an outstanding order accounted for the 20 AEC Regal single-deckers placed in service in the Bath Tramways Motor Co fleet under BTCC ownership in 1937. They had bodywork by Eastern Coach Works Ltd, that firm having been formed in 1936 as a subsidiary of Eastern Counties to continue the bodybuilding business at Lowestoft originally founded by United. These were the first products of that works to join the Bristol company's own operational empire, apart from one double-deck body built at Lowestoft on a Bristol GO5G demonstrator just as the factory changed hands,

A distinct AEC influence on BTCC was evident from 1936 to 1938, feeding into chassis production to a minor degree. In terms of vehicle purchases, this may have been influenced by the gaining of control of Bath Tramways Motor Co Ltd, though comparative tests of AEC engines had begun before then and were evidently part of the general study of the subject in hand at the time. This AEC Regal with 7.7-litre engine was one of three with Weymann coach bodywork added to the Bath fleet in 1938 – numbered 2249 and registered in Bath as GL 5833. It is seen in wartime in that city with destination blind set for Salisbury – note the temporary panelling replacing the window glass, probably a consequence of blast damage from an air raid.

Eastern Counties had three engine variants among Bristol J-type models added to its fleet in 1937. Eighteen were coaches with Eastern Coach Works bodywork to this curved-waistrail sloping-pillar style conforming to the fashion of the period and of these, twelve were JO5G models with 30-seat bodywork, including LJ22 (BVF 102) on chassis JO5G.488, seen here and delivered in July. Six, outwardly almost identical, were JO6A models with 28-seat bodies and AEC engines, believed to be of the A173 7.7-litre direct-injection type. In later years, some of the JO5G received AEC engines and some of the JO6A were fitted with 5LW units.

For bus work, Eastern Counties chose the JO4D, with Dennis four-cylinder oil engine, for its delivery of six vehicles in September 1937. They had Eastern Coach Works bodywork to what by they had become Eastern Counties bus style – the basic structure had much in common with the 1935 Royal Blue coach. It has been suggested that these engines were of the Lanova type as used on some Dennis vehicles of about 1935 but by 1936 Dennis had adopted its O4 design of direct-injection engine and this seems much more likely by this date. Even so, Gardner engines were fitted to this batch between 1943 and 1947 – they were withdrawn in 1953-4.

this being added to BTCC's own fleet in 1937 after it had spent its first year with the Chatham & District fleet.

Also entering service in the spring of 1937 were twelve more JO6A chassis. Six received Duple coach bodywork and were added to BTCC's own fleet. These had 7.7-litre AEC engines, and it seems probable that these would have been A173 units of the early direct-injection type, as built. Later in that year AEC introduced a modified version of this engine with toroidal cavity pistons, this soon becoming AEC's standard engine for much of its range, many earlier engines, including most A171 units, being subsequently converted. The remaining six JO6A delivered later in the year were for the Eastern Counties fleet, receiving ECW coach bodywork.

Further AEC Regal vehicles were purchased by BTCC in 1938, this time all coaches and including eighteen with Duple bodies for the company's own fleet and three for Bath with Weymann bodies, but otherwise the purchase of AEC vehicles or engines ceased until the special circumstances of wartime re-opened the connection.

The final year for the G and J series chassis was 1937, work then being in hand on new designs, but output

remained strong, particularly of the JO5G, of which 245 were delivered during the year. Most of these went to Tilling-controlled companies, United taking 60, West Yorkshire and subsidiary 48, Eastern National 34 and United Counties 25, plus 32 for BTCC itself. There were also eight for Rotherham Corporation and three for Doncaster, plus a pair for Western Welsh, a BET-controlled company and mainly a Leyland user. There were also the JO4D, JO6A and JO6G examples supplied that year and already mentioned, which brought the total of J-types supplied in 1937 to 277. The JO5G thus became by far the most numerous Bristol model of its era, with a total of 562 produced, not including JO5G.206 which became JO6A.2 before delivery.

The double-deck output was not so strong, amounting to 60, all GO5G, BTCC's share being 22, the remainder being supplied in small groups to nine operators. At that stage, many of the Tilling-controlled fleets operated relatively few double-deckers, tending to serve more rural areas than those under BET control (the latter often having tramway origins). The total number of GO5G models delivered was 211 and, as with the JO5G, almost all were built in the 1935-37 period.

In the short period from 1935 to 1937, Bristol's position in terms of the buses to be seen in different parts of the country and their operators had altered greatly, mainly as a result of its new status as main supplier to a growing number of the fleets under Tilling influence.

United took a total of 125 JO5G models in that period, and with the 50 J.NW of 1935 and 35 H models of 1933-34 as well as the 130 B-types of 1929, approaching half its single-deck fleet was of Bristol make. Bearing in mind that the remainder included various older classes largely of ADC make, many buses and coaches from acquired businesses as well as more modern coaches, where Leyland continued to be the preferred make, the extent to which Bristol had become the 'front-line' bus make was remarkable. Seen here in Scarborough in 1937 are BJO44 (BHN 239) on chassis JO5G.175, one of 60 JO5G delivered in 1936, and BH20 (HN 9050) on chassis H146, one of the 20 H models dating from 1933, both having Eastern Counties 36-seat rear-entrance bodywork of United's evolving standard styles of the period.

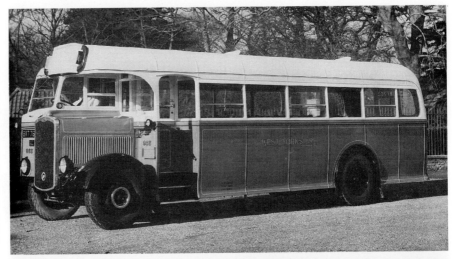

A little further south, West Yorkshire had graduated to this style of body for its 1937 batch of JO5G buses, totalling 48 including three for Keighley-West Yorkshire, delivered between January and May. ECW continued to build to individual company designs, though the desired overall design was generally achieved by using alternative basic framing modified by alternative styles of front-end or other details. This photograph of No.965 (BWT 760) on chassis JO5G.356 was used in an ECW advertisement ten years later praising their performance, in some cases having run over half a million miles by then; 20 of them were seventeen or eighteen years old when withdrawn.

North Western Road Car Co Ltd, based at Stockport, on the other side of the Pennines but, like West Yorkshire, a former Tilling-Stevens and then Dennis Lancet user, switched to the JO5G as its standard single-decker with an initial 24 in May 1936, including No.729 (JA 5529) on chassis JO5G.210 seen here, followed by 50 later in the year – thereafter, Bristol was the standard make for this fleet until ended in the post-war era, following a switch of control to the BET group. Here ECW built to a quite different style – the half-canopy cab then had quite a following for single-deck buses in the north west of England generally.

Bristol's sales to its small band of faithful municipal customers continued, but accounted for only 30 of the total of 562 of the JO5G model, and supplied to only two operators, illustrating how the core of its business had shifted to the group company sector. Rotherham Corporation took batches of eight in 1935, 1936 and 1937, all with Cravens 32-seat centre-entrance bodywork. The vehicle shown was one of the 1937 vehicles, No.136 (AET 636) on chassis JO5G.480 – note how the traditional Rotherham centre-entrance bus had developed by then, with 'streamline' paint style and half-canopy cab, this latter feature having spread to a few municipalities.

Doncaster Corporation preferred a more conservative style, its three 1937 JO5G buses having what was basically the standard Roe single-deck body of the time, most often built on Leyland Tiger TS7 or TS8 chassis and very similar to, though not quite the same as, the British Electrical Federation design used by several BET companies. It was adapted to the JO5G chassis with its higher driving position by setting the underside of the front canopy slightly above the cantrail level of the remainder of the body.

The United Counties Omnibus Co Ltd had a long tradition of using Leyland buses – its roots going back to a venture supported by Leyland management – and this continued for a few years after it came under Tiling control in 1931, but the JO5G was adopted as the standard single-decker from 1936, the initial eight being followed by batches of seven and then the final eighteen in 1937. Number 460 (VV 6258) on chassis JO5G.547 is representative of the last batch, having an ECW 35-seat body exhibiting another combination of features producing a distinctive 'company' style. It was rebodied by ECW to post-war style and remained in service until 1958.

This view of the chassis of GO5G.56, built in 1935, shows the form in which chassis were sent the bodybuilders at that stage, with no full-width panel to form the front bulkhead, as was normal practice for Leyland and AEC models. The Autovac fuel-lift device was mounted on a temporary support stencilled 'To be returned at once to Bristol', implying that bodybuilders were apt to forget to do so. The mounting of the dynamo, by then outside the nearside sidemember, can be seen – it was driven from the JS four-speed gearbox by a cross-shaft in an arrangement different from that introduced in 1933 on the KS five-speed unit. Also visible in this view is the rear mounting arrangement used for the engine on early GO5G and JO5G chassis, with widely-spaced thick rubber pads attached at each end of a rear engine crossmember passing just in front of the enclosed clutch unit. It was considered unsatisfactory and by 1937 a simple arrangement with the engine bolted to the frame was adopted, as explained in the text.

'Bus & Coach' ran a series of articles reviewing the design of various chassis in the 'thirties, and the GO5G was examined in the January 1937 issue. Considered by contemporary standards, it was an intriguing mixture of some ideas that had become quite old-fashioned with others aimed at up-to-date efficiency, but the firm discipline on the designers of operating experience was clear in many ways. The main features and layout were orthodox, with the engine and separate gearbox mounted so as to give a straight, slightly inclined, transmission line to the underslung worm-drive rear axle. The laden frame height was quoted as 1ft 10 7/8in and the price as £1,100, this latter rather less than most competitive models at the time, though discounting was so common as to make comparisons difficult.

The description makes a virtue of the 'comparatively recent' adoption of a rigid engine mounting after the rubber-cushioned design used on the early GO5G and JO5G, on the grounds that, at certain speeds 'unsteadying influences become so evident that firm anchorage is rendered imperative'. The engine was simply bolted to the banjo-shaped frame cross-member at its rear end and, at the front, a saddle bracket attached it to the tubular front crossmember. This very simple system was to remain standard on Bristol buses until 1948, and although the 'Bus & Coach' reviewer P. M. Sanders tactfully said in regard to vibration, 'I found little to complain of when travelling on the road', he was referring to a chassis with test load; the passengers in completed vehicles might well have differed. Ironically, the gearbox continued to be rubber-mounted, and such gear whine as there was, low-pitched in tone, was barely audible above the racket of a 5LW when working hard. Another refinement from the passengers' viewpoint was the ingenious spring bracket design which gave a progressive action by reducing the effective length of the leaf springs as loading increased which had been used on earlier models. This was a concept derived from ideas developed by BTCC in the 'twenties.

There were occasions when the GO5G was involved in problems related to overall height, but it was possible to produce a lowbridge body of what seems to have been about the accepted overall height for the type – indeed the chassis shown at the top of the page became West Yorkshire 337 (AWW 42), of the same batch as the unidentified bus shown below. The problem may have related to the amidships gearbox and when ECW used a version of its post-war standard lowbridge body for rebodying GO5G chassis, it was mounted slightly higher than on K-type chassis.

An instance of 'high' lowbridge' bodywork on GO5G chassis was that of six vehicles delivered to the United fleet in October 1936. They were given the fleet numbers BDO11-16 when new, 'D' in this fleet signifying double-deck lowbridge, and following on from ten earlier GO5G which had bodies very similar to that on the West Yorkshire bus shown on the previous page. They were of the normal sunken side-gangway layout but were about 6in or so taller than other lowbridge buses in the fleet and quite soon were given fleet numbers in a new series BOH1-6 until rebodied with post-war standard lowbridge bodies in 1949 when they reverted to the original numbers. This seems to indicate that the extra height justifying the fleet number change lay in the bodywork itself; the writer has a recollection that headroom on the upper deck was less restricted than the normal lowbridge standard. BOH6 (CHN 106) on chassis GO5G.160 is seen in Newcastle bound for Throckley in immediate post-war days.

The tall radiator meant that a fan was thought unnecessary, despite Gardner's usual caution in such matters. A feature a little reminiscent of London Transport practice was the removal of the dynamo to an under-floor location with its own shaft drive, though the GO5G version mounted it sideways, attached to the outside of the frame side-member where it was accessible through the body skirt panels. The drive was taken from a bevel-gear unit at the front of the gearbox through a small hole on the sidemember.

Generous brake lining areas were another characteristic, the front brake shoes being 6in wide and the rear ones 7½in wide, both exceptional dimensions, and although the shoes were fairly short because of the worm-drive adjuster provided for each shoe, the total effective area was 725sq in. The open construction of the brakes, so that lining condition could be readily seen when the vehicle was over

an inspection pit was another reflection of operator influence on the product. The brake system was of the so-called three-servo type, with a large vacuum slave cylinder mounted on each front stub axle, linked by vacuum pipe to the main Clayton-Dewandre servo, which operated the rear brakes via mechanical linkage. Bristol was not influenced by the trend to vacuum-hydraulic brake actuation as adopted on equivalent AEC, Daimler and Leyland models of that period. Significantly, there was a general trend back to triple-servo brakes in later years.

In the cab, the hand brake lever was still on the left, but layout was otherwise quite orthodox, there now being quite a large organ-pedal type of accelerator pedal to suit the rather heavy action caused by the Gardner governor. The steering column angle was more inclined, with the wheel set slightly higher, than on subsequent models. The steering gear is described as of worm and quadrant type.

The Southern Vectis Omnibus Co Ltd, operating on the Isle of Wight, was another Bristol 'conquest', albeit on a modest scale, after a period when Dennis chassis had been favoured. Number 700 (BDL 100) on chassis GO5G.189 had highbridge 56-seat bodywork by ECW, being one of a pair of buses delivered in March 1937. The body style, with deeply arched roof was showing a touch of Roe influence, arising from Bill Bramham's arrival at ECW from the Leeds firm. Two JO5G with ECW bodies were also supplied.

The last JO5G, numerically, was on chassis JO5G.563, seen here after completion as United Counties 476 (VV 6256) by ECW and ready for delivery on 14th September 1937. The body was a 31-seat coach variant of the standard UCOC body style of the time. The 41st sanction J-type chassis introduced some changes in design with revised front and rear axles, introducing 10-stud wheel fixing, a foretaste of the K and L design. The wheelnut guard rings hitherto fitted to G and J chassis when new (though quite rapidly discarded in almost all fleets) were no longer provided.

The GO5G chassis weight is given as 4tons 6cwt, which at that date was relatively heavy for a two-axle double-deck model, but it is not made clear as to whether this was a 'dry' weight or with fuel and water, and the fact that some seated 56 implies that weight was not a problem, for many buses of that time had to have seating capacity reduced because the gross weight limit was tight.

During the period between the latter part of 1935 and 1937, the sanction system settled down to a more regular pattern. Sanctions 32 and 33 were each for 50 J-type chassis, Sanction 32 covering J.NW.73-97, JO5G.42-55, J.JW.217-226 and JO6A.1, while Sanction 33 covered JO5G.56-104 and J.PW.1. Then Sanction 34 was for 50 vehicles, GO5G.64-113 and Sanction 35 and 36 covered 100 and 98 J-type chassis respectively, covering JO5G.105-205/7-294 between them though JO6G.1-8 and JO6A.2 were also included in Sanction 35.

Then there was a regular pattern of Sanctions covering 50 double-deck or 100 single-deck models from mid-1936. Hence Sanction 37 covered GO5G.114/7-147/9-64, GO6L.1 and GO6G.5; Sanction 38 included JO5G.295-394; Sanction 39 covered JO5G.395-486 and JO6G.9-16, while Sanction 40 was for GO5G.165-214, the last of that type to be built.

The final J sanction was No. 41, covering JO5G.487-563, JO6A.3-14 and JO4D.2-13. This not only covered the last J-series chassis but also brought the system of numbering chassis in series related to type rather than sanction that had been in force since early days to an end. These 41st sanction JO5G and related chassis introduced some changes in specification. There were new front axles, JE instead of GE as on previous J types, new rear axles, PM instead of GM or JM.

The last GO5G was supplied to BTCC's own fleet in the autumn of 1937. The intake of double-deckers had increased since 1936, often for the growing Bristol City Services fleet though this final batch of twelve were for country services and thus their fleet numbers 3070-81 had no 'C' prefix. The final vehicle, 3081 (EAE 598), GO5G.214, is seen here in post-war livery at Marlborough on the Swindon service. Like the rest of the batch, it was rebuilt with PV2 radiator and a new ECW body, in this case in June 1950, continuing in service until 1956, when the 1950 body moved to a later K-type chassis.

Two new models appeared in time for the Commercial Motor Show of November 1937, the first to be held at Earls Court. They replaced the G and J range and were initially offered with the Gardner 5LW engine as standard, the K5G being a double-decker and the L5G the corresponding single-decker – note that 'O', to signify oil-engined, was now dropped as superfluous, in contrast to the previous Show display, in 1935, when petrol engines had still been in the majority.

The general appearance of the new models was quite similar to that of the GO5G and JO5G they respectively replaced, with tall radiator of similar outline to the previous JV type, though the surround of the new KV unit was less slim, somehow helping to convey the rugged nature of the design as a whole. In fact, an extensive redesign had been carried out, covering most aspects of the new models' specification.

The management changes of 1935 inevitably had their effect on the Motor Construction Works, Major Chapple having his own ideas on bus design and, at Chairman level, John Heaton was keen to pursue his rather centralised ideas of bus group organisation, including quite extensive standardisation. In addition, there was a significant change in the management of the works itself.

Hitherto, there had been a Works Manager, Major C. G. Nevatt, M.I.Auto.E., having held that position since 1922, though his title was also sometimes quoted as Chief Mechanical Engineer. He had left his mark on the firm's products, and although many aspects of the B, G and J models which had formed the bulk of the output during that time could be regarded as conservatively orthodox, there had been occasional sparks of quite radical ideas. Not all of these were his own, as with the Redrup axial engine, but clearly he had been influential in following them up and persuading management of the value in pursuing them. The G & J were basically very sound chassis and with the Gardner 5LW engine, the Tilling-controlled operating companies had a source of reliable and economical vehicles, the latter aided by the five-speed gearbox found on most oil-engined J-types, itself a feature well ahead of general practice elsewhere.

Major Nevatt's retirement signalled the end of an era. He had been the second Works Manager, in succession to D. H. Duff, who had been appointed in 1913, though

Above and facing: A clear indication of a new, down-to-earth, policy was the Bristol stand at the Commercial Motor Show held in November 1937, the first to be housed in the then new Earls Court exhibition building in west London. Bristol's stand, No.45, was quite a modest one, at one side of the main hall, in a position leading to the displays of various trailer makers and smaller goods vehicle manufacturers. In place of the array of models that had been at the 1935 Show, there were just the two new K and L types, all of the two chassis and the two bodied vehicles on display having Gardner 5LW engines. Nearest the camera in the scene above was a K5G double-decker chassis, priced at £1,185, the example shown being 42.23, which later joined BTCC's fleet as C3094 (EHU 229). Alongside it, and seen more clearly on the opposite page, was an L5G chassis, possibly 43.3, complete with mudguards and dash panels. Behind, both the complete vehicles were bodied by ECW, reflecting the increasingly close association with that firm – this was the first time bodywork of that make was displayed on Bristol's stand. The single-decker was 43.2, the second L-type chassis built, for Western Welsh. The K5G double-decker, partly visible on the right, but more clearly seen on the opposite page, was 42.29, for the West Yorkshire fleet. Note the use of facsimile radiator outlines as a basis for the brief notes identifying each model.

briefly, in that first year at Brislington, there had been an Engineer in Charge, E. Serex.

In 1936, Arnold J. Romer, M.I.Mech.E., M.Inst.T., was appointed as General Manager (Works), a new title relating to the Motor Constructional Works as such. He had come from the Eastern Counties bodybuilding establishment at Lowestoft, where he was Works Manager, having held that post since about 1928, when the premises were in the hands of United Automobile Services Ltd, then an independent company – his career had begun with J. I. Thornycroft & Co Ltd, and there had been a spell as assistant engineer with Midland Red before the move to United. Although so long associated with bodybuilding, he had been trained as a mechanical engineer and was to

play quite an important role in the Bristol vehicles story.

The most obvious difference between the K and L chassis and their predecessors was the switch to unit construction of engine and gearbox, as by then well established as the majority choice for British bus chassis except where the dimensions of a Wilson-type epicyclic gearbox forced the retention of the mid-chassis position. The problem of clutch life was tackled by increasing the frictional area from the 227sq in of the G-type unit to 300sq in and the lining thickness from $^3/_8$in to ¾in, it being claimed that it shared in the general rule that the vehicle should give reliable service without any individual unit requiring major overhaul at less than 100,000 miles.

With this, the simplification of attaching the gearbox

It was appropriate in more ways than one that the complete double-decker on the Bristol stand at the 1937 Show was numerically the first of a batch for West Yorkshire Road Car Co Ltd, No.347 (BWY 979) on chassis 42.29. This picture taken by the bodybuilders shows another of the batch, No.351 (BWY 383) on chassis 42.33, which left ECW a couple of days earlier than the Show bus, on 26th October 1937. One of the aspects of the new regime was the degree of standardisation, not only of the K5G chassis but also the main features and appearance of the standard ECW lowbridge body which was to be supplied to group companies operating in most parts of England. The seating capacity in this case was 53 and the unladen weight 6tons 13cwt 3qr, about average for a double-decker of that period.

West Yorkshire was the company of which Major Chapple had been General Manager before he moved to Bristol in 1935, and the new K5G and L5G models, with the plans for their standardisation in Tilling-managed fleets, could be regarded as the fruit of the policies then adopted. This view conveys the character of the model quite effectively. The tall radiator was of much the same height as on G-type models, but the driving position was also quite high and forward vision for the driver better than might have been thought. The ECW body style suited the chassis quite well, as did West Yorkshire's red and white livery with traditional lining-out – the type was to appear in a variety of liveries – the era of standardisation in that regard was yet to come.

to the rear of the engine became an obvious step. The gearbox itself was basically simple, with straight-cut gears, though constant-mesh engagement for third gear was achieved by a twin-fork arrangement sliding the third-speed wheels on both main and lay shafts in a manner akin to that used by AEC since 1931. Particular care was taken in the design and machining of the gears, and the new gearbox was relatively quiet despite being mounted solidly with the engine, which gave a clear path for noise to be transmitted via the frame to the vehicle interior. The actual tone of the gear noise, barely audible above the 5LW's clatter, was relatively low in pitch and quite mellow in character. The four-speed MS version was standard for the K and the five-speed PS version usual for the L, and in the latter, a mild 'crooning' sound was evident to some degree when the overdrive fifth was engaged.

The K5G wheelbase was 16ft 3in and the L5G 17ft 6in, for the contemporary maximum lengths for two-axle double- and single-deck models of 26ft and 27ft 6in respectively. The frame designs, PA and QA respectively, were new, though quite orthodox, with tubular cross-members in most positions and bolted-on rear extension for the platform. At the front, cast dumb-iron brackets formed the front spring anchorages and supported the radiator on rubber mountings, the form of construction at this point being a little reminiscent of the Leyland Titan TD4 pattern, with similar gussets formed in the each side of the cast aluminium radiator casing, though the dumb-irons were deeper.

The triple-servo brake system was similar in principle to that of the G-type chassis, with the main Clayton Dewandre vacuum servo on the offside of the frame and two slave cylinders operating the front brakes. The rear brakes retained the 7½in wide shoes in 17¼in drums as used on the G type, but the front brake dimensions were now 3½in wide by 17in diameter.

Kirkstall forgings were used for the front axle beam and rear axle casing, but the units were of Bristol design, the rear axle as used on early K and L chassis being of generally similar design to that of the previous models. The steering was of Bristol worm-and-sector type. It was mounted with the column a little more upright than on the previous generation of models, and with the handbrake lever now mounted to the right of the driver, the cab layout became quite orthodox.

Drivers with experience of the model in this early form reported that it was considerably more agreeable to drive than might have been thought from the passengers' seats, where the noise level was greater than in any other contemporary production type of bus in Britain, only marginally eased by the effect of the standard overdrive on the L5G. The precision of the controls, with accurate steering, a particularly smooth clutch, a gear change that needed care but was agreeably precise once mastered and brakes that inspired confidence added up to a satisfying model from the driver's viewpoint. With hindsight, the tall radiator might have been thought intrusive into forward vision, but the driver sat quite high and had quite a good view forward, though vision when pulling out from behind another bus was not as good as on some other makes of chassis.

With the introduction of the K and L, a new method of chassis numbering was introduced. Hitherto, the chassis

number and the sanction allocations were separate, as indicated in previous chapters, but the 42nd sanction marked the beginning of a new system, for the first K-type was given the number 42.1 and this sanction, all of K-types, continued to 42.101. Similarly, the first L was 43.1, beginning a series running to 43.100. A further sanction for L-types followed, the 44th, running from 44.1 to 44.105, and then 45.1 to 45.153 were further K-types. After that, a general pattern of 'odds' and 'evens' emerged, in pre-war days the succeeding sanctions for L-types being the 46th, 48th, 50th and so on up to the 56th, while K-types were covered by the 47th, 49th, etc up to the 57th. With occasional exceptions, the number of chassis covered by each sanction tended to be a round figure, usually 100 for K-types and varying for L-types, there being 150 in the 46th sanction and 200 in the 48th, though settling back to 100 thereafter until wartime circumstances to be explained later curtailed the 56th and 57th sanctions.

The original system of numbering individual chassis sometimes caused confusion if the dot sometimes used to separate the sanction number from the individual serial number within each sanction was omitted, since 429 was followed by 4210 and 4299 by 42100. From the 48th and 49th sanctions, the number series began at 48001 and 49001 to overcome this problem, and this was to remain the system used for Bristol chassis until the mid-'sixties, apart from a brief departure during the latter part of the wartime period also to be explained later.

The first K5G, chassis 42.1, was completed as a prototype and after test running was fitted during the late

For the first few months, emphasis on production of the new models was on the K5G double-decker, and so the Show example of the L5G exhibited at Earls Court in November 1937 was on the second chassis of the type to be built, 43.2. It was the only one completed with bodywork at that stage as chassis 43.1 was a prototype retained as a development vehicle and not entering service with BTCC until July 1938. The choice of Western Welsh Omnibus Co Ltd as the customer may have reflected a hope that business could be attracted from British Electric Traction Co subsidiaries; the ECW 32-seat body was to British Electrical Federation design, as favoured by several BET companies. Western Welsh had taken delivery of two JO5G models (JO5G.391 and 392) with generally similar bodies in May 1937, numbered 401-2 (KG 9640-1), but with the L5G, No. 403 (AKG 330), they were to be the only single-deck Bristol buses of that era to join the WW fleet, bulk orders continuing to be for Leyland Tiger chassis.

Summer of 1937 with the 52-seat Bristol (BBW) body from one of a batch of GO5G buses for BTCC dating from early that year, retaining the fleet number C3063 that bus had received, and being registered EAE 280, the first number in a batch allocated to some of the final batch of GO5G models, also built for BTCC. It ran in this form until December 1937, when the body was refitted to its original chassis (registered DHT 942) and a new body, again 52-seat, was built by BBW for the prototype K-type chassis which returned to service now numbered C3082 in May 1938.

The first batch of K5G models, numbered immediately after the prototype 42.1 retained by BTCC, were 42.2-11, all fitted with Beadle highbridge 56-seat bodies, of which the first eight were supplied to Western National and the last two to Southern National. They continued a registration batch which had begun with some GO5G chassis with similar bodies. Seen here in Weymouth in September 1949 is Southern National 244 (ETA 989) on chassis 42.11, substantially as originally built in 1937. The following year this was among seven of the type which received new Beadle lowbridge bodies.

Hants & Dorset Motor Services Ltd was one of the companies in the TBAT group in which, up to 1938, BET influence on vehicle policy had been strong. The first sign of strengthened Tilling influence came in April 1938, when the first ten of a batch of 23 Bristol K5G models entered service. Among them was TD628 (BTR 307) seen here when new. At that date the fleet was almost entirely based on Leyland chassis and, from 1933, Brush had built the bus bodywork, this last feature continuing on this initial K5G batch.

More unusually, eighteen Titan TD4c double-deckers bought by H&D to replace Poole's trams in 1935 had petrol engines and torque-converter transmission, the latter an early step towards today's automatics, chosen to simplify retraining of tram drivers. The contrast of the K5Gs with the TD4c buses was immense, though doubtless the saving in fuel costs was equally so. Bristol did not depart from conventional clutch and gearbox transmission until 1966, and H&D converted its torque converter Titans to conventional gearboxes between 1938/46, some also receiving Gardner 5LW engines.

12 The K and L go into production

Numerically the first production K5G delivery, in 1937, were ten vehicles with chassis numbered 42.2-11, supplied to the Western National and Southern National fleets, all having bodywork by Beadle.

However, ECW was busy with batches of lowbridge bodies on K5G chassis, including five for Westcliff (42.24-28), 21 for West Yorkshire etc (42.29-49), sixteen for Eastern National (42.51-66), and eight United Counties (42.70-77) all of which were delivered in 1937. There were also three (42.67-9) for Brighton Hove & District, bodied in its own workshops. The intervening numbers were for BTCC itself, bodied by BBW but not placed in service until 1938. Thus the model got off to a flying start, with more in service within the first few months than the G had in its first four years, and the 1937 Commercial Motor Show exhibit was representative of production.

The first signs of a general Tilling policy of standardisation, not only of chassis types but make and basic design of bodywork, began with the first K5G buses with ECW lowbridge bodywork, of which 50 were built and delivered to four operators between 20th October and 15th December 1937. Uniformity did not at that stage stretch to seats, destination equipment or livery and so there was still a degree of variety even among this group.

By that period, the Eastern National Omnibus Co Ltd specification was quite a bit different to that of the Southern and Western National concerns, despite their common origin as part of the former National Omnibus & Transport Co Ltd. ENOC had stuck to a two-tone green and cream livery and fleet numbering system which followed on from that of NOTC, and the seats in No. 3735 (FPU 515) on K5G 42.58, like the rest of the sixteen for this fleet, were almost coach-like in form, with high backrests and the seating capacity as delivered was 50, though reduced to 48 almost immediately. Two-panel destination display was also a feature, though as usual, ECW used this space to advertise its product on delivery, in this case on 15th November. This bus, newly rebodied by then, was transferred to United Counties in 1952 when the company took over part of ENOC's services in the Bedfordshire area, surviving until 1959.

United Counties favoured a more basic specification and also used the 55-seat layout, with 28 seats on the lower deck, that was to become accepted as the typical Tilling lowbridge standard on K-type chassis right through to the 1950s. The vehicle shown was No. 480 (VV 6348) on chassis 42.73, ready to leave Lowestoft on 7th December 1937. It was to remain in service with UCOC until 1956, in largely original condition except for a change of fleet number to 604 in that company's renumbering scheme of 1952.

The first quantity order for L5G models to emerge from ECW was for North Western Road Car Co Ltd, for which concern 50 were completed in exactly a month, the first delivered on 25th January 1938 and the last on 25th February. The body design was as built on JO5G chassis and followed this operator's standard practice in having 31 seats to virtually coach standard, and the overall interior finish, complete with curtains, was in keeping. The word 'bus' is perhaps too utilitarian for such a body design, and 'saloon', sometimes favoured at the time, was perhaps more apt. The unladen weight was 6tons 5cwt 2qr.

The vehicle shown, No. 899 (JA 7799) on chassis 46.51, was the first of the next order for 45 similar vehicles, delivered towards the end of 1938. North Western was one of several operators which booked long blocks of registration numbers in those days, in this case in round hundreds. This was the last in a series had begun at No. 801, JA 7701, almost at the end of the final North Western JO5G batch, there also being some Leyland coaches and North Western's first ten K5G buses in the series; the next bus, continuing the same order, was No. 900 (AJA 100), the batch running to 943. A final eleven L5G, of the same pattern, were delivered in 1941, these being 984-994 (AJA 184-194), and bringing the total in the fleet to 106. Number 799 ran until 1961, being rebodied in 1950.

Evidently early emphasis had been on the K type, the L being slightly slower off the mark. It appears that the first chassis, 43.1, an L5G, spent some time as a development vehicle before joining the BTCC fleet with BBW 32-seat two-door body in July 1938, along with 43.3 and 43.64-8, the seven vehicles becoming 2082-8 in the fleet, registered FAE 56-62. Only one L5G seems to have been bodied in 1937, this being the Show 43.2 built for Western Welsh and fitted with ECW body to BET Federation design, much the same as on two JO5G models supplied to the same operator earlier the same year. It took

the next number, 403, in that fleet, being registered AKG 330, and was new in November 1937. It seems possible that an attempt to interest BET in the model may have been intended, paralleling ECW construction of bodies to Federation design, on Leyland Tiger or other chassis, for several BET-controlled companies. In the event, apart from Maidstone & District and its subsidiary Chatham & District, this was not successful.

Early L5G production comprised a batch of ten for Southern National with Beadle bus bodywork (43.4-13) and then 50 for the North Western Road Car Co Ltd, which

Following hot on the heels of the first North Western L5Gs out of ECW, in February 1938, were Eastern Counties' first L-types. Here four-cylinder engines were again favoured, but this time of the Gardner 4LW type, an engine not fitted to Bristol chassis previously, there being 36 in this order. Seen here is the first one, fleet number LL1 (CNG 201) on chassis 43.90 – the first twelve had 32-seat bodies with sliding roofs, the remainder being 35-seaters. The non-standard engine created no external difference; the bonnet could have been shortened if the driving position had been moved forward, as on Leyland and Dennis four-cylinder bus chassis, but Bristol evidently preferred to maintain standardisation – Eastern Counties later had some L5G of similar design. LL1, latterly LL501, remained in service until 1950.

had become a Bristol user with two batches of JO5G totalling 74 vehicles in 1936. These and the L5G models supplied to NWRCC up to 1941 all had ECW bodywork to the operator's distinctive half-canopy style, with seating virtually to coach standards for 31 passengers. All of these early production L-type buses entered service early in 1938, as did the remainder of the 43rd sanction.

The last eleven vehicles of that sanction, and the first 25 of the 44th, were of type L4G, with Gardner 4LW four-cylinder engine, a power unit that had not figured in Bristol production hitherto, even though such a version of the J had been offered with what seems to have been this engine in 1934. They were for the Eastern Counties Omnibus Co Ltd, whose terrain was largely quite flat, and the smaller engine was considered to give adequate power. Even so they had the overdrive gearbox, as usual for L-type chassis, and it was apparently quite an experience to travel through East Anglian villages in fifth gear at about 20mph, at which the firing of individual cylinders could almost be counted. Although it would have been possible to shorten the bonnet, this remained at standard length as used with the 5LW, so there was no external difference.

This was not possible with the L6G, with the relatively long 6LW unit, this being the next variant to appear, two chassis, 44.26 and 27, being built for A. & R. Graham Ltd of Kirkintilloch. They entered service in July 1938, having received coach bodywork by Pickering. They were to prove the last Bristol vehicles for this operator, for the firm was taken over by W. Alexander & Sons Ltd that same month. Although a fresh class, with prefix letter G, was created by Alexander for the nine Bristol coaches taken over, extending from two B-types dating from 1930, through D, J and JO5G models to the pair of L6G, all were sold off by 1944. Alexander was not to become a purchaser of new Bristol vehicles until 1955.

The main recipient for the L6G in its original form was Black & White, for which fleet six, with chassis 44.48-53, were built in 1938, receiving 31-seat bodywork built by ECW to the same style, of Burlingham origin, as those on JO6G chassis. A further six, on chassis 48.115-20, followed in 1939, this time with bodywork built by Duple, though again to much the same style, and a final three, 54.018-20, again by Duple, in 1940. These fifteen L6G models, plus the sixteen JO6G models with similar bodywork, constituted Black & White's main coach fleet until post-war additions began to arrive in 1948, the combination of Bristol chassis with 6LW engine and distinctive bodywork in the livery appropriate to the name making it widely respected.

Only one further operator chose the L6G in the pre-war period, this being West Yorkshire Road Car, to whom six chassis, 50.064-9, with ECW bodywork were delivered, though not until October-November 1939 and thus, like the three built in 1940 for Black & White, strictly speaking wartime vehicles, and having little opportunity for use before express service operation was shut down.

Thus the total number of L6G built up to 1940 was a mere 23, and the model was virtually unknown in the industry at large, yet they could be regarded as amongst the most impressive coaches of their period. The 6LW engine with overdrive gearbox gave remarkably relaxed performance, the engine hardly ever seeming to have to work hard, and even though rigidly mounted, the six-cylinder unit gave much smoother running than the more familiar 5LW. The engine length meant that 31 was considered to be the maximum coach seating capacity practicable within the 27ft 6in overall length then permissible, and indeed it was not until the later era of underfloor engines that the six-cylinder Gardner unit came into its own as a coach power unit.

The L4G also remained a minority choice, though the

Black & White followed up its JO6G coaches by choosing the L6G for the additions to its fleet made in 1938, 1939 and 1940. The order for the 1939 and 1940 batches went to Duple, but the design, as with those built by ECW on both types of chassis, followed the style of the Burlingham bodywork on the original JO6G batch of 1936 quite closely. This can be seen in this view of No. 105 (DDF 49) on L6G chassis 48.120, the last of the 1939 batch, which had a distinct Burlingham 'flavour' despite their origin.

West Yorkshire Road Car Co Ltd had tended to favour rebodied Leyland Tiger coaches in the 1930s, but in 1939 ordered six L6G models with ECW curved-waist coach bodies not unlike the style favoured for some years by both Eastern Counties and Eastern National, though with full-width canopies. The writer still clearly recalls being much impressed by a journey from Newcastle to Leeds in one half a century ago. They were delivered just after the war had begun, in October-November 1939, though there is no evidence of that in this pre-delivery view of the first one No. 640 (DWU 138) on chassis 50.064. The extended bonnet to accommodate the 6LW engine can be seen though, as with the Black & White examples, the design of the body helps to disguise the effect.

takeover of the Gloucester Corporation undertaking, which had converted a Thornycroft BC with a 4LW engine in 1935, followed by the allocation of six JO4D after takeover, led to the construction of two batches of L4G for this section of the BTCC fleet – there were seven in 1938 on chassis 44.76-82, and six in 1939 (48.058-63). With the Eastern Counties batch mentioned above, there were thus a total of 49 L4G models built in the pre-war period.

After the wide-ranging experiments with alternative makes of engines in the G and J types of chassis, the adoption of Gardner units for all the K and L chassis built in the 1937-42 period is striking. Indeed, notwithstanding the four- and six-cylinder batches produced for particular needs mentioned, it was the 5LW that was very firmly established as the standard power unit for Bristol vehicles during that period. However, it would be wrong to suggest that the Gardner had been accepted as the only choice for the future, for the Bristol engine design team was busy on the company's first venture into diesel engine design, a six-cylinder unit, the first prototype of which was fitted in March 1939 to a 1938 K5G in BTCC's fleet, C3215, with chassis 45.136. Other prototypes were built, some going to associated companies for trials which were unexpectedly extended by the war – more on that development will figure later in the story.

The nature of the output of the Motor Constructional Works during this period is perhaps best conveyed by looking at the successive sanctions. References to numbers for major operators includes vehicles allocated to subsidiaries where applicable.

42nd sanction. 101 chassis, all K5G.
All for Tilling-controlled companies, including 35 for BTCC itself and 21 for West Yorkshire. Delivered late 1937 to early 1938.

43rd sanction. 100 chassis, 89 L5G, 11 L4G.
All but one for Tilling companies, delivered early 1938. Largest batch 50 for North Western. One L5G for Western Welsh (BET-controlled), delivered late 1937.

44th sanction. 105 chassis. 65 L5G, 32 L4G, 8 L6G.
Mostly for Tilling companies, but eight L5G for Rotherham Corporation, six L6G for Black & White (BET-controlled) and two for Graham (independent). Delivered 1938.

45th sanction. 153 chassis, all K5G.
Of these, 99 were for BTCC itself, the remainder mainly for Tilling companies, but two for Pontypridd UDC. Delivered 1938.

46th sanction. 150 chassis, all L5G.
Mostly for Tilling companies, including 45 for North Western, 28 for BTCC itself and 28 for Eastern National, but twelve for Rotherham Corporation. Delivered 1938-39.

47th sanction. 100 chassis, all K5G.
Mostly for Tilling companies, including 33 for BTCC itself and 27 for West Yorkshire, but sixteen for Maidstone & District (BET-controlled). Delivered 1938-39.

48th sanction. 200 chassis – 188 L5G, 6 L4G, 6 L6G.
Mostly for Tilling companies, including 40 for West Yorkshire etc and 40 for United, but nine L5G for Rotherham and six L6G for Black & White. Delivered late 1938 to 1939.

49th sanction. 100 chassis, all K5G.
Mostly for Tilling companies, including 34 for BTCC itself and 30 for Hants & Dorset, but fourteen for Chatham & District (BET-controlled). Delivered 1939.

Maidstone & District Motor Services Ltd and its subsidiary, Chatham & District Traction Co, were TBAT companies which remained under BET influence until they passed to the BET group in 1942. Even so, they chose Bristol buses for part of their needs from 1936. The initial delivery that year was of sixteen GO5G models (GO5G.130-47 and 149-54), all with Weymann metal-framed 48-seat bodywork. Most unusually, the chassis were traded back to BTCC in 1938 and the bodywork, retaining the same fleet numbers, transferred to new K5G chassis. The four buses for the Chatham fleet had highbridge bodywork, as seen (right) on No.354 (DKN 45) on chassis GO5G.145.

The new K5G chassis were 47.69-84, and M&D No.279, now on chassis 47.76 and registered FKL 606 is seen below in post-war days, this being a lowbridge bus. The GO5G chassis were rebodied by Bristol and transferred to Bath Electric Tramways Ltd, forming part of the fleet which replaced the Bath tram system. In 1948-50, they received a third set of new bodies, this time by ECW, at the same time being equipped with PV2 radiators, and remaining in service until 1955-58.

Hants & Dorset had purchased part of its bodywork needs from Beadle for several years, notably that on Leyland Tiger coaches in 1935-38, and chose this make for the Bristol L5G buses supplied, eighteen in 1938 and nine in 1939. One of the latter, on chassis 48.148, registered ERU 517 and originally numbered TS706, is seen here in post-war days, by which time it had been numbered 753. The body style was not unlike some of the contemporary ECW designs though the sliding roof originally fitted had been panelled over and some simplification of the mouldings had occurred by the time this photograph was taken; a quick-action radiator filler cap of the early post-war type had also been fitted.

In the period of roughly two years from the introduction of the K and L in 1937 to the outbreak of war with Germany on 3rd September 1939, the chassis included in the foregoing sanctions, totalling 454 K-types and 555 L-types, plus 50 or so from each of the 50th (L-type) and 51st (K-type), were built, bodied and delivered in the normal way.

The beginning of the war makes a convenient point to take stock of what had been achieved. Roundly 1,100 of the new models had entered service, the total of about 600 L-types at that point being roughly equivalent to that of oil-engined J-types, but the 500 K-types were more than double the total of oil-engined G-types. This had been done in a shorter period than that from the beginning of 1935 to late 1937 during which most of these earlier models had entered service.

The increase in numbers of double-deckers was due to a combination of factors. The most obvious was the conversion programme for the Bristol tram system, 31 new K5G buses having replaced trams on the first stage of conversion on 8th May, 1938, followed by 51 more in July 1939. The numbers supplied to BTCC and associated fleets was considerably more than the above, for general

expansion of double-deck services was occurring, and in addition, fourteen buses helped to replaced the Bath trams in May 1939, these being owned by Bath Electric Tramways Ltd. This expansion of need caused the bodywork for part of the deliveries to BTCC to be supplied by ECW rather than built entirely by BBW, as had been usual for most of the company's own needs. ECW supplied what was basically its standard 56-seat highbridge design for these buses, there being initially 54 such, based on 45th sanction chassis, delivered in 1938.

Most K5G buses supplied to other Tilling-controlled companies received ECW lowbridge bodywork to what was basically a standardised design, although sometimes varying in minor details, an early pointer to the much more rigorous standardisation applied to Tilling new vehicle deliveries from 1946.

There was an expansion of orders for such fleets, for a combination of reasons. One was increased use of double-deckers – for example, North Western, which had run only six double-deckers (Leyland Titan TD1 models of 1931) during the mid-'thirties, took 64 K5G with ECW bodies in 1938-39 – incidentally the Titans were purchased by BTCC and could thus almost be considered as taken in part

The United fleet was well established as a major Bristol user, and this continued with the L5G, classified BLO in that fleet. The first 20, on 44th sanction chassis, delivered in 1938 had what had become this company's traditional rear-entrance style, much as used since 1934. For the next 70, delivered between March and June 1939, this new body style was introduced, with front entrance, though retaining the same capacity of 35 seats as on the later rear-entrance bodies. The overall effect was quite well-proportioned and the author has a vivid recollection of the good impression on seeing one for the first time, brand new, outside Jesmond depot in Newcastle, quite near his school.

The body design was slightly higher built than the earlier style, allowing all seats to face forward, though those over the rear wheel arch were not very comfortable. The chassis were produced in an initial batch of 40 in the 48th sanction, including 48.159 seen here, which was BLO29 (EHN 529), and then two of fifteen each in the 50th sanction. Basically the same design, save for separate number and route destination display, was used for a further 50 placed in service in 1940-41, taking the fleet numbers up to BLO140, based on chassis numbered in smaller runs in the 52nd and 54th sanctions – by then the war was disrupting production.

The replacement of Bristol's trams by buses helped to swell the demand for the K5G, and batches for the fleet were being built in every sanction. Almost 200 had been built for BTCC and its Bath subsidiary by the time war broke out, roundly two years from the beginning of production, and the total was to rise to 285 before the war cut off normal production. Representative of those with Bristol bodywork is No. 3800 (GL 6601) on chassis 47.47, one of the fourteen placed in service by the Bath Electric Tramways Co in 1939 as part of the fleet replacing that city's trams in May 1939. It is seen in that city with part of the original paintwork replaced by matt grey. It remained in service until 1952, being owned by the Bath Tramways Motor Co Ltd from 1949.

To meet the needs of the tram replacement, ECW began to supply part of BTCC's body requirements for the K5G chassis, for the first time where the Bristol fleet itself was concerned. The body design was basically the Lowestoft factory's standard 56-seat highbridge of the day, with strongly curved profile contrasting with the sloping style favoured by BBW – the Bramham/Roe influence on this ECW product was more obvious than the lowbridge equivalent. The initial 54 supplied in 1938 were followed by 24 delivered in August-September 1939, all for the Bristol City fleet, as indicated by the C prefix of the fleet number C3296. Registered GAE 494 and on chassis 51.066, the bus is seen at Lowestoft before delivery on 15th August, showing off the merit of the dark blue and white livery. It remained in service until 1954.

Double-deck expansion was not confined to Bristol, and North Western became a substantial double-deck operator after running only six such buses since 1931 when 64 K5G with ECW lowbridge bodies were added to the fleet in 1938-39. Seen here is No. 887 (JA 7787) on chassis 45.152, one of the second batch of twelve supplied in September 1938. Much the same philosophy as for North Western's single-deckers was applied in regard to the interior, the coach quality of which meant that only 47 seated passengers could be accommodated, with 23 on the upper deck. The unladen weight quoted reads 6tons 19cwt 3qr, unusually high for a prewar double-decker and only possible within the gross weight limit because of the low seating capacity. They were highly regarded by North Western and all 64 were rebodied by Willowbrook in 1951-2, some surviving in service as late as 1965.

exchange, though in fact acquired via Millburn Motors, the dealers, of Preston.

Another factor was an increase in the number of operators which came under Tilling influence, generally due to changes in shareholdings. Hants & Dorset had followed a more BET-like policy until 1938 and even its first batch of 23 K5G buses had Brush bodywork of a pattern used by this operator on Leyland Titan chassis in the mid-'thirties.

A third factor was a delayed consequence of the general switch to Bristol chassis for Tilling-controlled fleets, as many of them had adopted the Leyland Titan TD1 for their initial double-deck purchases, sometimes relatively large, in the 1928-31 period, and many of these vehicles had become due for replacement, by K5G in such cases. In the event, most of these TD1 buses survived for much longer than anticipated, though quite often moving from their original fleets, being used for conveying workers on

various defence-related projects, such as the construction of airfields.

The single-deck deliveries on L-type chassis, mainly L5G, were more similar to the pattern that had applied with the JO5G, for although most bodywork was by ECW, the designs continued to vary, each of the major users such as United, Eastern Counties, North Western, West Yorkshire and others having their own distinctive styles. There was thus still no such thing as a complete standard Tilling-group single-decker at this period, even though ECW characteristics and alternative minor variations that could be applied in a 'pick-and-mix' way gave clues to the common origin.

The intakes of the various fleets in question also did not greatly alter. There were one or two new names among the users, such as East Midland Motor Services Ltd, which briefly became a Tilling-controlled company in the 1939-42 period, receiving one batch of five L5G buses, and

Single-deck deliveries to associated companies continued in the pattern that had become firmly established. Westcliff-on-Sea Motor Services Ltd had come under Tilling control in 1935, and subsequent bus requirements were met by Bristol chassis with ECW bodywork, though AEC continued to be favoured for coaches. This L5G with 32-seat body was registered AJN 826 and based on chassis 48.064, entering service in 1939. The continued use of the engine-turned bonnet finish familiar on earlier Bristol chassis is noteworthy – it had become rare by this date. Westcliff was taken over by Eastern National in 1955, this vehicle remaining in service until 1959, unusually late for an L5G with original body.

Caledonian Omnibus Co Ltd, which switched from BET influence more permanently, taking its first Bristol buses, two L5G, in 1939.

Another similar case, though involving double-deckers at this stage, was the Thames Valley Traction Co Ltd, hitherto favouring Leyland chassis, but receiving one K5G, 51.094, with ECW lowbridge body in June 1939 – eighteen more were to follow in September-October. They were of interest in having five-speed overdrive gearboxes as normally fitted to L-type chassis and then an unusual feature for double-deckers, being chosen for this operator's London-Reading service.

East Midland Motor Services Ltd had its origins as an offshoot of United, and its livery continued that firm's pre-1929 beige and brown colours. When East Midland came into the TBAT group, its policy took a different course from United, with BET influence dominant until shortly before the war years, when it was one of a number of companies to swing towards Tilling, in this case briefly. Just one batch of five Bristol L5G buses was delivered in January 1939, including G4 (ERR 604) on chassis 48.078. These had ECW 35-seat bodywork with frontal design to a style with projecting peak over the windscreen, by then generally out of favour, in accordance with the taste of EMMS management. When East Midland found itself in the BET group from 1942, these buses were exchanged for some Leyland Tigers with North Western.

Doncaster Corporation continued to order Bristol chassis for much of its single-deck needs, though double-deck orders had been going to AEC, Leyland or, in one case, Daimler. Number 17 (BDT 225), on chassis 50.051, was one of four L5G models with Roe 32-seat bodywork delivered in May 1939. However, when a need for three more arose under wartime circumstances, chassis earmarked for BTCC's own use were supplied and delivered, again with Roe bodywork, in 1941. Subsequently replacements were built and supplied to BTCC's operating department bearing duplicate chassis numbers but with a /56 suffix to signify that they were built as part of the 56th sanction.

Having arrived at the combination of K5G chassis and Weymann metal-framed body which suited its needs, Chatham & District took delivery of 37 further such buses in 1939. They had bodywork to the curved-profile style by then usual from Weymann and seated 54. Nos.896 and 897 (GKE 90 and 91) on chassis 51.027-28 are seen here with 353 (FKL 613) on chassis 47.74 of the 1938 batch with bodywork transferred from GO5G chassis. The Luton shown on the destination display was a terminus of one of the local routes based on the former tramway network – Chatham & District Traction Co was a statutory company which became a Maidstone & District subsidiary when the trams were replaced by Leyland buses in 1930, surviving as a separate entity until 1955

Although Bristol had become mainly a supplier to associated company fleets, a limited core of municipalities, centred on Yorkshire and south Wales, remained faithful customers. Among these was Pontypridd Urban District Council, where the small fleet was mostly of Bristol make, then largely B-types, of which four had been bought second-hand from BTCC, two GO6G double-deckers and two K5G 54-seat buses bought in 1938. Three more K5G were added in 1939, including No. 30 (ETG 140) on chassis 53.046, seen here in post-war days. All the double-deckers had Bristol bodywork, by this period rarely specified except for BTCC's own use, and on these 56-seat additions to the Pontypridd fleet the specification was very similar to those being built for the tram replacement fleet in Bristol.

Thirteen miles north of Pontypridd, Merthyr Tydfil Corporation operated some B-types but had favoured Dennis vehicles, bodied by Dennis or Park Royal, in the 1930s. In 1939 an order was placed for six K5G models and that for the 56-seat highbridge bodies went to Northern Coachbuilders of Newcastle-on-Tyne, at that time a concern little-known outside the north-east of England, though to become better known from 1942 as one of the main bodybuilders chosen under wartime rules to rebody existing bus chassis. Three of the vehicles, Nos.27, 30 and 31 (HB 5875/8/9) on chassis 53.082/4/1 are seen in later years.

The Western National and Southern National companies had continued to use bodywork by Beadle for K5G and Mumford for their L5G fleet addtions in 1938-39, but switched to ECW for a delivery of K5G models in 1940. The seven buses for Western National, including No.313 (DOD 502) on chassis 55.003 seen here at Nailsworth were delivered between July and September, having been delayed by the evacuation of ECW's Lowestoft factory because of the threat of invasion at the end of May – the four for Southern National had arrived just before that event. Unusually among ECW bodies for the K5G in that period, they were of non-standard frontal appearance, resembling the Beadle design particularly in the cab and windscreen shape, the latter deeper than the ECW standard for this chassis and swept sharply downwards to the offside in typical Beadle style.

13 The war years

The outbreak of war brought about some immediate and obvious changes, such as those related to the blackout immediately enforced, but, at first, output of new buses continued at the Motor Constructional Works and the bodybuilders. Many vehicles were 'in the pipeline' at stages varying from material or components on order, in process of being built at Brislington, chassis at bodybuilders (themselves with a similar momentum of work in hand) and at various stages of completion. Clearly buses were going to be needed and so this work continued.

When war broke out, most if not all of the 100 K5G chassis in the 51st sanction were complete and most for operators other than BTCC itself (largely for North Western and Chatham & District) had been bodied and entered service or were soon to reach this stage.

The final stage of the Bristol tramway conversion had been due in October 1939, but the decision was taken that this should be postponed, and 66 trams running from three depots were retained. This meant that new buses intended for their replacement were not required. It is known that 24 K5G buses delivered back to BTCC from ECW in

August-September 1939 were not put into service until 1941 and it seems that the intention was simply to store them for the time being. At that stage, of course, there was no idea how long the war would last and after the initial expectation of immediate heavy air raids did not materialise, there was a period of about six months when there was very little activity in western Europe, sometimes called 'the phoney war'.

A rather similar pattern applied to the 50th sanction, which covered 100 L-type chassis, including 94 L5G, of which just over half had entered service in the summer of 1939, largely with United and Eastern Counties, but also including the first two for Caledonian, as well as four (50.048-51) with Roe bodywork for Doncaster Corporation delivered in May. Most of the remainder followed normally enough later in the year, including a batch for United Counties, four for Southern Vectis, and the six L6G coaches for West Yorkshire already mentioned.

Here again, however, a batch of 21 for BTCC's own fleet (50.072-92), was put in abeyance until 1941, but in this case, it seems that some chassis had not reached the

Although the Bristol tram-replacement programme was put in abeyance at the outbreak of war, limited numbers of buses for the Bristol City Services fleet entered service in 1940. Among them was C3336 (GHT 154), a K5G on chassis 53.035 and with Bristol 56-seat body. It was one of a number of which the bodies were reconstructed by the company in 1951, though it was withdrawn from service two years later. It was sold to a fairground proprietor but fortunately was subsequently purchased for preservation and restored, using the distinctive original dark blue and white livery, as seen here, and conveys the unusual proportions of this body design.

Among the buses completed in the early months of the war were four L5G models for Southern Vectis, delivered in December 1939 and entering service in the following year. The ECW 35-seat bodywork incorporated touches of Harrington practice, that concern having bodied a previous batch. Seen here is No. 825 (DDL 51) on chassis 50.093. Some vehicles were photographed before application of wartime items, but here the lifeguard rail and tips of the front mudguards were painted white and a headlamp mask had been fitted to meet blackout requirements. The nearside mudguard appears to be of the rubber type then being sold by Dunlop, the strips visible covering spring steel supports – the war ended this development as the need to conserve rubber became more urgent.

stage of bodying when urgent requirements were received from the Doncaster and Rotherham Corporation fleets for three and two L5G chassis and chassis 50.081/2/4 were diverted to Doncaster and 50.090 and 092 to Rotherham, receiving Roe and East Lancs bodywork respectively. These were completed, as were the remainder of the BTCC order, in 1941-42. Five replacement chassis were built for BTCC and received these same chassis numbers, as originally intended, but with the suffix /56, since by that time current production had reached the 56th sanction.

Apart from the special case of BTCC itself, deliveries were remarkably normal during the early wartime period. The 52nd sanction, of 100 L5G chassis; the 53rd, of 100 K5G; the 54th, of L-types (97 L5G and three L6G for Black & White) and the 55th, of 101 K5G, were all built, apparently much as usual, so far as Brislington was concerned. Some of the earlier ones were probably already at the bodybuilders, but output seems to have continued undisturbed for a time. Most of the vehicles were for

familiar customers, but there was another newcomer to the ranks of Tilling-controlled companies and Bristol users – Wilts & Dorset Motor Services Ltd, hitherto under BET, and in particular, Southdown, influence received twelve K5G with largely standard ECW lowbridge bodies (though with minor features to similar pattern as on previous Park Royal bodies on Titan chassis) in January 1940.

However, by the Spring of 1940, the war situation had altered dramatically for the worse. The German armies invaded Holland and Belgium, not only threatening France but causing the military authorities in East Anglia to consider the risk of an attempted landing to be great enough to order the closure of ECW at a day's notice and the removal of all vehicles, lest they fell into enemy hands. Up to that point, output from there had been almost normal, and many vehicles of the above sanctions had already been bodied. About 160-170 vehicles, largely on Bristol chassis from the sanctions mentioned above, were in hand and in states ranging from bare chassis to being

Wilts & Dorset Motor Services Ltd was a new customer for Bristol, having been closely associated with the Southdown company, of which it had been virtually a branch in earlier times. Leyland chassis, with bodywork built by such firms as Park Royal to a specification almost identical to that of Southdown, had been standard. The company came under Tilling influence, and twelve Bristol K5G models with ECW lowbridge bodies were added to the fleet in January 1940. However, the bodies were trimmed and finished to the operator's traditional style, with seating for 26 on each deck, and livery and lettering in virtually Southdown manner save for the use of red as the main colour rather than green. Seen here is No. 188 (CHR 487) on chassis 53.021.

A departure from normal practice was the placing of an order for Roe bodywork for five K5G buses for United Counties, a Tilling group subsidiary and, under normal circumstances, firmly in the pattern of taking ECW bodywork by then. Production of buses had been slowed to some degree as a result of the outbreak of war in September 1939, but Bristol/ECW output had not been seriously affected up to the time these were delivered in May 1940; Roe itself had completed no buses in April of that year. The design resembled the standard ECW lowbridge body in such respects as the six-bay construction (Roe normally standardising on five-bay) and the 55-seat capacity with 28 in the lower deck. Even the slightly raised window sill line at the cab found on most ECW bodies for the K5G was reproduced, yet Roe used its usual teak-framed construction and retained its normal profile, more strongly curved than ECW's, with no step in the cab front. All in all, it seemed a surprising effort for so small an order at that time, though possibly it was meant as an exploration of alternative supply. The first of the batch, No.567 (BBD 811) on chassis 55017 is seen ready to leave Roe's works in Leeds. All five remained in service until 1958.

almost completed, and they were all moved out within 24 hours beginning on the morning of 28th, after a telephone call the previous day.

Many were at first moved to various operators' depots, notably of the local Eastern Counties fleet, but gradually arrangements were made for their completion, in some cases by the operator to whom they were to be delivered. ECW itself moved its bodybuilding operations, reduced in scale, to Irthlingborough, in Northamptonshire, where a United Counties depot that had former workshops, redundant after the building of new premises, was available. Inevitably, output virtually stopped for several months before resuming on a more limited scale. As a result, the delivery of some batches of vehicles was disrupted quite severely, but eventually all the chassis in these batches were bodied and delivered, although this process was not completed until 1941 or, in a few cases, 1942.

Even so, the general character of these vehicles was, for the most part, remarkably little affected by war conditions, apart from such matters as the adoption of modified liveries, some operators adopting styles using grey in place of cream to make buses less readily visible from the air – for the same reason, roof panels were usually in grey or other dull colours.

Although the invasion feared from 1940 never occurred, the war situation worsened. With the fall of France, air raids by German bombers on British cities became more numerous from the Autumn of that year, and Bristol was now within quite easy range. On 4th January 1941, Bedminster tram depot received a direct hit, most of the rolling stock therein being put out of action, and thus ending operation on two of the remaining routes.

Then, on 11th April, St Philip's Bridge was hit, collapsing into the floating harbour and in doing so, severing the main power cables feeding the system at Old Market Square, and this ended tram operation in Bristol for good. Hence, the conversion delayed from October 1939 was brought about by enemy action in 1941. The buses mentioned above as being stored were put into service, and indeed quite a number of buses were destroyed or seriously damaged in various air raids from December 1940 until 1942.

With Britain effectively alone in continuing the battle against Germany, apart from support from the Commonwealth, from mid-1940, it was not long before almost all non-essential manufacture was stopped and for a time this applied to bus manufacture. As a result, quite a number of orders for Bristol chassis were not fulfilled.

Some involvement in military production had begun even before war began as what was called the aircraft expansion scheme was put into effect in the early part of 1939, when some machine shop capacity at Brislington – doubtless available as the result of the cessation of engine production for bus chassis from 1936 – was used to make engine components for the Bristol Aeroplane Co. Immediate expansion of this had occurred when war was declared. Bristol radial aero engines were used in many Royal Air Force machines of the time, by no means only in aircraft of Bristol make. Some 50,000 gears for aero engines and superchargers were made. The Motor Constructional Works also made large quantities of parts for Rotol Airscrew Co, the main makers of propellers for both Bristol and Rolls-Royce engined-aircraft.

The Chatsworth Road works built 1,300 main fuselage assemblies for the Bristol Beaufighter twin-engined fighter while BBW was busy with the nose and tail sections; additionally there were a variety of other items from shells to tank components going through the Brislington shops. Among these were 400 searchlight generator trailers while the quantity of 20mm cannon shells ran into hundreds of thousands. There were also tank transmissions as well as items for pontoons and portable bridges.

There was another threat to Britain, for, in those days, all oil was imported and severe shipping losses from U-boat attacks raised the prospect of insufficient fuel for road vehicles, despite severe rationing, even for essential purposes. All major bus companies were required to convert 10 per cent of their fleets to producer gas, using plant mounted on trailers which were towed by the buses converted, generally petrol-engined models which lent themselves to conversion more readily and offered larger savings. BTCC was one of the largest makers of such trailers, 2,500 being supplied to 92 operators from between 1942 and the latter part of 1944 when the scheme was abandoned as the shipping position improved.

It was also realised, even in the dark days of 1941, that some supply of new buses was essential, not least because of the sizeable numbers of vehicles that had been damaged, even though many that were originally considered to be beyond repair were eventually returned to service, often with new bodywork. As an initial step, it was realised that parts or even part-built vehicles existed, and these were 'unfrozen', a phrase that was used to identify such vehicles nationally.

The Bristol contribution was some 85 K5G and 15 L5G models, which comprised the 57th and 56th sanctions, respectively, with chassis specifications much as previously. By this time production, including the choice and specification of bodywork, was under the control of the Ministry of Supply, and the normal process of order by customers replaced by an allocation system run by the Ministry of War Transport. There were quite a number of operators with outstanding orders for these models who received none of the 'unfrozen' production, while others which had never operated Bristol buses of any kind received allocations. The Ministry of Supply issued its own numbers, and the 'unfrozen' K5G buses with chassis numbers 57001-85 had MoS numbers BD01 to BD85, in sequence.

There was a semblance of normality in most of the operators' names included in the 56th series L5G allocations, though understandably no operator got more than three examples, and the body makes were strange. This was also the case at the beginning of the 57th sanction K5G series chassis numbers, with two for Pontypridd followed by seven for BTCC's own use, these having BBW

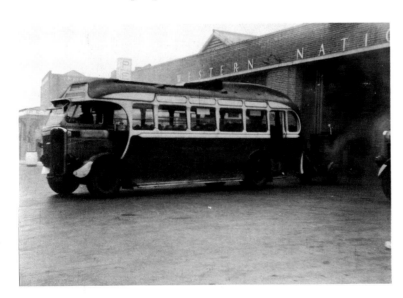

Producer-gas operation was the subject of a national scheme announced in May 1942 and the Tilling group, already active in experimental conversions, took it up with a level of perseverance rarely found elsewhere. Here Western National 167 (BTA 457), Bristol J.JW.178, dating from 1935 and demoted from Royal Blue duty (by then, express services had ceased 'for the duration') is seen leaving Taunton garage while running on producer gas, in a picture taken by the late John Parke early one morning c.1943. The trailer is wreathed in smoke as the fire begins to draw – driving such vehicles required a kind of skill somewhat similar to a steam locomotive fireman to keep the gas supply up, particularly before climbing hills. By no means all the 2,500 gas trailers made by BTCC were actually in use by the time the Government scheme was dropped in September 1944, and it seems unlikely that any bus operator reached the target of 10 per cent of their fleets, but several Tilling companies were among those nearest such a figure.

The 'unfrozen' bus scheme allowed manufacturers to produce chassis for which parts were in stock and an official internal works memorandum surveying war production after the event refers "to a batch of 200 which were assembled mainly from existing stocks in 1941". This quantity does not correspond to the total of 100 (85 K5G and 15 L5G) actually built, which reached operators mainly in 1942, but may indicate that there was a change of plan.

Among them were two for United Counties which received Duple bodywork to the 'utility' specification then introduced to economise on skilled manpower and materials, one being No.615 (BRP 233) on chassis 57.013. The 'shell-back' rear dome is clearly visible in this view, as is the lack of glazing in the upper-deck rear emergency exit, this also being laid down in the initial specification, though it did permit the use of rather basic upholstered seats. Duple was among the most successful in producing a well-proportioned vehicle under these rules, aided here by being painted in a near approach to normal livery, although lacking the traditional lining-out.

The earlier 57th sanction allocations were to regular Bristol customers, and the first two chassis went to Pontypridd Urban District Council. They were complete with Bristol bodywork, as were the following seven which went to BTCC itself, also in line with previous deliveries. The vehicle shown was 57.001, the first of the sanction, which became Pontypridd No.17 (ETX 763). The bodywork conformed to the utility specification in outline but was of six-bay construction, as usual in Bristol double-decker bodies of that period and it may be that, as BBW was not to continue body production beyond 21 vehicles of this sanction, it had been agreed that the five-bay layout set out in the utility scheme need not be followed. The squared-up foremost side window on the upper deck was also unusual and did nothing for the appearance, though a similar feature was found on the first Brush highbridge utilities.

The fifteen L5G buses built under the 'unfrozen' scheme were in sanction 56, and again there were elements of normal practice mixed with wartime austerity. United received two, which received bodywork by Burlingham, which had been selected to build single-deck bodies, in most cases as replacements for those on existing vehicles. This view of BLO142 (GHN 179) on chassis 56.015 shows that the body design, though conforming to the layout agreed for the 'utility' standard, had rounded front and rear domes and out-swept skirt panels, peacetime features not supposed to be found on new products of that period. When delivered in 1941, it had 36 seats, in line with the planned Ministry of Supply design, but this capacity was reduced to 32 in 1948. This bus was to become quite well-known as, converted for one-man operation, it was given, on behalf of the British Transport Commission, to Norman Fox, of Falstone in October 1956 to operate his remote Bellingham to Keilder Forest bus service.

bodies, and then followed buses for Western and Southern National, United Counties, Hants & Dorset, Thames Valley and Maidstone & District, though most of these were in twos and threes rather than the runs of longer sequences normally to be expected.

Perhaps the most obvious change was that in most cases the bodywork was to the newly-introduced utility specification intended to economise on skilled manpower, very 'basic' in nature and with angular outlines dictated by the edict that the normal shaped dome panels were to be replaced by two-dimensional curves not requiring panel beating. Opening windows were restricted to one on each side of each deck, though hinged vents were to be provided at the front. In practice, some bodywork already under construction to normal peacetime outlines was allowed to be completed, though usually with the restrictions on opening windows and the rather austere seats, though at that stage these continued to be upholstered.

Thames Valley was fortunate in that its total of five 57th-sanction K5G buses had ECW lowbridge bodies of normal style, the only ECW bodies to appear on these unfrozen chassis, apart from some experimental and prototype vehicles to be described later.

The allocations began to include unfamiliar names at 57.026 and 27, for Potteries Motor Traction, together with 042 & 043, 050 and 081-3. A minority of later numbers went to regular Bristol users but most went to other completely unexpected names including the municipal fleets of Liverpool (whose five examples received bodies based on Weymann shells intended for AEC Regents, completed by the operator), Colchester, Edinburgh (receiving one K5G, and also one L5G, the only comparable 'surprise' in the 56th sanction), Coventry, Derby and Plymouth, none of which had any Bristol buses in service. There were also independent operators such as Griffin, of Brynmawr; Silcox, of Pembroke Dock; Tilstone, of Stoke; Harper, of Heath Hayes, the Gosport & Fareham Omnibus Co and Moore of Kelvedon. Perhaps most surprising of all was the London Passenger Transport Board, which received nine, which it numbered B1-9, though the two for Northern

Ireland Road Transport Board broke new ground in several ways.

The bodywork, apart from those by BBW, was built by Duple (which built lowbridge examples for various fleets), Strachans (both lowbridge and highbridge), Northern Counties (lowbridge and highbridge, the latter, on the Edinburgh bus, to that firm's very rounded late pre-war style) and Park Royal, which bodied the nine for London Transport. Five of the single-deckers were bodied by East Lancs to peace-time outline, of which Rotherham received three, and which may have been the intended destination for one body of this make received by Aberdare and two by Caledonian. BBW bodied three (including Edinburgh's example), Strachans four and Burlingham three.

All in all, it was a strange distribution, clearly the result of a Ministry bureaucracy with little knowledge of the bus industry, and much the same happened to vehicles of other makes. In due course, some exchanges were made in a few cases to help operators to standardise, though most of the 'unfrozen' Bristol buses ran for much of their lives as allocated, even in fleets where they were the only examples – no doubt, their reliable nature and minimal maintenance needs were widely appreciated, especially in wartime.

Two special single-deck chassis were built at the end of the 56th sanction as a part of the national effort to investigate producer-gas operation. They differed from the conversions of existing buses then in hand in having the producer gas plant housed at the rear of the bus itself, rather than being carried on a trailer. Also, to compensate for the loss of power, Gardner 6LW engines were fitted.

Uniquely among Bristol installations of the 6LW, the extra length of 6in or so of this engine compared to the 5LW was accommodated by extending the frame forward, the radiator thus projecting forward of the cab front panel, rather than extending the bonnet rearwards as was usual Bristol practice in such cases. This might have been in an effort to help in balancing the extra weight of the gas plant at the extreme rear of the vehicle. Special permission was given for the overall length to be 30ft rather than the 27ft

The 'unfrozen' bus scheme produced several surprises, not only in the allocations of chassis makes to hitherto unlikely users but in the combinations of chassis and bodywork produced. In some cases bodies intended for other chassis as well as other fleets found unexpected homes. As well as producing new bodies to the utility specification, Duple fitted bodywork of pre-war design to some K5G buses, including chassis 57.051, allocated to Thomas Tilstone & Sons Ltd, of Burslem, Stoke-on-Trent in 1942. Generally similar bodies had been built on Albion Venturer CX19 chassis for Red & White Services Ltd and its subsidiaries up to 1941. It was still in grey livery when photographed by John Gillham in May 1952.

Left: At the time, and for many years afterwards, the only Bristol vehicles to have been exported to the island of Ireland were two K5G models allocated to the Northern Ireland Road Transport Board in 1942, chassis 57.057, registered GZ 304, being seen in early post-war days running as V340. The 53-seat lowbridge bodywork was built by NIRTB but resemblances to the Northern Counties utility design – see the picture below left – suggests that the structure may have been based on its framing.

Below: Strachans bodywork was fitted to some of the unfrozen K5G buses, some being to utility specification but others of pre-war design, in all probability intended for Dennis Lance buses to be operated by Aldershot & District. This example of one of the latter, chassis number 57.081, was allocated to Potteries Motor Traction Co Ltd, becoming its No.196 (HVT 912) but in 1946 transferred to North Western Road Car Co Ltd, as seen here, becoming No.1 in that fleet. It was part of a scheme under which all of PMT's K5G buses were exchanged for wartime Guy Arab and Daimler CWG5 buses from North Western's fleet.

Below: United Automobile Services Ltd received four K5G with Northern Counties 53-seat lowbridge bodywork in 1942, the first one, BDO27 (GHN 187) on chassis 57.030, being transferred to Bell's Services Ltd of Westerhope, a United subsidiary, and seen operating for that concern in about 1947.

A unique pair of buses were the L6GG types numbered 56.016 and 017, an attempt to make a satisfactory producer-gas bus not requiring a trailer to carry the gas plant, with its attendant problems. Also, to improve power output, a Gardner 6LW engine was fitted, adapted to run on gas, evidently with spark ignition and sounding very like a six-cylinder petrol engine. Unusually for a Bristol fitted with this engine, the extra length it needed was provided by extending the bonnet forwards, perhaps in an effort to minimise the tail-heavy effect of the gas equipment mounted at the extreme rear in an extended overhang – as built, they were 30ft long. They had been ordered by Western National but when delivered back to Bristol in April and July 1942 were numbered 2169-70 and registered HHT 459-60 as in the BTCC fleet before being sent quite soon to Eastern National and Eastern Counties respectively, although one ran for a time in 1945, still on gas, with Western National. Both were rebuilt to 27ft 6in length in 1946.

6in which was the normal maximum for a two-axle single-decker at the time.

The two chassis were numbered 56.016 and 017 and were bodied by ECW largely in accordance with the utility specifications, though with emergency exit at the offside front, the rear of the body being partitioned internally to leave room for the gas plant in a rear compartment – the seating capacity was 32. Both were officially for BTCC, given the fleet numbers 2169-70 and registered HHT 459-60, the first being delivered in April 1942, but they were respectively transferred to the Eastern National and Eastern Counties fleets in June of that year, and it seems that the latter vehicle may have gone directly to ECOC, since its delivery date from ECW is quoted as July 1942. These vehicles are of interest, quite apart from the gas propulsion, in that some aspects of the body design formed the basis of what eventually became the Tilling group's post-war standard single-deck design put into production in 1946.

Mention of the Tilling group makes it appropriate to mention the reorganisation of the Tilling & British Automobile Traction Co Ltd, which had been set up in 1928 in an effort to tidy up the complex investments of Thomas Tilling Ltd, on the one hand, and on the other, the British Electric Traction Co Ltd. The latter, originally largely a tramway group, then had many of its bus interests in the hands of a subsidiary called the British Automobile Traction Co Ltd. Tilling had shares both in BAT and

directly in some of its subsidiaries, so the creation of TBAT had seemed a logical step. The general pattern that had emerged was that a large proportion of the major bus companies in England and Wales were subsidiaries of TBAT, although in practice either Tilling or BET had a dominant shareholding, this being reflected in the vehicle policy.

Tilling also had direct shareholdings in other companies, notably Eastern, Southern and Western National, and also United Counties, as well as Brighton Hove & District, which was the direct successor to the local branch of Thomas Tilling Ltd. BET, on the other hand, also had direct holdings in companies which had tramway origins. So the structure was still very complex, and as the management of Tilling and BET, with strong personalities on both sides, tended to differ on many policy matters, the apparent joint control via TBAT did not work very smoothly.

So it was resolved to split TBAT into two quite separate holding companies, one run directly by Tilling and the other by BET, so that all the companies henceforth became subsidiaries of either Tilling or BET, eliminating cross-shareholdings between the two as far as possible. In the course of setting up this new arrangement, some companies 'changed sides'. The Tilling group gained Crosville, Lincolnshire and Cumberland (though in the last-mentioned case, the Meageen family which had founded the business still retained control). The BET group gained East Midland, which had briefly switched the opposite way, and North Western.

The effects of these changes, effective from September 1942, on vehicle policy did not become clear for a couple of years or so due to the overriding effects of wartime controls, but, in due course, the general rule already in effect that Tilling subsidiaries would standardise on Bristol chassis and, usually, ECW bodywork, became tighter. Conversely, the BET companies did not have an automatic choice of make – though there was widespread favour for Leyland and in some companies, AEC, but there were various exceptions to this. The high regard clearly held by Maidstone & District and, at that stage, especially its subsidiary Chatham & District, for the Bristol K5G was particularly relevant here. The departure of North Western from Tilling control was a particular surprise at the time and its future policy was awaited with interest.

During 1942, production got under way with utility buses based on new rather than 'unfrozen' chassis. For double-deck buses, operators were for a time offered no choice, the only make available being Guy, which was another wartime surprise, for Guy Motors Ltd had made hardly any full-sized motor bus chassis since 1936. When it was decided that this was to be the situation, Major Chapple offered Sydney Guy use of the K-type design but the latter, the founder of his business, preferred to produce an updated version of the Arab model that had been built from 1933. It is interesting to speculate on what might have happened if Guy had accepted the offer, which doubtless would have suited the Tilling group in maintaining supplies of what would have been virtually its standard model. In the long run, however, Guy was able to build up considerable post-war business by further updating

the Arab in a way that would not have been possible with a 'borrowed' design.

However, even though Bristol bus chassis production ceased for much of the middle period of the war, permission was given for the construction of a few post-war prototypes, Bristol and ECW building a pair of double-deckers. They were on K5G chassis, to a specification quite close to the contemporary standard, though the appearance was slightly altered by the use of mildly lowered radiators. Much more evident to the passengers was a very considerable reduction of noise and vibration by the use of flexible engine mountings of a design much more effective than that used on early GO5G and JO5G models. The bodywork was largely to the style that had been developed by ECW after its move to Irthlingborough and being used on a small scale to rebody existing chassis. Although based on the wartime specification in some respects, such as the use of five window bays between bulkheads, it was more rounded in outline and the functional lines were to form the basis of the post-war Tilling standard. The chassis were given numbers following on from the 'unfrozen' 57th sanction. The first, 57.086, received a highbridge 56-seat body and became Western National 350, registered JTA 271, being delivered on 1st November 1943, painted in a wartime grey livery. The second chassis, 57.087, was given a 55-seat lowbridge version of the same general body style, and was delivered to Eastern National as its 3885, registered JVW 430 on 17th January 1944, painted in green and cream. These two buses were given MoS numbers BD86 and 87 respectively.

The two spent periods with various Tilling group operators, giving a clear indication of the direction of the group's ideas for post-war bus design.

The two K5G prototypes produced as a basis for post-war production were readily distinguishable from the pre-war version by the radiator, modified in design so as to be set lower on the frame than previously, though not so markedly so as was to become standard from 1946. More fundamentally, the engine was flexibly mounted, making these buses much less noisy than their predecessors and largely vibration-free internally, and thus greatly improved from the passengers' viewpoint. The ECW body design was based on those built in small numbers to rebody existing buses, conforming to the wartime utility scheme in being of five-bay layout and in some minor details, yet having an agreeably functional outline that was to be the basis of ECW double deck bodywork styles in the post-war period. Seen here is the first of the two to be completed, on chassis 57.086, which became Western National 350 (JTA 271), with highbridge 56-seat body delivered from Lowestoft on 1st November 1943. During the next two years or so, this bus, and its lowbridge counterpart, JVW 430 of Eastern National, operated for various Tilling companies. In 1955, JTA 271 was fitted with a new ECW lowbridge body and a PV2 radiator, thereby conforming outwardly to postwar standard.

The first of the K6A models built under wartime arrangements had chassis number W1.001, becoming BTCC's 3642, registered HHY 586, one of a pair which were the only new buses entering the Bristol fleet that year. They had Strachans 55-seat lowbridge bodies and, as delivered, conformed to the full rigours of the utility specification, with wooden slatted seats and unvarnished grey paintwork. This early post-war view shows that by then upholstered seats had been fitted, the standardised green and cream Tilling livery had been applied and a quick-action radiator filler had been fitted in place of the original screw-down type.

The AEC A202 engine used in the K6A was very similar to the A173 unit which had become standard in most of the AEC range from 1939, of 7.7-litre nominal size and with direct injection using toroidal cavities in the pistons. So as to allow its use in place of the Gardner 5LW engine under wartime production allocations, the A202 was modified in regard to mounting arrangements and a detachable bell housing. This also had the effect of making subsequent switches from AEC to Gardner 5LW relatively simple, and these were not uncommon among K6A buses in some Tilling fleets. The inclined lubricating oil filler cap, slightly domed and mounted relatively high near the front, where it was readily visible through a large access hole in the bonnet side was an obvious identification point, as was the splined shaft for a starting handle which projected slightly through the hole provided in the radiator grille, though a handle was not fitted as standard. Neither of these features were needed to identify the type as soon as the engine started, when the sound was both smoother and much less staccato than the 5LW's clattery bark. Engines for Bristol chassis generally had Simms fuel injection pumps, as seen here.

The Gardner 5LW engine, Bristol's standard oil engine since 1935 though temporarily not available to Bristol in 1944-5 under wartime allocations, had not altered significantly since its introduction in 1931. Its standard output of 85bhp remained unaltered until 1950, and even then the changes in design did not alter the main features and could be applied retrospectively. Gardner, as proprietary engine builders, had not been as conscious of the desirability of compact design as concerns which also made chassis, and thus Gardner's five-cylinder engine was of about the same length as most other makers' six-cylinder bus engines of similar bore size. Among other factors, the timing case at the front, and associated items such as a device giving automatic advance in the injection pump drive, were bulkier, and hence the first cylinder was set well back from the radiator. Gardner's lubricating oil filler was horizontal and set lower. When used in post-war models, this and part of the linkage controlling the injection pump governor could be seen through the bonnet hole.

14 Production resumed – the W-series chassis

By 1943-4, the war situation had improved and it became possible to allow the producer gas scheme to be scaled down – in September 1944, it was abandoned completely.

The Government permitted bus manufacture to be expanded – Daimler had been allowed to resume production of double-deck chassis, deliveries having begun during 1943. It became possible for Bristol to resume chassis production in mid-1944, this also being of double-deck models only. The chassis was the K-type, with design largely as before, but no supplies of new Gardner engines could be released as they were fully taken up by other needs, including the Guy Arab double-decker. It seems clear that the Tilling group acted upon the knowledge of the forthcoming resumption of production, as group companies took only limited numbers of Guy Arab buses, ceasing to do so after about the end of 1943.

AEC had engine-building capacity available, and a special version of its direct-injection A173 engine of nominal 7.7-litre capacity (the actual swept volume being 7.58 litres) was put into production with features to facilitate its use in chassis which normally employed the 5LW with minimum modification. This was type A202, having the same 105mm bore and 146mm stroke and most main design features as the A173. The difference lay in the mountings, flywheel dimensions and detachable bell housing that made it directly interchangeable with the 5LW in its installation into the chassis, though the exhaust, on the opposite side of the engine, and control linkage differed. The A202 unit was used by Atkinson, ERF and Maudslay in wartime goods chassis as well as by Bristol in the K6A, as the resulting model was known.

The maximum power output was quoted as 98bhp at 1,800rpm, substantially higher than the 85bhp at 1,700rpm of the 5LW at that date, but in wartime many AEC 7.7-litre engines were derated to an economy setting of 86bhp, which made them only marginally more powerful than a full-rated 5LW, though the slightly broader speed-range and less sharp governor cut-off still left them with quite a responsive performance.

There was some confusion in regard to the name of the model in contemporary press reports, in which it was described as the W1 series or type, but this was the designation of the sanction covering the first 150 chassis. The Ministry of Supply allocated its own parallel series of numbers, beginning at B001, which was W1.001, and kept in step throughout this sanction; thus B116 was W1.116.

Generally, the chassis design changed only slightly from that as built in 1937-42. As was usual AEC practice, access holes were provided in the bonnet sides to allow engine oil levels to be checked and replenished without their removal, and this also became a feature of subsequent K and L models with other engines. At first, the radiator had a painted finish and the headlamps were of the small type as fitted to military vehicles, the black-out restrictions still requiring that they be masked.

Wartime restrictions on the use of aluminium or other light alloys generally made wartime buses appreciably heavier than their predecessors, and the description of the model in 'Bus & Coach' magazine of December 1944 quotes the chassis weight as 4tons 15cwt 3qr, dry and less batteries, but by February 1945, that in *Modern Transport* was down to 4tons 2cwt. This description refers to release of aluminium, of which advantage was taken 'at a very early stage', enabling a saving of weight of 10cwt to be made in the first production batch of the new series. The figure quoted in 1937 for the K5G was 3tons 18cwt 2qr, and as the 5LW was about 2cwt lighter than the 7.7, it seems that the chassis of the K as being built early in 1945 was only marginally heavier than as originally introduced. As completed, with utility bodywork, the difference was rather greater, taking the complete unladen weight from the usual figure below 6tons 15cwt applicable in 1939 to over 7 tons, and this continued in the post-war period.

Other aspects of the chassis remained much as introduced in 1937, with triple-servo brakes, the same Bristol-designed 17in clutch, four-speed gearbox and rear axle, the standard ratio in the latter being 6.0 to 1. On the road, the combination of this and the AEC engine married up very well, with noticeably livelier performance despite the extra weight. From the passenger compartment, there was a noticeable reduction of noise and vibration despite the AEC engine being solid-mounted in just the same way as the 5LW, this having the effect that the gearbox whine became clearly audible instead of being largely drowned out as hitherto. However, the Bristol gearbox as used in the K had an agreeably mellow tone, more so in the opinion of the author than the AEC crash gearbox normally associated with this engine, and the combined effect was quite pleasing to the ear, even if still relatively noisy by later standards. However, it has to be said that the standards of balance of wartime AEC engines were sometimes suspect, and the occasional K6A would have an unpleasant 'thump' at the higher end of the engine speed range in much the same way as applied to the similarly-powered wartime Daimler CWA6.

The system of bodying and allocation of production utility buses continued in much the same way as applied to the unfrozen examples, except that body production was

Bus production was under Ministry of Supply control during much of the war, this being in full swing when Bristol resumed production in 1944 and continuing into 1946, though gradually the degree and extent of such control was eased. This view in the works of Park Royal Coachworks Ltd shows an example of that concern's standard pattern of highbridge body to the 'utility' specification in force at the time, nearing completion. The maker's body number chalked on the registration plate, B28690, identifies it as being on K6A chassis W1.046, completed in November 1944 for Luton Corporation, where it was to be No.86 (DMJ 86). Buses were generally delivered in matt grey paint at that date, the precise shade depending on the bodybuilder. Although looking rather artificially posed here, women were directed into factory work in quite large numbers at that date, to some degree replacing men called up into the armed forces, though skilled craftsmen were generally retained.

less widely spread. Officialdom tended to work on a basis of 60 per cent highbridge and 40 per cent lowbridge, failing to recognise that this was as out of line with demand in one direction for Bristol as it had been in the other for Daimler. The W1 sanction included 90 Park Royal highbridge and it seem probable that originally there were to have been 60 Strachans lowbridge, though in the event one chassis, W1.147, received a Duple highbridge body, possibly as a prototype, for Duple was to take over from Park Royal as the standard highbridge supplier from about a third of the way through the second wartime sanction.

The wartime body specification applicable when output for the W1 chassis began was about at its most austere, with the slatted wooden seats that had been introduced for double-deckers in the latter part of 1943 in place of the upholstered type provided previously. On the other hand, a minor improvement that had appeared at the same time was the glazing of the emergency exit at the rear of the upper deck in place of the steel-panelled version as specified on earlier utility designs, including those on unfrozen chassis. Generally exterior panelling had been in steel as part of the earlier wartime policy, but aluminium was permitted again from July 1944, and this change was just beginning to come into effect as the early W1 models were being bodied. Much more noticeable in its effects was the 'relaxed' specification announced at the end of 1944, when upholstered seats and domed panels at the front and rear of the roof were once again permitted, together with two opening windows (instead of one) on each side of each deck. In practice, for supply reasons, these latter changes came into effect in a piecemeal fashion, spread over the earlier months of 1946, bodybuilders differing sharply in the way they were introduced.

Park Royal's utility body design was very much as it had been in 1941-42, and even its relaxed version on Bristol chassis looked very largely as the 1942 version on unfrozen chassis. The Strachans utility body was perhaps the most box-like of all in its outline, this applying to early examples on W1 chassis, but the rear view was greatly improved in relaxed form as introduced in the Spring of 1945, with a rear dome shape almost to peacetime outline. Duple's wartime utility bodywork was among the better-proportioned in appearance, and the relaxed version as built on W2 and early W3 chassis was one of the least austere-looking of the designs conforming to the utility specification.

Allocation of the W-series chassis was still under the Ministry of War Transport's system, which meant that chassis numbers were allocated in quite small runs, rarely exceeding three at a time. There was a little more responsiveness to operators' preferences and thus the lowbridge buses in particular mostly found their way to Tilling companies. Even so, there were some unfamiliar names among the recipients. Thus W1.001 and 002, with Strachans lowbridge bodies, were supplied back to BTCC as 3642-3 (HHY 586-7), being the fleet's only new buses

placed in service in 1944. Then followed W1.003-5 with Park Royal highbridge bodies for Maidstone & District, a Strachans pair for Southern National, three more Park Royal for M&D, two Strachans for Hants & Dorset, then three Park Royal but this time for Cardiff Corporation, and so on. Deliveries of completed W1 series chassis continued until about July 1945.

At that stage, the AEC engine was the only unit on offer – indeed early in 1945 it was reported that the production rate of chassis was governed by the delivery of engines from AEC, then being allocated at eighteen per month. However, the easy interchangeability of engine types allowed the possibility of the 5LW being substituted with minimal difficulty. It is understood that some operators were able to send 5LW units that were available from spares float or removed from other vehicles which were then built into new chassis, and thus a few of the W1 and W2 chassis began life as K5G models – in addition, there were quite a number of instances where such units were fitted in later years. In many Tilling fleets there were numbers of 5LW engines available from scrapped buses, and even quite an old engine could be brought up to later standard at overhaul, Gardner making a point of so designing minor improvements to allow parts to remain interchangeable. So far as is known, the following W1 and W2 chassis were built as K5G – W1.011-2 (Hants & Dorset), 049 (Southern Vectis), 132-3 (Western National), W2.081 (BTCC).

The W2 sanction, of 100 chassis, followed much the same pattern as W1, though the 57 highbridge versions had bodywork divided between 20 Park Royal and 37 Duple, there being 43 with Strachans lowbridge bodies. Deliveries to operators extended over the period from July 1945 to about the end of the year, though some of the later

A similar bus to the one shown opposite, in fact the next one for the Luton Corporation fleet, No.87 (DMJ 87) on chassis W1.054 with Park Royal body B28695, is seen here in service still in virtually original condition in the 1950s. This was the last of the four with similar bodywork allocated to Luton, which had standardised on Daimler buses pre-war but that undertaking was to receive four of the W3-series chassis with Weymann bodywork of peacetime style in 1946 before turning to Crossley for its next ones did not enter service until early 1946. The chassis design continued virtually unchanged, this being the last sanction to have the tall radiator as introduced on the original K and L in 1937. For most of this sanction, the Ministry of Supply numbers continued in sequence, so that B151 was W2.001, running to B237 (W2.087) but then the order began to be out of sequence, and became intermingled with the next sanction, W3.

Taken together, the W1 and W2 production thus amounted to 250 vehicles, and apart from orders from what could be counted as regular Bristol users – at this stage, the pattern of allocations did reflect operators' preferences to a greater degree than earlier – notable recipients included some hitherto unfamiliar names. Among the most significant of these was Crosville Motor Services Ltd, now a member of the Tilling group instead of a BET-influenced member of TBAT, and hence obliged to switch from Leyland to Bristol as its main supplier of chassis, the initial vehicles being twelve K6A with Strachans bodywork as supplied to other lowbridge users.

Among municipalities, and in addition to four Park Royal examples for Luton Corporation (following on from its single unfrozen K5G), Cardiff Corporation, then having a largely AEC fleet, took a total of eighteen, of which thirteen had Park Royal bodywork and five Duple. Wigan Corporation, normally a Leyland user, received three K6A from the W1 sanction with Strachans lowbridge bodywork, though those with longer memories would recall that, in 1927-8, eleven B-types had been purchased. St Helens Corporation, another lowbridge user, also took three examples, but from the W2 sanction, which also included a pair for a Yorkshire independent operator, T. Burrows, of Wombwell, another such recipient being Tilstone of Stoke, which received a single example, all these having Strachans bodywork. Tilstone had been allocated an unfrozen K5G, and hence the repeat order suggests that was another case of the K being well regarded.

With the resumption of bus chassis production at Bristol, the Tilling group was able to resume its normal standardisation on the make, though quantities, especially of lowbridge versions, were generally limited at first. Crosville, hitherto a TBAT company under BET influence and standardising on Leyland chassis, now found itself coming under Tilling's centralised policy on such matters. Deliveries of Bristol vehicles to this fleet began in 1945-46 with 22 K6A models with Strachans lowbridge bodywork in the W1 and W2 sanctions, an unusually large allocation at that date. They also introduced Tilling green livery – up to that date Crosville standardised on maroon, favoured since its period under LMS railway ownership.

Among them was the vehicle shown, originally numbered M176 ((FFM 315) on chassis W1.102, and seen here in Liverpool in early post-war days. Crosville's M series of fleet numbers was at first issued only to oil-engined Leyland Titans but Guy and then Bristol models were added in wartime – in 1946, the prefix MB was adopted for the K6A buses, as shown. Like others of the batch, it received a new ECW body and PV2 radiator in 1953, continuing in service until 1967.

Quite a large proportion of the highbridge K6A buses from the W1 and W2 sanctions went to municipal fleets. Pontypridd was able to resume its normal choice of chassis, even though with unfamiliar engine and body makes. Number 39 (FNY 932) was on K6A chassis W1.050 and had Park Royal bodywork, entering service at the end of 1944. The body was rebuilt in post-war days and the four buses of this type in the fleet remained in service until the 1960s. Visible behind is No.56 (HTX 611) a K5G dating from 1949 on chassis 68.014 and with body by Beadle.

United was typical of Tilling companies that had been users of Bristol buses pre-war in applying for allocations of K6A models for its fleet as soon as they became available. There were ten from the W1 and W2 sanctions, all with Strachans lowbridge bodywork – indeed, save for a total of nine examples for municipal or independent fleets as mentioned in the text, the entire Strachans output of 102 such buses went to Tilling fleets. United was typical in that a small number, seven in this case, of Guy Arab buses had been added to the fleet in 1943, but none were purchased in 1944, the group evidently preferring to wait until the K-type became available.

This scene outside the United headquarters works and depot in Darlington shows BDO34 and 37 (GHN 634 and 837) with chassis W1.145 and W2.055, both dating from 1945, in company with post-war L5G single-deckers circa 1949. The slightly earlier of the two buses, BDO34, on the left, had bodywork to full utility pattern at the front though having a rounded rear dome, whereas the slightly less angular form shown by BDO37 had been reached later in 1945. Both had large destination apertures as being standardised by Tilling companies, though with a blind of more limited width in one case, and they had received the early post-war type of filler cap, as extensively adopted by Tilling fleets. It is also noteworthy that starting handles had been fitted, presumably to simplify maintenance – hand-starting an AEC 7.7-litre engine would be quite a feat, though this unit's response to an electric starter was normally very rapid. Both received later bodies before withdrawal in 1960 and 1958 respectively.

Duple became the normal highbridge body supplier in mid-1945, about a third of the way through the W2 sanction. This example for Colchester Corporation on chassis W2.042 received a lower registration number than three buses on chassis W2.020-22 for this fleet with Park Royal bodywork – it was not uncommon for bodybuilders to be out of step to some degree. Duple had built only small numbers of double-deck bodywork before the war but became one of the larger producers in wartime, largely on Daimler chassis, though there were also a few Guys – its designs had the merit of good proportions and tended to last a little better than most utility bodies despite the slender pillars used.

Maidstone & District seems to have been well satisfied with the Bristol-AEC combination, having had chassis of both makes prewar, receiving no less than 63 out of the 250 K6A models built in the W1 and W2 sanctions and then going on to standardise on the post-war version for its post-war double-deck needs until 1950. Duple bodywork was fitted to the last thirteen of the W2 vehicles for this fleet, as seen here.

Wartime introduction to Bristol chassis because the normal choice was unavailable sometimes led to post-war orders. Cardiff Corporation probably opted for the K6A when it became available because of its AEC engine, the pre-war fleet being largely composed of AEC buses. Number 79 (CKG 583) on chassis W1.015, new in 1944, had Park Royal utility bodywork, being seen here during an Omnibus Society visit in 1952 – it remained in service until 1962. Bristol was awarded a contract for 20 K-types delivered in 1948-9, though then the choice went to the KW6G model, 8ft-wide and with Gardner 6LW engine.

For its Bristol buses supplied under wartime arrangements from 1942, London Transport revived the class letter B, previously used by its predecessor, the London General Omnibus Co, for its famous pioneer type as introduced in 1910. The wartime Bristol fleet had begun in 1942 with nine unfrozen K5G buses with Park Royal bodywork, followed by 20 K6A models, beginning at the start of the W3 sanction and thus having the new lower-mounted radiator and bonnet. They had Duple bodywork and were delivered between December 1945 and January 1946. Seen here is B21 (HGC 246) on chassis W3.012, working on the route 92 and bound for the Hanwell garage terminus, its home base, which was only a few hundred yards from AEC's factory at Southall. The K5G buses were fitted with AEC engines in 1948-9. When withdrawn in 1951-3, all 29 were taken up by Tilling companies – B21 went to Lincolnshire Road Car Co, remaining in service until 1960.

15 Peace – and a new look for the K and L

The end of the war, firstly in Europe in May 1945, and then with Japan in August, brought normality nearer, though, as at the beginning, there was some delay before new vehicle deliveries showed evidence of these events. At first, the manufacture and allocation of buses remained under Ministry of Supply and Ministry of War Transport control and deliveries continued to show some indications of this until well through 1946, even though, gradually, peacetime standards returned.

Deliveries of W3 sanction buses began in December 1945, and here there was quite a dramatic change in appearance, with a new style of radiator, soon to become well-known by its designation PV2, mounted considerably lower than the previous standard, with bonnet line to suit. The radiator outline at the top was virtually unchanged but the sides curved gently inwards towards the bottom instead of being parallel. It was a simple change, but remarkably effective in giving the model a fresh appearance without losing its rugged character. Circumstantial evidence suggests that it was influenced by the similar bonnet level of the London Transport RT-type version of the AEC Regent, which had pioneered this feature from its introduction in 1939 – one vehicle, RT19, had visited many operators as a demonstrator, including Brighton

A dramatic difference in appearance resulted from the switch to the PV2 radiator from the beginning of sanction W3. The earlier K and L types, from their introduction in 1937, and indeed the G and J before them, had among the tallest radiators of contemporary British bus chassis, so the adoption of a bonnet level amongst the lowest on offer made a remarkable contrast. This view taken in the Autumn of 1945 shows the first chassis of the 'low' version, W3.001, alongside W2.094, representing what had gone before – both were K6A models, the AEC engine being the only one on offer at the time. The front axle, frame, and steering were all unaltered in height, save that the dumb irons became shallower, but the new PV2 radiator (replacing the KV type) and bonnet to match, plus new deeper front mudguards, gave a completely fresh and 'modern' appearance. Very often, a purely cosmetic revision of this kind is apt to turn out unsatisfactorily, but here the proportions achieved were particularly harmonious, possibly the most attractive ever achieved by Bristol. The external mounting of the Autovac fuel-lift device was beginning to go out of favour generally but Bristol continued with it and left it at the same level as previously, logical from a functional viewpoint, as fuel flowed by gravity from it to the injection pump, but it was to somewhat spoil the good view forward from the nearside passenger seat allowed by the new bonnet level.

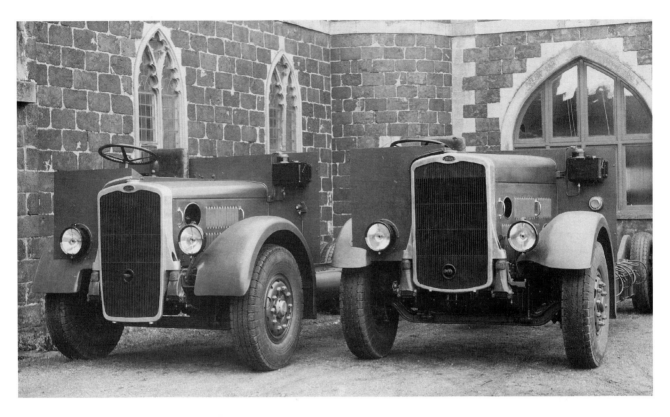

This three-quarter view of chassis W3.001 and W2.094, again posed amid the almost ecclesiastical surroundings of what had been Brislington tram depot, shows the effect on the bonnet side of the lower radiator level. The front access hole became positioned only just below the top edge of the bonnet side panel, the louvres and handles to lift it off being repositioned slightly lower. This high position was to be used for both AEC and the new Bristol engine then soon to be announced, whereas bonnet sides for Gardner-engined chassis had it positioned slightly lower to suit the position of the filler on that engine. There was also a rear hole, the top edge of which is just visible on the right-hand chassis, that being always set lower to suit the dipstick level. The pre-war models did not have access holes, this being an idea that had come in with the AEC engine, having been usual on AEC models of the period. This view also shows how the bonnet top had become low enough to reveal the top of the gear lever and, more important when pulling out from behind another bus, the driver was able to see almost to the bottom edge of the nearside mudguard. The two chassis went respectively to London Transport, W3.001, fitted with a Duple highbridge body becoming B10 in that fleet, immediately after its 'unfrozen' K5G buses, while W2.094 went to St Helens Corporation, being one of three with Strachans lowbridge body.

Hove & District, then still apt to be regarded as 'Tilling's own', where an official photograph taken in April 1942 showed it lined up in a carefully posed front view with one of BH&D's standard Regents and a 1940 K5G.

Initially, the engine for the W3 sanction version of the K continued to be the AEC 7.7-litre in its A202 form, and the bodywork choice remained restricted to Duple highbridge or Strachans lowbridge, in both cases still to the relaxed utility specification. The Ministry of Supply serial numbers continued, beginning in correct sequence at B251 for W3.001, though several buses among the first fourteen had numbers which fitted into the late W2 sequence before reverting to a regular pattern from B265 for W3.015 and then continuing to B389 which was W3.139, at which point the system ended.

Breaking into the run of early W3 chassis for London Transport was W3.015, a K6A which received a Strachans lowbridge body and became United BDO41 (GHN 841). It was photographed at Whitley Bay by the author a few minutes after he had ridden in it from Newcastle in May 1946, apparently very newly in service – note the shiny tyres – although this bus has been recorded as dating from 1945. It was unusual in having the combination of W3 chassis and 'relaxed utility' body for a Tilling fleet, BTCC being the only other recipient of buses with such a combination. It had the new Tilling ultra-large destination display in its early form.

Despite its remnants of wartime practice – note that the headlamps were of the small 'military' type, unusually on a W3 chassis – it had given a favourable impression, not matched by BDO42, on chassis W3.055, also sampled at about that date, which reverted to United's normal practice in being a K5G and was disappointingly noisy despite its stylish new style of ECW body. The flexible engine mounting on the two wartime prototypes was not adopted for production until 1948-9.

St Helens Corporation was another operator whose allocation of K6A buses with Strachans lowbridge bodywork spilled over from the W2 to W3 sanction and thus included examples with both radiator heights. Seen here is W3.022, St Helens No.48 (DJ 9270), new in March 1946, which joined three buses with similar bodywork but on W2-series chassis, including that shown before bodying on the opposite page. It is seen here after repainting into the livery with cream upper panels adopted after the arrival at St Helens of R. Edgley Cox as General Manager, better known for his introduction to that fleet of buses built to the London RT specification. It had also acquired a quick-action radiator filler cap of the type fitted to later models. Most bus bodies built under the wartime 'utility' scheme suffered to varying degrees from the poor timber available at the time, and by the mid 1950s a Strachans body of this type had become a rarity. This picture also shows wiring for the town's trolleybus system, part of which briefly outlasted this bus, withdrawn in 1957.

As it happened, the change in style coincided with the supply of 20 buses to London Transport. These were given the fleet numbers B10-29, which followed on from that organisation's nine unfrozen K5G models – they had chassis numbers W3.001-14/6/7/20/1/4/5, entering service in December 1945 and January 1946. They had the Duple body, which was one of the best-proportioned of the utility designs, and naturally attracted quite widespread publicity. Other single early W3 buses went to United, Doncaster and St Helens Corporations, and a Welsh independent operator, Bryn Melyn of Llangollen; there were also eight for BTCC, all of these having Strachans bodywork.

An important landmark was the return of Eastern Coach Works to body construction on new chassis. In February 1946, production of the post-war standard 55-seat lowbridge design began with a batch of eight for Crosville Motor Services Ltd, henceforth a major Bristol user. The first vehicle was on chassis W3.033, which received ECW body 1001 of Series 2, the first in its post-war sequence, and the remainder comprised W3.040-6 with bodies 1002-8. The body was quite similar to that on the prototype supplied to Eastern National in 1944, but the design was most noticeably altered to suit the lowered radiator.

The reappearance of Eastern Coach Works as a bodybuilder was another key step in the return to something akin to the prewar production pattern. The immediate post-war standard lowbridge body was well suited to the design of the revised Bristol K chassis, giving a functional overall effect apt to make some other designs of the time look dated. This example for Thames Valley Traction Co Ltd on chassis W3.112 has the 1946 style of glazing, with square-cornered sliding vents which clashed stylistically with the radiused corners of the rubber-glazed main windows beneath them, but that was tidied up the following year. Thames Valley, which had favoured six-cylinder Leyland models prewar, apart from its first Bristol buses which arrived just as war broke out, turned to the K6A and the corresponding L6A in the period just after the war. A similar pattern tended to be followed by Crosville and Lincolnshire, also previously Leyland users.

ECW initially concentrated on lowbridge bodies and hence BTCC took some of its early post-war K5G buses with Duple highbridge bodywork, still to the 'relaxed utility' specification; elsewhere among the traditional Bristol users within the Tilling group the return of the Gardner 5LW engine was linked to that of ECW bodywork. Seen here at the Marlborough stop for the Swindon service apt to be favoured by bus photographers is 3674 (JHT 123) on chassis W3.070. It is in the modified version of the postwar Tilling green livery with cream window surrounds adopted at the time of the 1951 Festival of Britain. A complex body and engine transfer exercise in the mid-1950s caused this bus to acquire an AEC engine and a 1948 ECW body previously on a 1937 GO5G and it ran in this latter form until 1964.

Intermingled with them were further Duple-bodied highbridge buses to relaxed utility specification, for BTCC, all the W3 chassis up to 048 being K6A models. From W3.049, the K5G reappeared as a regular production option, and was promptly restored, at least for the time being, as the usual choice of most of the longer-established Tilling group users. Eastern National took W3.049-50 with ECW lowbridge bodies and similar buses were supplied to Eastern Counties, United, Western National, Wilts & Dorset, West Yorkshire and Hants & Dorset.

However Maidstone & District continued with the K6A, but reverted to Weymann as its regular body supplier, the latter supplying metal-framed highbridge bodywork to its standard post-war outline, the first examples, on W3.062-4, being delivered in June-July 1946. The K6A-Weymann combination was to remain the standard M&D double-decker, built in both highbridge and lowbridge forms, until 1949, a noteworthy instance of continued favour for the K chassis from what was now a BET subsidiary with not even a minority Tilling shareholding.

Duple continued to build its relaxed utility highbridge double-deck design well into 1946, and as ECW was slightly later in restarting highbridge double-deck production, BTCC took deliveries of the Duple body on twelve further chassis, now K5G, numbered W3.053/4, 060/1, 070/1/6/7, 084/5 and 092/3. Body supply followed

St Helens took a further three K6A, ordered in May 1945 initially via the Ministry of Supply, along with the previous four which had arrived early in 1946, but these were not delivered until July 1947. They had 53-seat lowbridge bodywork by East Lancashire Coachbuilders Ltd, by then released from its wartime role as a 'rebodying' concern. Seen here when new is No.44 (DJ 9837) on chassis W3.168. East Lancs had adopted a four-bay layout for some of its double-deck bodywork, as seen here, being among the earliest bodybuilders other than those under London Transport or AEC influence to do so, these being among the first known examples on Bristol chassis. Unladen weight was 7 tons 11 cwt 2 qr, fairly typical of the period. They remained in service

The first K6G buses were four built in the W3 sanction for Stockton Corporation, having Massey 56-seat bodywork and delivered in 1947. The logic of using the six-cylinder Gardner 6LW engine to power buses which were often almost a ton heavier than their pre-war counterparts and more often running with full loads was clear, but the extra engine length implied a shorter lower saloon than with other engines. Stockton also bought Guy Arab III models with 6LW engines and similar bodywork, though later turning to the Leyland PD2. Seen here when almost new is No.11 (HPT 432) on chassis W3.185.

much the same pattern up to W3.139, the only additional make to appear before then being Roe, producing one highbridge body for Doncaster on W3.101, a K6A. After W3.140, when the MoS system had ceased, East Lancs came back into the picture, with four highbridge for Rotherham (W3.140-1/97-8) and three lowbridge for St Helens (W3.168-70). Four buses for Stockton (W3.1836) were noteworthy for being the first K6G models and having Massey bodywork.

Meanwhile production of single-deck chassis had restarted, and as the wartime system was still in force, the

sanction in question was numbered W4. The chassis were equivalent to the W3 double-deckers in having the PV2 radiator and largely being split between the AEC 7.7-litre and Gardner 5LW engine, the former creating a further new type, the L6A.

The first two chassis were delivered to ECW on 22nd December 1945, receiving prototype bodies to the standard post-war Tilling group single-deck outline with rear entrance, though not delivered to their respective operators until some time after early production examples were entering service. Of these two, W4.001, an L6A, was

Production of L-type single-deck chassis resumed with sanction W4, using the same revised front-end design as the W3 K-type double-deckers. Of the 50 W4 chassis, 32 were L5G models, including the first nine of a batch of 35 for North Western Road Car Co Ltd, a BET company since 1942, though these chassis were a partial fulfilment of an order outstanding since 1939. The body order went to Brush, this firm being willing to produce a design based on North Western's characteristic pre-war outline, with half-canopy cab, though updated in detail design and with outswept skirt panels. The seating capacity was 35 instead of the pre-war 31, but the type of seats were higher-backed than ECW's post war standard. Seen here in Buxton bound for Manchester is No.130 (BJA 430), one of the later vehicles in the batch, on chassis 63.012. The bodies proved fairly troublesome, requiring attention to a structural weakness around the front end, though this one lasted until 1958 when the chassis received a Willowbrook body dating from 1952, the bus being withdrawn in 1964.

The Government's export drive in the immediate aftermath of the war led Bristol to build a special export version of the L5G, with long wheelbase and accordingly designated LL5G. One of the first of the initial delivery of ten chassis to South Africa was W4.016, sold to Penguin Bus Service as shown here, the body being constructed locally.

completed to the 'express' form with 31 coach seats some time in the Spring of 1946 though not joining the Crosville fleet as its KB1 (FFM 469) until January 1947, while W4.002, an L5G, became the first example of the much more numerous 35-seat bus version. This latter, delivered in February 1947, was for United, being given the fleet number BLO223 and registered HHN 223, these following after that company's first post-war batch of similar buses, which began with BLO143 (GHN 943), on chassis W4.005, delivered in July 1946, regular deliveries of the type having then just begun.

The W4 sanction comprised only 50 chassis, and most were supplied in small numbers to Tilling companies, complete with standard ECW 35-seat bodies, following a similar pattern to the double-deckers. They were generally on L5G chassis though Crosville favoured the L6A, and two of these were also supplied to Aberdare UDC, again with ECW bodywork, now tending to be taken up on Bristol chassis for non-Tilling users in cases where Bristol bodywork might have been more likely hitherto. However, North Western, now a BET company, took Brush bodywork

to a style a little reminiscent of its pre-war standard as built by ECW for a batch of L5G, of which the first nine were on W4 series chassis.

A very significant development was the construction of some special export single-deckers. There was strong pressure from the Government to build up exports to redress the serious financial position in which Britain found itself after the enormous outflow of funds during the war. The initial Bristol contribution to this was the construction of a version of the L which was longer than permissible in Britain at the time, and fitted with the Gardner 5LW engine, thus being designated LL5G, and ten chassis, W4.011/2/6, 023/4 and 041/2/5/6/9 were of this type, exported to South Africa via J. A. Ewing of London, acting as shipping agents, and bodied on arrival. They were sold to various operators – W4.011 to Van Zyls Bus Service, W4.012/23/4 to Benoni Municipality (these having Welfitt-Ody 39-seat front-entrance bus bodies), W4.016 to Penguin Bus Service, W4.041/2/5 to Vaal Transport, and W4.046/9 to Thatcher, Hobson & Co.

Pontypridd UDC placed this L5G in service in 1947, one of four with Beadle 32-seat bodywork showing the influence of post-war Tilling ideas in its proportions and the wide destination display, even though the bodybuilder's fondness for curved outlines was also evident. No.50 (GNY 914) was on chassis 61.133.

16 Bristol's own oil engine

A further engine option introduced at this time was Bristol's own six-cylinder diesel and it is opportune to trace its development. As mentioned in Chapter 12, the original prototype unit was fitted to a K5G in BTCC's fleet in 1939. Work had begun in 1938 to develop a six-cylinder unit as an alternative to the Gardner, six experimental units being built. Some were supplied to other operating companies, among them United, which fitted its BDO17 (EHN 617), a 1939 K5G, chassis 47.88, with one that the author noted as beginning operation on a hilly route out of Newcastle in September 1945, finding both its performance and smoothness of running as much improved on the 5LW. These prototype engines were designated XOW, evidently signifying 'experimental oil', the final W being the usual Bristol engine suffix number.

The war gave an opportunity for the trials to last long enough to give an indication of the unit's durability. Only slight modifications in the light of operating experience, and to meet manufacturing requirements, were found necessary and the unit was given a preliminary production code of VW, evidently before WW was issued as an internal code for the AEC A202 unit as used for the W1 sanction chassis in 1944. A pre-production run of twelve engines to this design was produced in 1946, of which six went into W3 sanction chassis, the earliest numerically being W3.072 for Hants & Dorset and W3.078 for Crosville, the chassis being designated K6B. It was then publicly announced in production form as the AVW type, with unchanged 110mm bore and 143mm stroke, giving a swept volume of 8.153 litres. The direct injection system was of the toroidal-cavity type, by then becoming quite widely favoured. Bearing in mind its pre-war design, the AEC and Dennis versions of this layout may have influenced its choice, as examples of both were to be found in BTCC's own fleet. The AEC was the better known, and had the more usual two valves per cylinder, as on the AVW, but the latter's vertical and centrally placed injector was reminiscent of Dennis practice, used in that case with four valves per cylinder and in turn derived from Saurer designs.

However the AVW had a form of induction system intended to improve the engine's breathing and without the complexity of four valves per cylinder. This was the subject of a patent taken out jointly by BTCC and the company's designer, F. J. Buswell and published in June 1941. The inlet ports were extended by 8in-long external pipes linked to a manifold and the ports in the head shaped to promote air swirl. The output quoted was 100bhp at 1,700rpm.

The design was otherwise quite conventional, with separate cylinder block and crankcase, and two cylinder heads each covering three cylinders. Care was taken to minimise the length from the front of the timing case to the back of the cylinder block, and keeping this down to 43in meant that the unit was interchangeable with the 5LW or AEC 7.7, fitting directly into the same bonnet length. The oil filler was in a similar position to that of the AEC unit and thus the access hole for it near the front end of the bonnet side was set higher than with the Gardner engine. The Bristol unit could be visually identified from the AEC by the corner of the polished aluminium induction manifold of the AVW visible just inside the top of this hole. At first the oil filler itself was quite similar to the AEC type, but later Bristol adopted the quick-action swing-over type, also used, on an inclined base, for the radiator filler of all Bristol models from 1947.

On the road, the AVW was readily identified by its deep induction roar, doubtless partly related to the patented design, but it was a relatively smooth-running unit giving acceptable levels of refinement, even when mounted in the

The Bristol 8.1-litre oil engine, in the form as adopted in 1946 for production as the AVW. The lubricating oil filler was in much the same position as on the AEC engine, at first having a conventional screw-on cap, and the access hole in the bonnet side was similarly placed, but the front corner of the inlet manifold could also be seen through it, giving a simple identification guide.

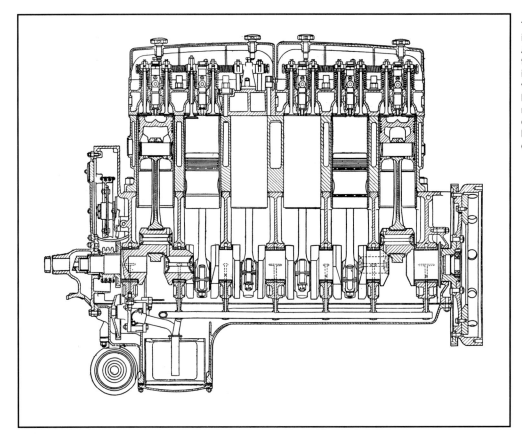

This cross-section shows the internal construction of the AVW engine, including the toroidal-cavity pistons – the injectors were mounted vertically on the cylinder centre-lines. The curved outline of the rocker covers was reminiscent of the short-lived HW engine built for the C-type six-wheeler of 1929.

simple bolted-down way common to all Bristol production models of that early post-war period. In practice, performance on the road seemed much the same as with the AEC engine.

A new pattern of more variety of engine types was emerging, even though the standardisation on Bristol chassis and group specification for ECW bodywork was tighter than even in late pre-war days, within Tilling companies. In addition to Crosville, Thames Valley generally favoured the K6A (instead of reverting to the K5G, as used in 1939-42) and Lincolnshire was another operator to favour the K6A from the beginning of post-war deliveries. The common factor for all of these was a history of general standardisation on Leyland six-cylinder models while under BET management in the late pre-war period and it seems that the AEC engine was favoured as a more suitable successor than the 5LW in the K5G.

Production of the Bristol engine took a little time to gain momentum as was apt to be the case generally with new products, as manufacturers struggled to cope with shortages of materials and equipment in huge demand as peacetime reconstruction got under way. In later years it was to play a larger part in overall chassis production. Ultimately, 2,828 AVW engines were built, production continuing until 1958. The AEC engine faded from the scene after 1950, but the Gardner continued as a major supplier. It was the inability of Gardner to meet the demand for its engines that fostered Bristol's 'multi-engine' policy in the early post-war years.

The latter part of the W3 sanction, which ran to 200 chassis, reflected a little of this new element of variety, even though the K6B figured only marginally. Some of the

later K5G and K6A chassis in this sanction received ECW highbridge 56-seat bodies, this version having been put into production slightly later than the lowbridge. Luton took four K6A, this time with Weymann bodywork basically similar to the Maidstone & District ones.

There were the four K6G, with Gardner 6LW engines, for Stockton Corporation. Of course these required a lengthened bonnet, the Massey bodywork being proportioned to suit, the bulkhead set back by about 6in from the standard position. They were the first K-type chassis to have been produced with the 6LW, a combination later to become widely favoured, though at first restricted to certain municipal customers.

Performance curves for the AVW as put into production.

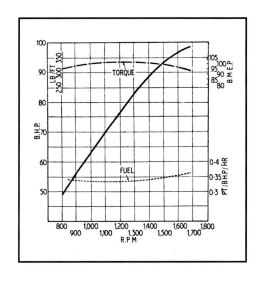

17 Post-war development of the K and L

As has been made clear, the W3 and W4 sanctions represented a transition from wartime methods, laying the foundations for the expansion of output to meet the demands for large-scale deliveries of new vehicles. The range of chassis produced within those sanctions covered most of the main types to be built by Bristol over the years up to 1950, even though various improvements were to be introduced from time to time. Now the emphasis swung to maximising production, helping operators to catch up with overdue fleet renewal and the need for more buses and coaches to carry the rising demand for travel of all kinds.

A return to the pre-war sanction numbering system was made, the 61st sanction being for L-type chassis, and the 62nd of K-types, of which deliveries to operators began in the latter part of 1946 and ran into 1947. It was clear that the series picked up the threads from the 'unfrozen' 56th and 57th sanctions of 1941-42, yet the 'missing' three sanction numbers 58 to 60 did not match up to the four W series that had been built.

A new pattern of L-types with odd-numbered sanctions, and K-types with even-numbered ones, the reverse of the pre-war sequence for these types, was established. It was to continue, with rare exceptions, to the end of regular production of these models, and indeed a similar routine was then followed for later types to a large degree. The level of demand made it logical to increase the sanction

quantities, and after the 61st and 62nd, which were for 150 chassis each, the usual quantity became 200, and this too continued with rare exceptions for the remainder of K and L production and beyond.

Although the Tilling group's philosophy was one of standardisation and the operating companies were given less freedom to follow their own managements' ideas on bus specification than the BET group, the Bristol L or K was reliable and efficient. As well as taking the pressure off hard-pressed companies by enabling them to run services with no more than routine servicing, it was particularly well-suited to the situation where operating economy was essential on rural services which, even in the generally favourable economic climate of those days, barely paid their way – many of the Tilling companies had large areas in which this was so.

Among the details revised during the early post-war years, the original type of radiator filler cap used with the low-set PV2 radiator was an orthodox flat type much as used since 1937, but from circa late 1946 an inclined filler with quick-action swing-over cap was introduced, often subsequently being fitted to earlier types, and indeed other makes of chassis within Tilling fleets, at overhaul. The design of this was further altered slightly from circa 1948 to a neater, less obtrusive design.

A revised design of rear axle was introduced from circa

The long-awaited fleet renewals for Tilling companies got under way in the early post-war years. The first new single-deckers for United's fleet since early in the war period began to arrive in 1946, when seventeen L5G with ECW bodies of the new Tilling standard 35-seat rear-entrance pattern arrived, taking the BLO class fleet numbers from where they had left off in 1942 at BLO142. In 1947 a further 83 were delivered, including BLO190 (GHN 990) on chassis 63.073, seen here dealing with holiday crowds as a relief vehicle at Scarborough in July 1950. By that time, the BLO-series fleet numbers being issued by United had passed the 500 mark, largely to this standardised design and mostly on L5G chassis, though from 1948 a proportion of L6B began to appear and some of the bodies were to the 'express' 31-seat pattern, with a minority of other body types from 1949.

Rotherham Corporation had run a bus fleet composed only of single-deckers (apart from an initial four Daimlers of 1913), but double-deckers were re-introduced in 1947, when four Bristol K-types with East Lancashire 56-seat highbridge bodies were added to the fleet. They were on W3-series chassis, two being K6B and two, as here, K5G, though the latter were later fitted with Bristol engines.

1947. It was readily distinguished by the appearance of the rear hub, which altered from a domed to a flat shape. More significantly, within, the new type of hub gave a strengthened form of drive from the half-shaft.

The wider choice of engines to be found in the W3 and W4 sanction chassis has been outlined in Chapter 16. Even so, after the standardisation on Gardner engines in the pre-war K and L, the continuing level of variety during the late 'forties came as something of a surprise, especially in relation to the Tilling group with its tendency for decisions to be taken at headquarters and uniformity to be favoured. This was being reinforced in other respects, as from 1946 the entire group received bodywork from ECW having none of the individual company variations seen in pre-war days. Apart from a few special cases, complete uniformity was imposed in such details as destination display, with very large units at front and rear of all vehicles, and livery, with choice confined to basically red or green versions of

the same design, even the upholstery being of an ingenious red, green and grey mix applied throughout the group.

The only general exception to this overall uniformity of body specification was in regard to coaches, for ECW did not offer a full luxury coach in the early post-war years, even though what was called the 'express' type, based on the standard rear entrance bus body shell, was quite widely used. Tilling companies were permitted to place orders for coach bodywork elsewhere and, in consequence, quite a variety of bodybuilders and individual designs were to be found on Bristol L-type chassis delivered to Tilling fleets in the 1946-49 period. Beadle alone built several different designs for different operators, but the list of participants included Duple and Harrington as well as several hitherto unfamiliar firms which had entered the coach bodybuilding business as a result of the strong post-war demand, such as Windover, Dutfield, Portsmouth Aviation and Vincent of Reading.

By 1947, the Bristol AVW engine was in regular production, and the highbridge 56-seater shown here ready for delivery from ECW back to BTCC on 16th September of that year was chassis 62.123, one of a run of nine chassis for BTCC all so powered and thus of type K6B. This was among the first instances of numbers of such buses getting beyond ones and twos. As was typical practice at that date for BTCC vehicles, it had received its registration plate KHT 518 but was otherwise unlettered, some of the batch being for the city and others for the country fleet, including this one, becoming 3695. The picture shows how the front of the polished inlet manifold of the Bristol engine was visible through the front bonnet hole, though once the engine was running the deep note of the AVW was readily identified. In 1958, this was one of a number which received slightly later ECW bodies of similar style but metal-framed, then remaining in service until 1965.

It must also be remembered that Bristol, though primarily concerned with supplying Tilling group needs, was still competing in the general market in the immediate post-war period, with BET group, municipal and even a few independent customers. Maidstone & District favoured Bristol chassis, generally K6A, for its early post-war double-deck needs while adopting AEC chassis for single-deckers coaches and buses at that stage.

Another important fleet now in the BET group was North Western, transferred from Tilling control in the

The Royal Blue fleet operating express services across the south of England and shared between the Western and Southern National companies continued to convey a high-grade image. In the late 1930s, some AEC Regal coaches had been purchased and in 1941 one of these was rebodied by Duple, setting the body style for postwar additions to this fleet. Those delivered between 1947 and 1949 consisted of 45 Bristol L-type coaches, with 31-seat front-entrance bodies of similar appearance to the 1941 style, but built by Beadle, 35 being on L6B chassis and ten on L6A.

Seen here in Worthing is No.1217 (JUO 982), on L6B chassis 65.023, a Southern National vehicle dating from 1947. Like others of the type, it was rebodied in 1958 as a bus designed for driver-only operation with full-fronted bodywork by ECW.

Maidstone & District Motor Services Ltd, had no financial link with Bristol in the post-war era, having become a BET subsidiary in the split of TBAT in 1942, but chose the K6A as its standard double-decker in the 1946-50 period, there being a total of 143 and one K6B, mostly in combination with Weymann metal-framed bodywork, though 40 had bodies by Saunders. The example seen here, DH250 (KKK 856), on chassis 66.166, was the first of a batch of 42 with 56-seat highbridge Weymann bodies placed in service in 1948-49. This body style, more usually associated with AEC chassis, suited the post-war K-type particularly well and in the dark green and cream livery looked strikingly attractive. After Bristol chassis could no longer be purchased, M&D turned to the Leyland Titan PD2 for its double-deck needs, as represented by the vehicle behind.

In the post-war era the bulk of Bristol chassis received ECW bodywork and went to Tilling operating companies; until 1950, this output was entirely to the standardised outlines. The nearest approach to a coach as generally understood was the 'express' version of the single-deck body, as seen here. Within, there were comfortable coach seats for 31 passengers and batches were supplied to several companies in 1948, often on L6B chassis, as shown here. United Counties received two examples, of which No.107 (EBD 234), on chassis 71.023, is seen here in Nottingham on the London service.

1942 split. In practice, North Western almost behaved as if still within the Tilling group in regard to its early post-war single-deck deliveries, continuing to favour the Bristol L5G, though the first post-war batch received bodywork built by Brush to an outline rather like the late pre-war variation of ECW bodywork favoured by this operator. Later vehicles had ECW bodywork of standard post-war outline though with different seating and destination boxes. In this case it was the double-deck needs that were taken from another maker, the Leyland PD1 being chosen, though oddly enough even these had a Tilling-like flavour, having ECW bodywork.

Mention of this calls to mind the appearance of 200 new Leyland buses, 150 Titan PD1 and 50 Tiger PS1, divided among some Tilling fleets in 1947-48, that concern being able to supply chassis rapidly enough to boost deliveries to fleets beyond the capabilities of Bristol alone.

At that stage, the output of the Motor Constructional Works, at about 750 chassis per year, was above the previous peak of 630 in 1938 but was still rising, so reinforcement was welcome.

Most ironical was the supply of 50 Titan PD1 models to the Bristol Tramways & Carriage Co itself – a notable case of 'coals to Newcastle'. No doubt their design and behaviour in service was studied carefully by the company, but no indication of Leyland influence from this episode was evident in subsequent standard Bristol products – the days when the fate of Bristol commercial vehicle manufacture was to become bound up with that of Leyland were not to begin until 1965.

A further, and important, means of aiding the operating companies had been announced by the Tilling group early in 1945. This was a reconditioning programme for about 900 G and J type buses dating from 1934 to 1936. A production programme had been laid on for this work, planned to bring the chassis up to date as well as being reconditioned, at a cost equivalent to about three major overhauls. Some gearboxes and front axles were replaced and the brakes brought up to K-type standard – in some cases new frames were provided. The reasoning was that, as they were going to have to run for at least six more years while the arrears of production was made up, it was sensible to invest in making them almost as good as new. This philosophy, typical of Tilling practice, was extended to later types in due course.

Post-war municipal orders for Bristol buses often

It had been realised that new bus output would not catch up with the needs of the Tilling companies until several years after the war and a rehabilitation programme for about 900 buses of the G and J types dating from 1934 to 1936 had been announced by the group early in 1945. This work was put in hand alongside new production and was subsequently extended to later buses. Some had bodywork similarly rebuilt but others received new bodies. Western National 207 (ADV 113) on chassis JO5G.94, dating from 1936, is seen here in September 1949, soon after receiving a new Beadle 36-seat body to what could be described as a pastiche of post-war ECW style. Here a new front axle and the characteristic style of bonnet side fitted to the rehabilitated buses can be seen.

Traditional municipal Bristol users continued to take new buses in the post-war years, even though the numbers were small. Pontypridd UDC went to Beadle for bodywork in 1947-50, including that on six K5G buses delivered in 1948-9, the style used being much as built by this concern under the wartime rebodying programme. Here No.55 (HTX 610) picks its way through traffic entirely composed of the Council's buses and one of its trolleybuses, this being a Karrier W with Park Royal body built to 'relaxed utility' pattern in 1946 – the splashes of grease on the rear panels had come from the overhead wiring, a not uncommon problem, though here it looks as though someone had been over-enthusiastic in its application. The single-decker partly visible in the right foreground was one of three L5G buses with Bristol bodywork dating from 1941 acquired from BTCC in 1952. Pontypridd, unable to buy new Bristol buses by then, turned to Guy from 1956, perhaps influenced by wartime Arabs in the fleet – one with Northern Counties body is just visible here in the background.

tended to come from traditional users. Three of the smaller Welsh undertakings continued as regular purchasers. Aberdare followed three wartime K6A buses by eight L6A and five K6A in 1946-8, all these latter with ECW bodywork, now in effect the 'standard' offering, even outside the Tilling group. Merthyr Tydfil reverted to Gardner power, with three L5G with ECW bodies in 1946 and following up the five K types in the W3 sanction by three K6G with Massey bodywork in 1947 and twelve, split between Duple and local bodybuilder D. J. Davies, in 1948. Pontypridd also took Gardner-engined Bristol buses, but with Beadle bodywork, four L5G and two L6G in 1947, six K5G in 1948-9, four K6G and two L5G in 1950.

Among other traditional municipal users, Rotherham tended to favour the Bristol engine for post-war examples, following up its W3-sanction buses by a series of batches of K6B and L6B in 1948-50, all with bodywork of East Lancashire design, though some were built by associate companies of that concern. Doncaster continued its practice of buying small numbers of Bristol buses among a mixed intake into the early post-war years, with a final four K6A having Roe bodywork in 1947-48.

Cardiff Corporation, which had received allocations of K6A models under wartime arrangements but had not been a peacetime user, placed an order for 6LW-engined K-type chassis to 8ft width, this being permissible for use

Warrington Corporation divided its post-war bus orders between Bristol, Foden, Guy and Leyland but the first pair of K6G buses in 1947 was followed by two batches, a dozen and then ten, in 1949 and a final five in 1950, outnumbering all other purchases in the period. This view of No.66 (GED 62), on chassis 76.174 of the second 1949 batch in the town centre in March 1954 shows the longer bonnet needed for the Gardner 6LW engine, there being a gap of about 6in behind the near-side front mudguard. The bodywork was built by Bruce Coachworks, a Cardiff firm which, in effect, acted as a branch of East Lancashire, building to that firm's designs.

in Britain on approved routes from 1946. These 20 vehicles, bodied by Bruce Coachworks, a local concern which built bodywork to East Lancs design, and delivered in 1948-9 were designated KW6G, being the only home-market 8ft-wide Bristol vehicles built before approval for general use of vehicles of this width in Britain was given in 1950. However, another municipal user of the K6G was Warrington Corporation, again with East Lancs or, mainly, Bruce bodywork, an initial two in 1947 being followed by 22 in 1949 and then five in 1950. Also in Lancashire, St Helens Corporation took eight L6A with Roe bodywork in 1948, but possibly the most remarkable municipal order received by Bristol in that period was one from Edinburgh Corporation, for many years a Daimler stronghold, for twelve L6B with Brockhouse bodywork, supplied in 1950.

Independent customers for Bristol chassis in the 1946-48 period tended to be very few and far between, but it is significant that introduction to Bristol chassis in wartime was apt to be a common factor. Dodds of Troon had acquired the two 1938 L6G coaches originally supplied to Graham of Kirkintilloch when they were sold off by Alexander's in 1944 and, impressed by their qualities, placed an order for three post-war chassis of similar type, these, with Burlingham bodywork, entering service in January 1948. W. L. Silcox, of Pembroke Docks followed up an 'unfrozen' K5G by post-war orders, including six L5G and three K6G, while Bryn Melyn Motor Services of Llangollen followed a W3-sanction K6A with an L6A coach order notable for the choice of bodywork by Yeates, the only example of this combination.

Clearly the development of the Bristol AVW engine and its adoption for production was bound to alter the overall picture in terms of engine choice, but the Gardner, especially in 5LW form, was so strongly established that

its continued favour was hardly a surprise.

The continuance of the AEC 7.7-litre A202 unit as a regular option beyond the completion of contracts made under wartime conditions was more unexpected, though, as has been seen, there was a tendency to favour it for post-war deliveries to companies hitherto favouring six-cylinder buses, mainly of Leyland make, that had been brought into the Tilling group in wartime. This continued through much of the period up to about 1949, K6A and L6A models being found as a regular choice in such fleets as Crosville, Thames Valley and Lincolnshire. What was noteworthy was a tendency for certain longer-established Bristol users, notably Hants & Dorset and to a lesser degree Southern and Western National to switch to the K6A in 1948-9 after initial post-war deliveries of K5G buses. The Royal Blue coach business run by Southern and Western National also took L6A chassis for part of its post-war needs, in this case following pre-war deliveries of some AEC chassis.

In practice the pattern of engine choice that emerged was quite complex and varied as time progressed. Hardly surprisingly, the Gardner 5LW often reverted to being the usual choice among most of those companies, Tilling-controlled in pre-war days, that had standardised on the L5G for what were often substantial parts of their fleets. Notable in this category were United, West Yorkshire and Eastern Counties, though the last-mentioned did cause the revival of the L4G variant with four-cylinder Gardner 4LW engine for part of its post-war deliveries, initially to receive pre-war bodywork which had been built to rebody old chassis.

The Bristol engine began to be chosen for a proportion of K-type buses in certain Tilling-group fleets and for many of the group's L-type coaches, of both 'luxury' and

The Chatsworth Road chassis assembly shop became a hive of activity in the post-war years. This photograph dates from late 1946, it being possible to identify four chassis in the foreground by the time-honoured practice of chalking chassis numbers on the dash panels, useful to workshop staff at the time and invaluable to historians half a century later. All those readable in this view were for United Automobile Services Ltd, nearest the camera on the left being a K5G, 62.091 (which became BDO55, registered HHN 55), while alongside it was an L5G, 61.144 with, in the row behind it, 61.141 and 145 (respectively BLO 167, 166 and 168 and GHN 967/6/8) all receiving ECW bodywork to standard Tilling specification and entering service in 1947. That year, Bristol's output of chassis passed its pre-war peak of 630 attained in 1938, reaching 798. There was a slight fall to 752 in 1948 but in 1949 it reached an all-time peak of 1,002.

express varieties, as it came into larger-scale production from late 1946. Even in some fleets that had strongly favoured the 5LW, a need for more power for double-deckers, often carrying full loads in those days, was accepted, especially in the more hilly areas, West Yorkshire switching to the K6B for all double-deck deliveries from 1948, while United also largely took the K6B, though reverting to the K5G for a time in 1949-50.

There were also some switches from the AEC engine to the Bristol, the latter becoming standard with Thames Valley from 1948. Crosville's intake became more mixed, with some batches of Bristol engines among a majority of AEC units in both K and L chassis until 1949. On the other hand, post-war renewal of the Royal Blue coach fleet began with L6B vehicles in 1947 but, as mentioned above, some L6A as well as further L6B were added to the fleet in 1948-9, all having Beadle bodywork to the distinctive style favoured for this fleetname.

Quite apart from the preferences of operating company management faced with varying circumstances, availability of engines in sufficient quantity was an important factor at a time when output was being expanded and demand on engine suppliers could be the governing factor on chassis

output. Gardner was under particularly strong pressure as its regular pre-war customers, both in the sense of chassis makers and, indirectly, operators came back, augmented by others who had discovered the merits of its products in wartime models. Even though Bristol had been one of its most important users, the output was insufficient to keep up with demand and delivery delays built up from time to time.

AEC, with its own civilian chassis production restarted and fast expanding, was also not short of uses for its engines, but its output capacity was considerable and this may, at least in part, be why Bristol continued to be supplied with quite substantial numbers of A202 engines until 1950. Bristol gradually expanded its own engine production – it took a little while to build up output, but this itself was not easy when orders for machine tools were often slow in being fulfilled. In addition, operators may have wanted to try examples under their own operating conditions before deciding whether to take larger numbers of vehicles so powered.

The result of all this was a three-way split between these engine makes, the numbers from each varying according to circumstances though most sanctions included

In India, the Nizam of Hyderabad's State Railway had purchased British buses in sizeable numbers since the early 1930s, favouring Albion chassis up to 1946, but Bristol secured an important order for 100 L5G models, these being built in 1948 as the 69th sanction. The specification included a radiator which, at first glance, appeared to revert to the original tall KV design as standard on K and L models from 1937 to 1945. No doubt it was considered advisable to increase cooling capacity to suit the climate, but in fact the design was new, having sides that curved inwards slightly towards the bottom, as on the lower PV2 unit by then standard, and its mounting points were lower, to suit the post-war style of dumb-iron. A front bumper and towing eyes were also fitted and another special feature was the large oil-bath engine air-cleaner, mounted outside the bonnet, this being as also used on other makes of chassis with Gardner engines being exported to hot and dusty climates at the time.

All but one of the 100 were exported as chassis, but the exception, 69.035, was bodied by Park Royal to the 40-seat front-entrance design seen here – this firm had been the Nizam's usual choice of British bodybuilder since pre-war days. The body design was to a characteristically Indian specification, with jalousies to give ventilation and shade from the sun. It was to act as a prototype, particularly for the 50 to be bodied by the Hyderabad Allwyn Metal Works Ltd, Park Royal's associate company in Hyderabad. The others were bodied by McKenzies (25) and Simson (24), but the seating capacities and entrance position varied considerably even within each builder's share.

examples of all three in sufficient numbers to spread the load on production facilities in a way which helped overall output. In round figures, the total production rate during the 1946-50 period averaged nearly 800 chassis per year, a little over 25% higher than in the pre-war period of K and L production.

Viewed from half-a-century later, this seems an impressive figure, even though the whole British bus manufacturing industry was working virtually flat-out at the time. Clearly, it represented about the maximum then possible for Bristol, as indicated by the Leyland vehicle purchase mentioned above, and also smaller numbers of AEC single-deckers for some Tilling fleets although at that stage Bristol had not reached its full potential.

Limitation of supplies of materials was a problem faced by industry generally, and shortage of steel caused wartime allocation schemes to continue for some time afterwards. Because of the strong pressure for exports, manufacturers were apt to be quite severely restricted unless what was regarded as an adequate proportion of exports orders were obtained. Although there was world-wide demand in the aftermath of war, it was much easier for concerns with networks of well-established export agencies to expand such business, and firms such as Leyland or AEC, and even such smaller concerns as Guy or Albion, all with active export histories, were in a stronger position in this respect.

In this sense, Bristol, which had not engaged in exports at all in the 'thirties, was handicapped by having to start from scratch. An early start had been made with the LL5G, beginning with the W4 sanction as has been mentioned, but numbers were at first small.

A noteworthy export order came from India, where the Nizam of Hyderabad's State Railway also operated bus services. In prewar days Albion chassis, including some with Gardner engines, were favoured, and indeed further deliveries of these, though with Albion engines, had been made in 1946. It may well have been the availability of the Gardner that helped to attract this operator to Bristol, the order being for 100 L5G models, built as the 69th sanction. The hot climate was doubtless a factor in reverting to a tall radiator, very like the pre-war pattern, though in fact incorporating the post-war feature of a slight inward curve towards the bottom. Also related to operating conditions was the large oil-bath air cleaner, mounted externally alongside the bonnet. One vehicle was bodied by Park Royal, and 50 to similar pattern by the Hyderabad Allwyn Metal Works Ltd, a local subsidiary of Park Royal, the remainder by other concerns based in India – the final chassis was displayed at the 1948 Commercial Motor Show at Earls Court.

Meanwhile, the special long L-type chassis exported to South Africa in 1946 soon earned a good name, and repeat orders followed, there being eleven, this time mainly with

Above: The South African export business was also developing well, if at first less dramatically. The LWL6G chassis was built to 30ft by 8ft dimensions and among early users was Greyhound Bus Lines (Pty) Ltd, based in Johannesburg, using the same emblem and similar blue and cream livery as its American namesake. This example combines these transatlantic ideas with a very British-looking chassis and Afrikaans lettering. The early type of quick-action radiator filler cap dates it as among the earlier chassis of the type, probably from the 67th sanction. The builder of the coach body is thought to be Bus Bodies (South Africa) Ltd.

Right: Germiston Municipality was another LWL6G user, No. 43, seen here, having chassis 77.014. This sanction of 75 chassis delivered in 1948 was entirely of LWL6G models supplied via Trucks and Transport Equipment Ltd, of Johannesburg. Posed at what appears to be the same spot as the photograph above, the body seems likely also to be by Bus Bodies

6LW engines and thus LL6G, in the 61st sanction (61.023/ 30-3/47/8/72/88-90, all these numbers having an L suffix). Then the availability of an 8ft-wide version, type LWL6G, led to a switch to that type for subsequent orders, amounting to 100 chassis, of which 25 were built among other types in the 63rd, 65th and 67th sanctions, but the final 75 constituted the 77th sanction, built somewhat ahead of the normal sequence.

Trucks and Transport Equipment Ltd, was the Johannesburg dealer involved, the vehicles being sold on to a variety of operators, including municipalities. Among the later examples, 50 were to be exported complete with bodywork and ECW produced a special design which formed an initial step on its changeover to aluminium-

alloy-framed construction. They were bodied in 1948, the last example being displayed at the Commercial Motor Show that year. Apart from the dimensional differences from the home market model, they had a large oil-bath air cleaner fitted externally alongside the rear of the bonnet.

A 'Commercial Motor' road test report on a K6B published in December 1947 included mention of the availability of flexible engine mounting, although not fitted to the test vehicle. This feature began to appear on production vehicles, and in particular K5G and L5G models, during 1948-9. Although vehicles so equipped looked unchanged in appearance, unless one bent very low and peered under the radiator, the effect from the passengers' viewpoint was very considerable. The alteration

Of the 50 LWL6G buses supplied to South African operators complete with ECW bodywork in 1948, fifteen were for Benoni Municipality, some of which are seen lined up for a hand-over photograph. The leading vehicle was 77.003, No. 6 (TA 795), followed by 67.166, No.1 (TA 763) and 67.167, No.11 (TA 810). The two livery styles distinguished buses for European and non-European passengers.

not only reduced vibration but the reduction in noise level was, if anything, even more dramatic.

There can be little doubt that a K5G or L5G with the traditional 'solid' engine mounting was about the noisiest type of bus on offer in Britain at the time, but with the flexible mounting the characteristic sounds of a 5LW engine, though still evident, were much subdued and no longer unduly intrusive. Certainly the writer, who from experience of many headache-making rides, tried to avoid travelling in the earlier version whenever an alternative was possible, found the new quite acceptable, and a little superior to the similarly-powered Guy Arab, benefitting at speed from the overdrive gearbox, which from the passengers' viewpoint could now show its true value in reducing the general level of commotion to quite modest levels.

Two pilot installations were made in K5G chassis 66.151-2, placed in service in BTCC's fleet in 1948 as 3759-60 (LHT 720 and 901) with standard ECW 56-seat bodies. Among early examples to enter service were a batch of ten L5G coaches with Windover bodywork, built on chassis in the 67th and 71st sanctions, supplied to North Western in the latter part of 1948, and standard ECW-bodied K5G and L5G examples so equipped began to be delivered to Tilling companies by 1949, beginning in the 74th and 71st sanctions respectively. The Bristol engine used a similar system but evidently this changed a little later. The alteration did have one drawback, in that clutch judder, hitherto almost completely unknown on Bristol vehicles, could now be induced and drivers found that more care was needed to avoid this.

Three of the LWL6G chassis exported to South Africa in 1948, 77.052/68/9, were bodied as furniture vans, the latter two entering service in 1949. Medwood Furniture Removals (Pty) Ltd, of Durban, was the recipient of 77.068, registered ND 28788, and built the bodywork it carried. An item in *Buses Illustrated* in the March 1959 issue reported that it continued to be in regular use on journeys such as from Durban to Johannesburg, 494 miles, or Cape Town, 1,094 miles. Although other more powerful models in the fleet were faster on hills the ability to 'crack on' in overdrive saved time on long trips. The chassis had withstood a hammering on indifferent roads but the body had had to be rebuilt no less than three times.

18 Nationalisation and its effects

The Labour Government elected in 1945 included nationalisation of public transport in its programme, and the Transport Act, 1947 provided for the transfer of the railways to the newly-formed British Transport Commission on 1st January 1948, being run by the Railway Executive. The London Passenger Transport Board, created as a 'free-standing' public body in 1933, was also transferred on that date, becoming the London Transport Executive, though in reality continuing in much the same way, with general continuity of its policies. The railway shareholdings in most of the BET and Tilling group bus-operating companies passed to the BTC but at that stage control did not.

J. F. Heaton, who had been knighted as a result of the support he and the Tilling group had given to the wartime producer gas scheme, and had hence become Sir Frederick Heaton, had expressed views during the war years in favour of unification of public transport. Although he favoured a national transport authority owned by stockholders, not unlike the LPTB, rather than nationalisation, he felt that unification was so desirable that he was prepared to accept State ownership if this was the only way unification could be achieved.

With this background, it was not too surprising that negotiations with the BTC led to an agreement to sell it the road transport interests of Thomas Tilling Ltd, announced

in September 1948. It took effect on 5th November 1948, and though for financial purposes it was deemed to have taken place from the close of business on 31st December 1947 – clearly this could only be so in a financial sense. Sir Frederick retired from Thomas Tilling Ltd almost immediately, and died in April 1949.

It had been hoped that the manufacturing activities of the Bristol and ECW concerns would be excluded from the sale, in much the same way as AEC had been excluded from the transfer of the Underground group to the newly-formed LPTB in 1933. That would have been relatively simple for ECW, which had operated as a separate company since 1936, and even at Bristol, a step which might have facilitated such an arrangement had been taken in 1943, when Bristol Commercial Vehicles Ltd had been formed. Unfortunately, the transfer of manufacturing to it from Bristol Tramways & Carriage Co Ltd had not been made, and this proved too complex to achieve quickly enough to allow this activity to be excluded from the sale, and thus it was agreed that both Bristol and ECW manufacturing would be included.

This resulted in important restrictions being placed on these companies, for during the passage of the Transport Act 1947, provisions had been included as a concession to the Conservative opposition that forbade the sale of items

The main business of the Bristol Tramways & Carriage Co Ltd's Motor Constructional Works, that of supplying bus chassis for the Tilling group's bus and coach operating companies, was undisturbed in principle by the sale of Tilling's road transport interests to the State-owned British Transport Commission in 1948. Crosville, already well established as a Bristol user since 1945, was to continue receiving Bristol buses as long as they were being built. Here MW362 (KFM 238) on K6B chassis 72.043 with an ECW 55-seat lowbridge body, is seen in service not long after delivery in 1949. The Tilling group's efforts to improve destination display was somewhat negated by the use of a sticker in the bulkhead window in a way not untypical of this operator, though in this case the absence of proper blinds may have been the problem.

Although Bristol was forbidden to take orders from operators outside the British Transport Commission empire after 1948, the flow of work in hand meant that vehicles continued to be delivered to such undertakings in numbers which did not show any dramatic reduction for a couple of years. One of the more surprising was that from Edinburgh Corporation for twelve L6B buses, delivered in 1950. The Scottish undertaking had acquired one K5G and one L5G under the unfrozen allocations in 1941-2, but its standard make in pre-war and early post-war days was Daimler, augmented after the war largely by Guy, the common factor being a preference for Gardner engines, which might have been expected to be specified in this case. The 35-seat rear-entrance bodywork was by J. Brockhouse & Co Ltd, a Glasgow firm which may have been favoured to support Scottish industry – it had a period when its products were based on Park Royal structures, but there is no evidence of that in this case. Note the use of a sliding cab door and large single-panel windscreen. The vehicle shown was A175 in the fleet (FWS 168), on chassis number 81.100.

manufactured by the British Transport Commission or its subsidiaries to any other organisation. Thus, sales to other companies or even municipal undertakings were henceforth forbidden, although it was permitted that existing contracts could be fulfilled. In practice, some chassis for 'outside' users were delivered up to 1950, including models that had not even been legally permissible at the time of the cut-off – it seems possible that at least one operator, getting wind of the likely turn of events, may have hastened to get an order on the books before the restriction took effect.

The bulk of the firm's output had been for Tilling-controlled companies since the mid 'thirties, so the major part of output was not affected, and many of these fleets were still some way from catching up with the backlog of need for new vehicles, so there was no dramatic change of production. Yet, with the excellent reputation of the firm's products, it was sad that many important satisfied customers were henceforth denied Bristol chassis or ECW bodywork. The BET group was an obvious case in point, with Maidstone & District and North Western as two of Bristol's major users. The municipal market was also quite promising, with undertakings like Cardiff and Warrington

Output of L-types continued to be largely for Tilling companies. Crosville had departed from its initial concentration on AEC or Bristol engines to the extent of placing some L5G buses in service, KG115 (KFM 764), on chassis 79.015, dating from 1950 and seen here being a case in point. The standard L-type with ECW 35-seat body was to be seen virtually anywhere a Tilling company operated by that date. The long destination box helped readability when names such as Caernarvon were to be displayed but the overall effect here is spoiled by careless setting. Note the pre-war Humber and Austin cars, the latter still a very common sight in the 1950s.

added to traditional Bristol users as likely future customers – Cardiff was quite a substantial operator, running 170 motor buses at the time as well as trams and trolleybuses quite apart from the prestige attached to its status as the largest municipal undertaking in Wales. Sales to independents were quite small, but perhaps the unkindest cut was the destruction of the very promising export business with South Africa and India.

The Commercial Motor Show held at Earls Court, London, in October 1948 was the first since the war, and Bristol had a stand, even though the ban on sales outside the State-owned sector meant that, effectively, it could do no business. The ECW-bodied Show exhibits on display were a K6B, chassis 68.062, for Lincolnshire, 719 in that fleet, with highbridge body; an L6B, chassis 71.050, United BLO335, with 'express' ECW body, and an LWL6G, 77.056, for Benoni Municipality. On Weymann's stand there was a K6A, 68.028, Maidstone & District DH256.

There were three chassis on Bristol's stand, the last of the Hyderabad L5G models, 69.100, but the most interesting were two examples of a new M-type, one a double-decker with Gardner 6LW engine designated MD6G and the other a single-decker with Bristol AVW engine designated MS6B. It may have been the cut-off of normal commercial business which led to these, to be described more fully in the next chapter, never going into production, but a new design project already in hand was, in practice, so important as to supersede them. Bristol was thus prevented from exploiting its inventiveness on the open market, and though its achievements during the next few years were very considerable, they did not receive the publicity that would have been their due had events taken a different turn. Bristol did not exhibit at Earls Court again until 1966.

In practical terms, the first sign of the new link proved to be an ironic one. London Transport, though having very large numbers of new RT-type buses in course of delivery, had found itself with a severe shortage of serviceable buses, the problem being centred on the poor condition of bodywork of the surviving pre-war fleet. It was thus agreed that some of the deliveries of new Bristol K-type buses with ECW bodywork for Tilling companies would be temporarily diverted to operate for London Transport for the first year of their lives. They were painted in the liveries of their owning companies but carried no fleetnames, being temporarily identified by London Transport roundels attached to the radiators. Publicity mentioned 200, but the actual figure was 180 (145 lowbridge and 45 highbridge), though eleven replacements were made after a year, shortly before the scheme was wound down as London's bus situation improved. In terms of deliveries to London, it began in December 1948, early vehicles involved having chassis built in the latter part of the 68th sanction, and continuing with others from the 72nd, 74th and 76th, the scheme ending with the return of the last vehicles involved in June 1950.

The irony lay in the fact that many of the Tilling fleets still had substantial numbers of buses as old or older than London's oldest, and what some of the fleet engineers and drivers who found themselves having to persevere without new buses for a further year said when they heard is not recorded. The vehicles chosen were all K5G or K6A, on the grounds that the 5LW or AEC 7.7 were familiar engines in London, whereas the Bristol AVW would have introduced a new type. Accordingly, K6B deliveries were not diverted. So far as can be judged, the allocation of types was not distorted by this event, but it seems possible that output was stepped up, the 72nd sanction being unusual among the series at that time in being of 100 chassis, suggesting it might have been added to the schedule.

In the event. output of K and L models continued with the designs established by 1948 for a further two years, until 1950, when changes in legal dimensions caused the introduction of new variants to be described in a later chapter. Inevitably, the number of vehicles for operators outside the Tilling group diminished somewhat, though outstanding orders continued to figure among production until 1950.

There was an irony in the transfer of brand-new K-type buses ordered by Tilling companies to operate for London Transport for a year, in that the fleets that thus temporarily lost them often had buses at least as old as the oldest in London, long overdue for replacement by normal standards. Here United BDO105 (LHN 305), on K5G chassis 74.158, is seen at the Greenford terminus of the 97 service to Brentford in June 1949. Meanwhile some of United's Leyland TD1 buses dating from 1929-30 were to remain in service until 1951-53, despite being much older than anything in central London service by then. The loaned buses ran in their owner's liveries, in this case red and cream and thus not too far removed from LT colours, but devoid of fleetnames, and 'lazy' destination displays avoided the need for changes during duty.

The R-suffix chassis

Another consequence of nationalisation was a restriction on the total numbers of vehicles which could be built by subsidiaries of the British Transport Commission each year, also due to provisions in the Transport Act 1947 inserted as a concession to the Conservative opposition. The figures set were based on those shortly before the transfer from private enterprise. In general, this caused no undue problem, but the exceptional demand of 1949 led to a scheme which, in theory, provided for 'rehabilitation' of old buses, though in fact new chassis were built, identified by a suffix R to the chassis numbers, 73.133R to 200R and 79.189R to 200R. In some cases, existing Gardner engines may have been transferred, as even early LW-series engines could be brought up to date as well as reconditioned, and in some cases, old bodywork was remounted on the new chassis. Three operators were involved, United, Eastern Counties and BTCC itself; the approach differed somewhat between different batches.

The first numerically were United BLO356-399 and, of these, the first dozen were L6B, followed by 20 L5G, all with ECW standard 35-seat bodies; apart from the R-suffix chassis numbers they showed no outward sign of anything to distinguish them from other similar new buses coming into that fleet in sizeable numbers. However, 73.165R-176R, also for United, received Eastern Counties bodies removed from Bristol H chassis in that fleet. These bodies dated from 1933-34 but had been extensively rebuilt in the postwar period. All the foregoing received LHN registration numbers, but chassis 73.177R and 178R, which were to have been BLO400-1, remained unused until 1952, when they received new Roe bodies and joined the United fleet, being registered PHN 408-9 and becoming

BG13 and 14 as a consequence of a renumbering scheme, the Eastern Counties-bodied buses having become BG1-12. There was a reference in an internal United letter of July 1949 to 35 Bristol H and twelve B-type as 'rehabilitated', which was doubtless the basis of the above turn of events.

The Eastern Counties fleet received 73.179R-88R, which were L4G and had standard ECW 35-seat bodies, all placed in service in 1949. The most convoluted exercise involved 73.189R-200R, which were built for use by BTCC itself. Here the illusion that the buses were rebuilds was heightened by retaining the registration numbers of the B-type buses from which the bodies, built by Bence in wartime to utility specification, were transferred. Even the B chassis numbers were retained, with an L-suffix added – the 'real' 73rd R-suffix sanction numbers were not shown on the chassis number plates carried on these vehicles, though they were on R-suffix chassis supplied to United and Eastern Counties.

Finally, United received a further dozen chassis with the 79th sanction R-suffix numbers quoted above. Six of these received Willowbrook 35-seat bus bodies and the remainder Harrington 30-seat coach bodies for use on the Newcastle-London services. These latter were thus the pride of the fleet and about as far removed from alleged rebuilds of old vehicles as could be imagined.

In due course the R-suffix chassis fitted with bodies from old vehicles in both the United and BTCC fleets received post-war ECW bodies transferred from older chassis and the outward manifestation of the exercise diminished, though in the BTCC case the oddity of 1949 L5G chassis with registration and chassis numbers from 1930 B-type buses persisted.

Bristol L-type models with R-suffix chassis numbers were theoretically 'rehabilitations' of older buses. United BLO391 (LHN 591) with new L5G chassis 73.168R, placed in service in 1949, was officially a reconstruction of BHO9 (HN 9039), with H-type chassis H131 dating from 1933 (which, with most of its class, had been fitted with a Gardner 5LW engine). The bodies of twelve of the vehicles, including this one, were by Eastern Counties and had come from BHO-class vehicles, having been rebuilt, largely by Woodall-Nicholson, of Halifax, in the post-war period, gaining glazing similar to that of the 1946 type of ECW body. When transferred to the new chassis, new cab fronts were constructed, marrying a windscreen of post-war ECW style into the original body.

Easily the most glamorous of the R-suffix chassis were the six L6B coaches with Harrington bodywork added to United's fleet in 1950 for use on its Tyne-Tees-Thames long-distance services. United had switched to this bodybuilder for coaches on Leyland TS8 chassis in 1939 and there were elements of the styling of previous generations of bodies by Burlingham and Brush in the design. They were the only Bristol chassis with bodywork by this concern, based at Hove and much favoured for coaches by south-coast operators, most notably Southdown. This bodybuilder's view shows BLO476 (MHN 476) on chassis 79.195R – in the 1951 renumbering scheme it became BBT1. It was withdrawn with the others in the class in 1960, by which date half-cab coaches were regarded as unacceptably obsolete for such duty.

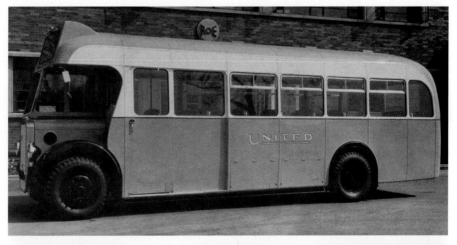

Two of the chassis purchased by United as part of what that concern called the 'one-for-one' programme remained unused until 1952, when they were sent, somewhat surprisingly, to Roe rather than ECW as was to be expected. They received 35-seat bodywork to a style which conformed to ECW frontal styling but were of Roe design in most respects and were noteworthy at that date in having front-entrance layout. United had introduced a renumbering scheme and they did not carry their intended numbers, becoming BG13 and 14 in the series then in use for Gardner-engined chassis, though an L6B-type bonnet side is evident in this photograph.

When this photograph was taken in March 1955, No.2299 of the Bath Services section of the BTCC fleet looked much like any other 1949 L5G, except for its registration number, HW 9493. In theory, it had been 'rebuilt' in 1949 from B636, new in 1930, but the chassis was new, though the Bence utility body dating from 1944 carried by this B-type was lengthened and fitted to the L5G chassis as part of the reconstruction. However, in 1954, the standard 1949 body shown was transferred from a J-type. This was a classic case of 'a new head and two new handles but still the same hammer'.

Coach design on Bristol L-type chassis showed quite wide variations of thought on the part of operators. However, Black & White Motorways Ltd was consistent in its preference for the L6G chassis, and indeed the 6LW-engined option was taken up unswervingly since the first JO6G models of 1936. The first post-war batch were delivered in 1948, consisting of ten L6G, including No. 113 (HDD 656) on chassis 67.047 seen here. The body order went to Duple, as it had in 1939 and 1940, but this time the 30-seat body design was based on Duple's post-war standard outline, though with four bays behind the entrance door (or, on the right, the emergency exit), one fewer than on most examples, a feature shared with a variant Duple built for the AEC Regal III chassis. The Black & White version also included a full-width canopy to carry this operator's winged emblem and destination box. This batch remained in service until 1960 and most, including this coach, were then added to the fleet of T. D. Alexander, of Arbroath and Sheffield, in this case operating until 1963.

The 1949 delivery to Black & White, another ten L6G and again with Duple bodywork, introduced a full-fronted version of basically the same body design. This revived an idea favoured for some early forward-control buses but which had generally given way to the half-cab style from the mid-1920s, so far as Bristol and most other British makes were concerned. By 1949, however, it had come back into fashion to some degree, partly as a result of the prospect of a switch to underfloor-engined models. Number 127 (JDD 498), on chassis 73.005, is seen about to leave Cheltenham on the London service. They were withdrawn in 1961 – Black & White, though a unique surviving example of a company with joint Tilling and BET involvement, followed BET policy in most respects, in those days working on a 12-year vehicle life basis.

North Western Road Car Co Ltd, a BET subsidiary since 1942, made a rather surprising switch to Bristol for some of its long-distance coach requirements. In pre-war days, under Tilling management control, even though Bristol chassis were strongly favoured for bus needs from 1936, the Leyland Tiger TS7 and TS8 had been chosen consistently for coaches, yet the first post-war coach order, delivered in 1949, was split with ten each of the Bristol L5G and Leyland PS2, all with Windover 32-seat bodywork.

A further order for another ten L5G, again with Windover bodywork, entered service in 1950, including No.288 (DDB 288) on chassis 83.063, seen here awaiting the return of the driver after a refreshment stop in Banbury on the Manchester-London service – note the pre-war Austin car in use as a taxi, very typical of the period. The contrast in power between the 125bhp of a PS2 and the 85bhp of an L5G must have caused some comment among North Western drivers, especially on hillier sections of the route, though the overdrive may well have evened the score by allowing cruising at up to 48mph with the L5G on the level, even though such a thing was quite illegal in those days of the official maximum legal speed of 30mph for a bus or coach anywhere. In practice, even modestly-powered coaches ran early, allowing stops such as this to be quite lengthy at times. Here again, these vehicles were withdrawn in 1961, though a factor in this case may have been quite severe deterioration of the wooden body framing.

After the flexible-engine mounting became standard in 1948-9, the K-type continued in production largely unaltered until 1950, still with the Autovac sited directly in the line of vision of the nearside front-seat passenger, though another minor change was the elimination of the bonnet louvres. This 1950 example, K5G 78.152, Western National 958 (KUO 971) had acquired a 1947-type filler-cap, probably as a result of a radiator exchange, when seen in Taunton, still in generally quite smart condition, in October 1963. A Ford Prefect of the early 1950s was following rather closely but a pre-war Austin Seven had yet to catch up.

A final development for the L-type chassis in original form was the introduction of a new coach body by Eastern Coach Works. This followed the curved waistline style still in favour at that date, ECW having built no bodies of coach outline since 1939, and reverted to traditional practice in being of wood-framed construction. The adoption of a fully-fronted cab may have been influenced by the Black & White Duple-bodied L6G batch of 1949, the profile being very similar. In all, there were 38 coaches with this design of body, all on L6B chassis with 27ft 6in length, 7ft 6in width and retaining the PV2 radiator within the curvaceous body design. They were delivered between May and November 1950, all being supplied to Tilling group subsidiaries. Seen here is the West Yorkshire Road Car Co's 662 (JWU 891) on chassis 81.151, in that company's bus station alongside Harrogate railway station.

Although the restrictions on sales to non-BTC operators prevented new Bristol buses being added to the fleets of former customers such as the North Western Road Car Co Ltd, they were to remain a familiar sight through the next decade. This scene in that company's Glossop depot in 1956 includes three L5G and a K5G, the last-mentioned, 890 (JA 7790), on chassis 47.2, seen after rebodying by Willowbrook in 1952, a course of action applied to all 64 of the buses of this type in the fleet, dating from 1938-39. On the right is 285 (DDB 285), on chassis 81.023, one of the second batch of L5G coaches with Windover bodywork dating from 1950. At the other end of that line, beyond 230 (CDB 230), a Leyland PD2, is 315 (EDB 315), on L5G chassis 81.063, a Weymann-bodied 35-seat bus of 1950, and on the left is 323 (ERR 603) on L5G 48.077, one of five 1939 buses acquired from East Midland Motor Services in 1946 and rebodied by Burlingham in 1950, receiving a PV2 radiator in the process. A Leyland Tiger Cub in the background and a 1954 Commer 8-cwt van complete the line-up.

19

Seeds of the Lodekka

The M-type

Setting aside the then very recent news concerning the transfer of the company's ownership, the appearance of a pair of new models, known collectively as the M-type, on the Bristol stand at the Commercial Motor Show in October 1948 had come as something of a surprise, particularly as the widely-respected K and L models had been developed with engine options and design improvements extending and updating their appeal.

John (B. J.) Cox, who joined the drawing office staff at the end of 1949, recalls that the impression he formed was that the M-type had been conceived under the influence of A. J. Romer as a beefed-up K-type, targeted largely on export markets, responding to the strong Government exhortations in that direction. A brief description of the type made in a letter from the Tilling Chairman to

The stand at the 1948 Commercial Motor Show was larger and more prominent than that in 1937, being in an almost central position in the main hall, indicating self-confidence when the stand was booked, with new emphasis on export business. However the new status of the company under the agreement reached the previous month meant that this was to be Bristol's last appearance at Earls Court until 1966.

In 1948 there were three chassis and three vehicles bodied by Eastern Coach Works. Nearest the camera were the two M-type chassis, destined never to progress beyond the prototype stage, the MS6B single-decker being displayed without mudguards or cab/dash structure and thus revealing its Bristol AVW engine. Alongside it was the MD6G double-decker, with these items, and thus revealing how the external appearance was the basis of that of the prototype Lodekka – indeed this chassis was dismantled and contributed many items to the first Lodekka prototype.

To the left can be seen the final L5G chassis of the 100 built for the Nizam of Hyderabad State Railway contract, 69.100, and beyond it a bodied LWL6G, 77.056, for Benoni Municipality. The double-decker almost directly beneath the stand banner was a highbridge K6B, 68.062, Lincolnshire 719 (FBE 323) and on the right was an L6B, 71.050, with 31-seat 'express' body for United, numbered BLO335 (KHN 435).

operating companies in June 1949 in relation to the MD double-decker refers to "improved wheel and tyre equipment, better springing and brakes, and an improved radiator and frontal appearance, driver's cab and control (with) bodywork reduced in weight and improved in regard to interior finish", while it was suggested that the MS could be made available for coaching duties. By that date, however, further ideas on both double- and single-deck design were being pursued and the M type never went into production.

In fact, there was not a great deal that was new about the MD and MS in terms of general layout and specification by comparison with the K and L in their latest form as on offer by late 1948, though the M-type's gearbox incorporated inertia-lock synchromesh. This, and some other details, suggested that there might have been a degree of following in Leyland footsteps on the part of the designers, not so much related to the Titan PD1 double-deckers in BTCC's fleet (save possibly the adoption of a wider radiator) but the PD2 model, with synchromesh gearbox and flexible engine mounting as standard, that had been announced in 1946 and went into production in 1947 – the use of a common initial type letter in combination with D or S to signify double- or single-decker was also in line with Leyland rather than previous Bristol practice.

A rather surprising feature of the M-types was the provision as standard of a front bumper, not usual on contemporary British full-sized bus models at that date, and perhaps an attempt to appeal to taste in some export markets. It was split so that the centre portion was readily removable and, with the front cross-member also arranged to be easily detachable, it was claimed that removal of the complete power unit was simplified, though this task was quite a simple one with a K or L, where there was no bumper to detach. Otherwise the general layout and frame design were quite orthodox and clearly intended for bodywork with typical floor levels of that period, much the same as since the mid-'twenties, with sidemembers having a drop in level over the centre section below the portions

over the front and rear axles, the latter unit a conventional underslung worm-drive type.

There were two examples of the new chassis on the Bristol stand at the Show. The single-decker model was of type MS6B, with Bristol AVW engine to similar specification as being offered in K or L chassis, developing 100bhp at 1,700rpm and with the five-speed synchromesh gearbox directly attached, the combined assembly being carried on flexible mountings. At the front, Metalastik rubber cushions were used and, at the rear, a Gardner-Silentbloc system was used to carry the assembly from an arched cross-member just behind the rear of the cylinder block – the use of part of a Gardner mounting system with the Bristol engine is noteworthy, and was part of a practical Bristol policy common to other models to facilitate the use of either make of engine.

The MS6B Show chassis had a wheelbase of 17ft 6in, 9.00-20 tyres being used all round, and the overall dimensions were quoted as 27ft 6in long by 8ft wide. The double-deck chassis was of type MD6G, with Gardner 6LW engine, but in other respects its general design was similar to that of the single-deck version, save for 16ft 4in wheelbase, tyres and springs to suit the contemporary British length limit of 26ft for such vehicles, the chassis weight being quoted as 4 tons 6cwt.

The MS chassis was displayed without bonnet or front-end sheet metal, but the MD was so equipped, allowing some idea of the appearance of a completed vehicle to be formed. The radiator height appeared to be much the same as that on the K and L, and its extra width might have looked quite well on an 8ft-wide vehicle. The detail design of the radiator differed in that it had a chromium-plated surround, slimmer than the PV2 version used on post-war K and L models, this being particularly so when viewed from the front. Space for the oval Bristol badge was given by gentle curves deepening this surround locally at the top, giving an outline which was adopted in varying forms on some later models.

Only the two chassis were built, and the MD was dismantled to provide parts for the first prototype Lodekka. The MS was used as an engineering department runabout and test hack for several years. It was fitted with the sawn-off rear-end of an old single-deck body with the front closed-in to act as an observers' cabin – it was invariably known and referred to in test reports as 'the Black Chassis'. After a time, it was given a PV2 radiator, evidently contributing the original to the second Lodekka prototype, and the close affinity of its general design to the K and L then became clear.

The MS6B had chassis number PT147 and the MD6G was PT148, apparently in a series which may have signified 'prototypes' although, apart from the number initially applied to the first Lodekka prototype described below, no others are known.

The former Show MS chassis was used as an engineering department test hack for several years, becoming known as 'The Black Chassis' and being given an observer's cabin made up from part of an old single-deck body. It also acquired a PV2 radiator and other associated front-end parts, as seen here, making it look much like an L-type.

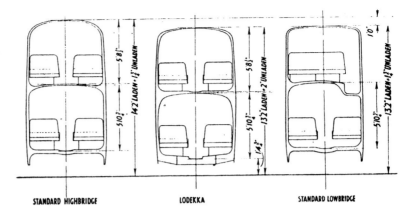

The basic idea of the Lodekka was to produce a bus as low as a lowbridge double-decker yet having the more convenient internal design of the highbridge type, with centre gangways on both decks and sufficient headroom for all passengers to reach their seats without having to crouch beneath low ceilings.

The first Lodekka prototypes

Specific design work on what was to become the Lodekka is said to have begun in October 1948, according to descriptions when the first prototype appeared a year later. That is an interesting date in relation to the agreement to sell the Tilling group's bus interests to the British Transport Commission which had occurred the previous month. Pinpointing the birth of an idea is always difficult, and there is clear evidence that initial thoughts on the subject went back to mid-1948 if not earlier. However, it is clear that a firm decision to pursue the idea was taken in the knowledge of Bristol's new position as part of the nationalised transport system, with the limitations on potential sales that implied.

Modern Transport of 8th October 1949 stated that both A. J. Romer, Director and General Manager of the works, and F. J. Buswell, Chief Designer, in conjunction with engineering officers of the Tilling group, were largely responsible for the new vehicle design.

The names of both Romer and Buswell as well as Bristol Tramways & Carriage Co Ltd appeared on the application for a patent, 659902, for the vehicle's basic layout allowing the low overall height with conventional seating arrangement. This went into considerable detail on the construction of both chassis and body, including the slim centre section of the upper-saloon floor, clearly based on work in which Eastern Coach Works was much involved though, rather surprisingly, ECW's name is not mentioned. This application was dated on the 28th January 1949, which indicates that by that date the project had reached the stage of formal application for its protection being thought desirable; by then both Bristol and ECW were nationalised concerns. This patent was granted on 31st

The prototype Lodekka chassis under construction, with AVW engine in place – the mounting arrangement, with two inclined Metalastik rubber cushions on an extended bracket at the front, and a Gardner system at the rear, was as devised for the M-type and provided for use of engines of either make with minimum chassis alteration. The specially shaped cross-members to allow the lower-saloon gangway to be as low as possible and with outriggers directly supporting the body sides at their outer ends are clearly visible.

This rear view of the chassis ready for delivery to ECW shows the original transmission layout, with gearbox set at a low level and close to the right-hand side-member, with a transmission line running from it to a chassis-mounted differential and then splitting into separate drives to two worm-drive units, one on each side of the rear axle.

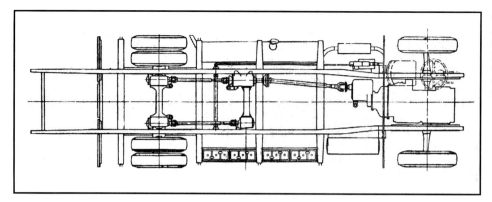

This plan view of the original Lodekka design shows the divided transmission layout. Items such the batteries, fuel tank and other units were sufficiently shallow to be accommodated below the outer parts of the frame.

October 1951, by which time two prototypes were being used as a basis for development of production models.

However, it has to be said that the Tilling group was an almost ideal 'market' for it, and the fact that Bristol could no longer build vehicles for general sale may not have cramped its success as much as might be thought. Under Heaton's influence, Tilling had put much more stress on centralised policy decisions for its operating companies, and indeed Bristol's position as supplier of bus chassis to the operating companies was largely based on group decisions taken during the 1930s. In a similar way, most of the companies standardised on lowbridge double-deckers.

To some degree, the reasons for this could be traced back to the original Leyland Titan TD1 model as introduced in 1927, indeed the word lowbridge had originally been Leyland's trade name for the standard body design with sunken side gangway. Together with its relatively low chassis, this reduced the overall height significantly compared to previous double-deckers. The lowbridge Titan was particularly well suited to routes linking country towns which often were major sources of revenue for many of the Tilling-controlled companies, several of which operated quite large numbers of the type.

From the mid to late 1930s, as explained earlier in this volume, Bristol chassis were generally adopted for new vehicles for these fleets but in most cases the bodywork continued to be of the lowbridge layout. To some degree, this was still necessary, where routes ran under low bridges, fairly common in some areas in those days of more numerous branch railway lines and industrial railways than survive today. However, and very much in line with Tilling fondness for standardisation, lowbridge vehicles were standard in many fleets where only a minority of routes called for their use. A justification of this was that unintentional use of a highbridge bus on a route which ran under a low bridge could be, and occasionally was, disastrous, but many other operators, and even a few within the group, coped with mixed highbridge and lowbridge fleets without undue difficulty.

The lowbridge bus did have drawbacks, and mainly these were concentrated on the upper deck. Entry to and exit from the four-seat rows via the sunken offside gangway was not easy and fare collection also had its difficulties. Particularly in winter, when most passengers would be wearing heavy overcoats, the space on these rows, especially in a 7ft 6in bus, as still universal in 1949 in Tilling fleets, was not enough for four average-sized passengers. The author can recall many journeys with barely more than half of his posterior poised on the right-hand end of a row upstairs on such buses, having to reach out over the gangway to the handrail attached to the offside windows to maintain balance. There was also the matter of the low level of the lower-deck ceiling on the right-hand side, directly under the sunken upper-deck gangway – despite the warning notices, passengers were apt to forgot about this as they rose to leave the bus, bumping their heads.

The idea of a bus of highbridge-style internal layout but with 'lowbridge' overall height thus had its attractions, and this is what Bristol, working in co-operation with ECW, set out to achieve. In effect, the idea was virtually to take a highbridge body and lower it by roundly 1ft (305mm) and, apart from altering the shape of the chassis frame to allow this, the main problem was to remove the obstacles in the form of the transmission line and rear axle – other minor chassis items could be repositioned more readily.

Another important factor was the way in which the chassis and body design were inter-related, Bristol and ECW engineers working in close co-operation. A combined plate quoted both Bristol chassis number and ECW body number, and on early production vehicles this bore the British Transport Commission's lion emblem, as displayed on British Railways locomotives of that period. The Lodekka was sometimes described as semi-integral, even though there was a separate chassis, the latter being designed to take advantage of the stiffness of the body structure. An important contribution to the height reduction was the absence of any separate body underframe, the lower-saloon floor being laid directly on the chassis, the crossmembers of which were shaped accordingly, with low level under the centre gangway and outriggers positioned to support the body pillars. This form of construction also helped to save weight.

In the early versions of the model, only the gangway level of the lower saloon was lowered to the full extent needed to allow 5ft 10¾in headroom there and 5ft 8½in in the upper deck, these figures being the same as in the contemporary standard highbridge ECW body as built on Bristol K chassis. The side portions of the frame, and hence the lower-deck floor, were slightly higher, with a drop of about 2in to the gangway. The overall height was 13ft 2in laden, the same as the standard lowbridge version of the K-type, the Lodekka's lower saloon gangway level being 1ft 4½in above ground level.

The first Lodekka prototype, as displayed to the technical press soon after its return to Bristol in bodied form from Eastern Coach Works in September 1949. The chassis was officially numbered LDX.001 by then, and it had been registered as LHY 949 but the Bristol City Services fleet number C5000 had yet to be applied. The proportions of the vehicle seemed very unfamiliar, the illusion being created that the radiator was tall though in fact the body, of similar proportions internally to a normal ECW highbridge design, had been set at a lower level on the specially modified chassis. The driving position had also been lowered slightly so that there was enough internal headroom in the cab, and the steering column was raked more than on the K, in a manner common to production Lodekka models. The livery was Tilling green and cream but applied in a different style, with cream window surrounds, adopted as standard for the BTCC fleet for a time.

The means of lowering the level of the mechanical units below the saloon floor on the Lodekka prototype was to use a set of input gears at the front of the four-speed gearbox which allowed the transmission line to be lowered 6.25in and offset 9.375in towards the offside from the crankshaft centre line. Then a conventional transmission line ran rearwards to the differential unit, which was a little over half-way along the distance towards the rear axle. There was a cross-shaft at this point, driven by a pair of bevel gears, and a second pair of bevels on the nearside. Two propeller shafts then ran rearwards to separate worm drive units on each side of the rear axle, each driving a rear wheel through a short fully-floating axle shaft. Thus there was no drive carried across the centre part of the axle, and this was set at a low level, being of I-section form akin to a front axle beam at this point.

A patent, No. 638426 for this transmission layout had been taken out by BTCC, the date of the application and filing of the complete specification being 7th July 1948, a clear indication that work had been in hand for some time before that, even if no decision to build a vehicle had been made at that stage, when even the M-types had yet to be announced. The object was stated, even at that early stage,

to be the lowering of the gangway level with a view to reducing overall height. The patentees in that case were the BTCC and F. J. Buswell, and it provided for alternative forms of the basic idea, such as with bevel rather than worm drive.

There was a precedent for this form of 'divided-drive' rear axle in a prototype double-deck six-wheel trolleybus built by Leyland in 1935, also having low overall height with full-length centre gangways on both decks. This had two motors and completely separate drive trains on each side of the vehicle, but the idea was not pursued and Bristol's Lodekka design using a single engine was quite new.

Hence the lower-saloon gangway was at the same level as the rear platform, though there was a pair of casings over the worm-drive units and the rear wheel arches carried a pair of longitudinal seats on each side, just ahead of the bulkhead, plus a small luggage space where the chassis frame reached its highest point.

At the front of the lower deck, a rearward-facing seat for five was used to cover the area where the sidemembers and gearbox casing would otherwise have intruded above the low floor level. With four rows of forward-facing seats and the pair on each side at the rear, the lower saloon

This interior view of the lower deck shows how the gangway was set slightly below the general floor level and the use of a rearward-facing front seat for five passengers gave enough room for most of the gearbox to lie beneath it, though a small protruding housing can be seen. The two worm-drive casings on the rear axle also required covers projecting above floor level, and the rear wheel arches, more intrusive than on a higher-built bus, were used as carriers for small items of luggage, with seats for two passengers each side facing inwards immediately to the rear.

seating capacity was 25, there being seats for 33 on the upper deck, making a total of 58, two more than most highbridge buses with the same 26ft overall length, the maximum permissible for a two-axle double-decker at that date. In keeping with Tilling policy at that time, the width was 7ft 6in – 8ft had been permissible in Britain since 1946, but only on specific approved routes and the lack of flexibility was considered by many company operators to make it not worthwhile.

The front-end of the chassis had clear affinities to the M-types and the 1948 Show MD chassis was dismantled to provide parts for the first prototype Lodekka. It had a Bristol AVW engine using a similar mounting arrangement, radiator and front bumper to the M-type. The gearbox had constant mesh on second, third and top gears and the brake system was of the triple-servo type, the main servo being mounted outside the frame. The driving position was lowered slightly so as to provide adequate headroom within the cab under the lower upper-deck floor level, and the steering column was given a greater angle of rake than on previous models, a feature to remain characteristic of subsequent production models.

In terms of general appearance, the body had an overall resemblance to ECW's standard highbridge body of the time in contours and detail design, but its new relationship in terms of height to the front-end of the chassis altered the overall effect considerably. The M-type radiator looked disproportionately large in its new setting, the prominent bumper adding to a look of heaviness, and the cab front panel, set back slightly, caused more of the offside mudguard to be exposed than was usual. A consequence of the form of construction was uneven spacing of the body side pillars, those fore and aft of the rear axle being slightly further apart than the others, a detail put right on later production versions.

In fairness, a great deal of effort and skill had been put into the more fundamental aspects of design and if the inheritance of some M-type chassis features and body styling originally intended to sit higher on a K-type chassis gave the effect of a mismatch, this was almost to be expected in the first example of a design which was laying down new standards.

The prototype chassis was at first given the chassis number PT149, following on from the two M-type chassis, but had become LDX.001 by the time the body was completed at ECW and delivered back to Bristol as a member of the company's fleet on 10th September 1949. Production Lodekka chassis had the prefix LD and the use of an 'X' suffix to signify experimental vehicles was subsequently repeated on other types. The unladen weight was 7 tons 9 cwt, only about 3 cwt more than a K-type with standard ECW body, despite the more complex transmission.

While the construction of this vehicle was in hand, the Tilling group was considering requirements for new vehicle deliveries to the operating companies in 1951-52, with a view to determining Bristol and ECW manufacturing plans. A questionnaire was sent out to the general managers of Tilling companies and the covering letter dated 7th June 1949 from Stanley Kennedy, Chairman of the Tilling Group Management Board, that was sent to A. T. Evans, General Manager of United Automobile Services Ltd, was no doubt typical in most of its contents. It began by noting the orders already in hand for K and L models for 1950 and that delivery of these chassis to the bodybuilders would probably spread into early 1951. It is clear that, at that stage, it was not planned to continue production of those models beyond that point.

In regard to double-deckers, it was anticipated that a "much larger proportion of this type may be used than in the prewar period" – in fact this was already happening in many Tilling fleets. It was proposed at that stage to offer a choice of the MD with either highbridge or lowbridge bodywork, or the Lodekka, the latter's ability to give 'highbridge' layout within a 'lowbridge' height being outlined. All three were to be of the 27ft overall length then known to be soon forthcoming but "the extent to which operation of 8ft-wide buses will be practicable during the next few years" was clearly considered to be in doubt. The questionnaire asked the Tilling operating companies for approximate numbers of new vehicles expected to be

The second Lodekka prototype, LDX.002, completed in April 1950, had the same style of radiator and frontal appearance as its predecessor, but the body design was revised, with taller windows. The latter seemed to suit the design better though the radiator still seemed disproportionately large. This vehicle was supplied to the West Yorkshire Road Car Co Ltd, being numbered 822 and registered JWT 712 though, like the first example, it was also much used by BTCC for development and demonstration work – it was painted in standard Tilling red and cream.

Here it is seen when on loan to the Notts & Derby concern, one of a group of companies which had come into State ownership as the result of nationalisation of the electricity industry but handed over to the British Transport Commission. It is seen on the Nottingham-Ripley route, then still served by trolleybuses though to be replaced by Bristol buses in April 1953 – at that stage the Lodekka had yet to go into full-scale production and the buses were based on KSW chassis of the type described in the next chapter.

required during 1951 and 1952 and the proportions of various types, the double-deckers listed being MD highbridge, MD lowbridge or Lodekka.

An idea mentioned in passing was the possibility of making a lowbridge version of the Lodekka, which would have had a height of approximately 12ft 6in. No such Lodekka was ever made, though one example of such a version of the Dennis Loline, which used the Lodekka principles and was made under licence from BTCC, was

built in 1960 with body by Northern Counties for the independent operator Barton Transport Ltd.

As will be explained later, the response and later events meant that actual production was quite different to these proposals, the MD never going into production while the K survived in a revised form and the Lodekka arrived somewhat later, though very successfully when it did appear.

A second Lodekka prototype chassis, LDX.002, again

At the Festival of Britain held in 1951 at the South Bank site in London, various transport vehicles were included among the exhibits, among them being the second Lodekka, seen here during its spell on display in August-September. A Jensen lightweight lorry is just visible in the left.

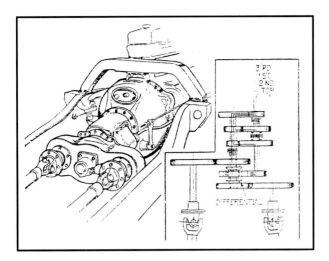

Alternative gearbox and transmission designs were tried on the two prototype Lodekka buses, among them this version, with differential built in to the rear of the gearbox and two full-length propeller shafts, one running down each side of the chassis. In the end, a single propeller shaft was adopted, with differential on the rear axle and a drive-shaft within a low-level hollow casing to convey the drive to the nearside, there being pairs of gears on each side to take it up to wheel-centre level.

with Bristol AVW engine was generally similar, but with a slightly modified body design incorporating taller windows in both decks, and was completed by ECW in the Spring of 1950. It was for the West Yorkshire Road Car Co Ltd, and was delivered from ECW on 3rd April, though initially back to Bristol and then spending a spell with Brighton Hove & District before arriving at the West Yorkshire headquarters in June.

Both Lodekka prototypes visited various Tilling companies as well as being engaged in development test work and other activities which interrupted their periods in service – the West Yorkshire bus was on display at the Festival of Britain on London in August-September 1951.

Meanwhile, further work was being done on the transmission in an effort to simplify its design. A key figure in this was E. H. (Ernie) Dine, whom John Cox describes as an absolute wizard on gearboxes and gearing generally. In one of two versions covered by patent 698895 taken out by BTCC, Dine and Buswell and with application dated 7th December 1950, the gearbox itself was more conventional but incorporated a differential mechanism in a casing mounted on its rear face, dividing the drive to two full-length propeller shafts taking the drive to the worm-drive units on the rear axle.

Subsequently, a more major redesign of the transmission was carried out. A single propeller shaft ran from a gearbox of the type much as used on the original vehicle but continuing, via an intermediate bearing, directly to the rear axle. This was of the drop-centre type, then a new idea, though it revived ideas from two famous much earlier bus designs.

The Milnes-Daimler buses, built on chassis supplied by the German Daimler company and much favoured in Britain in the period around 1904, had a rear axle using

gears which engaged with internally toothed rings attached to the rear wheel assemblies. This drive was exposed and rapidly became unacceptably noisy as grit got into the gearing, causing the idea to be dropped within a few years. No attempt was made to reduce height with this feature, but when the NS bus, made by AEC, was introduced by the London General Omnibus Co in 1923, an enclosed version of a similar mechanism was used to allow the differential and axle shafts to be at a lower level than the centre of the rear wheels. The NS was lower built than its predecessors but the underslung worm drive and differential casing was still positioned centrally, and similar floor height was achieved more simply in 1927 by the offset worm drive with straight half-shafts and no second stage of gearing on the Leyland TD1 mentioned earlier in this chapter, setting the pattern for subsequent British bus design in this respect among others.

Bristol's new rear axle as introduced during the development stage of the Lodekka prototypes used both an offset differential and secondary gearing. The latter allowed the casing surrounding the shaft conveying the drive to the nearside to be at a level low enough to pass under the gangway. It provided a simpler solution to the means of getting the drive to the rear wheels under a vehicle with 'one-step' floor line, and set a pattern followed in subsequent designs, not only by Bristol but across much of the British bus industry when a low-floor capability was required.

In this axle, spiral bevel drive provided the first-stage reduction, of 2.177 to 1, at the low level, situated on the offside so as to align with the propeller shaft running along that side of the chassis. The offside low-level drive shaft was very short, with a longer one running to the nearside within the hollow axle beam. At each end of this assembly, pairs of gears provided the second stage of the reduction ratio as well as taking the drive up to wheel centre level, there being alternative ratios of 2.05 or 2.25 to 1. The alternative axle ratios of 4.36 or 4.76 to 1 given by the combined sets of gearing have to be judged in conjunction with the step-down effect of the main gearbox.

The gearbox design was also tidied up, using a cleverly-arranged two shaft layout devised by Ernie Dine and also covered in patent 698895. The version adopted for subsequent production was available in four- or five-speed form, with all ratios except reverse in constant mesh. Because of the various stages of gearing in the transmission taken as a whole, with a 1.26 to 1 ratio applied at the input stage, the simplest way of comparing ratios with more conventional models is to take the alternative overall ratios in fourth gear, which were 5.5 or 6.0 to 1, much the same as the 5.4 or 6.0 to 1 found in most of the K or L type models.

It was not until 1953 that the Lodekka went into a pre-production stage with six vehicles, and larger-scale production did not begin until 1954. The intervening years were spent in painstaking testing and improvement of the basic design, which paid off as the production Lodekka soon established itself as fully upholding the excellent reliability and efficiency record of the K. The full story of later versions will be told in the next volume.

New models, and the changes in the maximum legal dimensions made in 1950 and described in the next chapter, were drawing the days of the standard K and L types to a close. These views show chassis as being built in the period up to 1950. That reproduced above had been mildly highlighted for use in advertisements or sales brochures and hence probably prepared circa1948. It has been described as showing a K-type chassis, no doubt because of the low-level rear frame extension visible. However the front tyres appear to be of the 9.00-20 size, as also used at the rear, rather than the larger 11.00-20 size used at the front of K-types and hence, with the high-set bonnet access hole showing just a glimpse of an AVW engine, the indications are that it portrays an L6B. The low-level rear-end, although looking like that used on K-types, was doubtless as provided on single-deck chassis when the bodywork was to have a luggage boot at the rear.

This three-quarter offside rear view shows one of the L5G chassis as built for the Nizam of Hyderabad's State Railway in India in 1948, identifiable as such by the taller dash and front bumper. It appears to be in Show finish and thus is almost certainly 69.100, the last of the batch, displayed at the Commercial Motor Show held at Earls Court, London, in October 1948. In this case the rear end of the frame was straight, with a spare wheel carried beneath it. Another item varying between the two models is the position of the batteries, mounted at a low level on the nearside of the frame in the version shown above but inside the frame, a little way ahead of the rear axle, on the Hyderabad chassis below, perhaps to better protect them from risk of damage when travelling over rough roads.

20

Longer K and L types

The legal length and width limits for buses had not altered since 1931, when new national dimensions were adopted as part of the aftermath of the Road Traffic Act, 1930. Operators had been pressing for increases for some time, and by June 1949 it was known that a small increase in length for two-axle double-deckers from 26ft to 27ft was almost certain to be granted, though at that date it was understood that the corresponding single-deck limit was only to be increased by 6in, to 28ft. Operators had been pressing for 30ft and, to their surprise, this was unexpectedly

agreed, this being announced early in 1950, both these increases coming into effect from 1st June that year.

In addition, almost immediately afterwards, the maximum width for general use throughout Britain became 8ft instead of 7ft 6in. It had been permissible to run 8ft wide buses from 1946, but only on routes individually approved by the Traffic Commissioners. Some operators took advantage of this, notably in the North West of England, where the attitude of the Traffic Commissioners' office seems to have been sympathetic but, characteristically,

The rapid successive altering proposals and then actual changes in legal length and width limits created great difficulties for bus manufacturers in the period before and after the change of regulations in mid-1950. Tilling group companies particularly welcomed the additional 2ft 6in in maximum length to 30ft for two-axle single-deckers, but some chassis were already built to the 7ft 6in width limit when the general increase to 8ft as the permitted dimension came through. Quite a number of vehicles were fitted with 8ft bodywork on 7ft 6in chassis, as seen here. West Yorkshire 424 (JYG 718), on LL5G chassis 83.201 received an 8ft-wide ECW bus body, entering service in 1951. Apart from the longer 19ft wheelbase, the L-type chassis to the 30ft length were not significantly altered in design, and the standard body was adapted to the extra length by the insertion of an extra bay behind the rear axle, giving space for an extra row of seats and raising the seating capacity to 39. It is seen just after arrival in Blackpool on a summertime express relief working from Yorkshire, for which such a vehicle, with its bus seating, was perhaps not ideally suited. Additionally, the performance over the Pennines would have been rather limited with the 5LW engine, though the internal noise level even when the engine was having to work hard was no longer excessive, in the way that it had been with L5G models up to about 1948.

Although only slightly longer than its predecessor, the typical KS was more obviously 'different' from the standard K than applied to the lengthened single-deckers. The longer bonnet, previously confined to the minority of K-types with Gardner 6LW engines, was now standard, giving freedom to fit this unit without affecting other aspects of the chassis or body. At first all production chassis had Bristol AVW or Gardner 5LW engines, and these shorter units were mounted as close to the radiator as previously, leaving a space of about 6in inside the rear end of the bonnet. ECW introduced a new four-bay body design with a slightly altered front profile for KS and KSW chassis.

This KS6B for Thames Valley, No.598 (FMO 980), on chassis 82.038, was one of six with coach seats for 53 passengers and platform doors for use on the London-Reading services, being placed in service in 1951. This operator had used five-speed gearboxes on its vehicles for this service ever since the first K5G models had been delivered to the fleet in 1939, when such units were very rare on double-deckers. The KS6B and, slightly later, even more so the 8ft-wide KSW6B coaches gave much improved standards of refinement and comfort compared to those earlier vehicles. Thames Valley built up a total of fifteen KS6B and 76 KSW6B, all lowbridge, in bus and coach-seated versions in the period up to 1955.

the Tilling group preferred to retain its freedom to use standard bus types, so had not pursued this option.

The overall effect of these changes, and the piecemeal way in which they became known, caused some problems for operators and manufacturers, not least Bristol. The extra length was widely accepted as desirable, and its adoption was more a matter of arranging production. There was less unanimity on width, some operators, particularly those with rural routes over narrow roads, being cautious in their acceptance.

Bristol's response to these events was a little different to that of other bus makers, though, as with most concerns, longer and wider versions of existing models were produced. It must have been tempting to defer changes until the Lodekka was ready for production, and no doubt the same applied to a new single-deck model to be described shortly, but neither would be ready for manufacture in quantity for a year or two at least. Even in the seemingly uncompetitive world of the British Transport Commission there was enough pressure to take advantage of the new dimensions to introduce new versions of the K and L. The plan to put the MD and MS models into production had been dropped;

it seems that the general view was that as the K and L had proved very satisfactory and were in service in large numbers in all Tilling fleets there was little point in bringing in new but basically similar models, especially as the Lodekka and a completely new single-decker were expected to become available within a year or two.

The new longer KS-series version of the K-type had its wheelbase increased to 16ft 8in from the earlier 16ft 3in, but was little altered in general specification, though it was decided to standardise on the 5ft bonnet length, as needed to accommodate the Gardner 6LW engine, for all KS models. At first, deliveries continued to have the Bristol AVW or Gardner 5LW, either of which left unused space within the rear of the bonnet space, but the 6LW became quite a widely-used option within Tilling companies from the 92nd sanction, deliveries of these reaching operators from 1952. Overall, the Bristol engine was in the majority for the KS and KSW types.

ECW, now the only bodybuilder on Bristol chassis, produced new four-bay body designs for the revised chassis, readily identified by the slight step in profile below the windscreen.

The LL6G was a very rare type, save for the South African examples built in 1946-7 before the switch to LWL6G for that market. When 30ft two-axle single-deckers became legal in Britain, the extended bonnet was not adopted as standard in the same way as with the KS and KSW, and the only home-market instances were for Hants & Dorset Motor Services Ltd, which had favoured the L6G for some of its coaches; this was an unusually mixed fleet in terms of engine types in the post-war years. The LL6G seen on the left in this view was No. 779 (KLJ 749) on chassis 73.132, the only 30ft model in that sanction, possibly already built late because of its specification and thus gaining the opportunity to be of the new length.

Portsmouth Aviation built coach bodies on L-series chassis for both Hants & Dorset and Wilts & Dorset, including this one seating 36 and of dual-purpose character – it was delivered late in 1950. Alongside is seen an L6A, chassis 73.060, delivered in 1949 with fleet number TC834 and registered JRU 66. Its body, also by Portsmouth Aviation, was to coach specification, seating 32 – it had been renumbered 366 by the time of this scene in the yard behind Bournemouth's bus station of those days, adjoining The Square. Behind can be seen two KS-series double-deckers with highbridge ECW bodies.

The passenger space within the lower deck was thus only lengthened by 6in by comparison with previous standard K models, and lowbridge buses continued to seat 55, as had been standard since production resumed in 1946, though the earlier vehicles' rather tight seat spacing was now eased. Highbridge buses now adopted the same 28-seat lower-deck capacity and, with an extra pair of seats upstairs, 60 became the standard capacity.

For the L-type the shorter, 4ft 6in, bonnet continued to be standard, and hence the engine choice was effectively the 5LW or the Bristol AVW. As 30ft models had been built for export since 1946, a suitable chassis design already existed, having a 19ft 3in wheelbase. If the width remained at 7ft 6in, the model code became LL. Deliveries of such buses, complete with the standard ECW body, in effect the previous design with a short extra window bay and now seating 39 passengers, began in late July 1950.

Because of the way in which short notice of the change was given, LL-type chassis began to appear part-way through the 81st sanction, intermingled numerically with L-types at first. Indeed it is understood that some chassis delivered to Lowestoft as L-type were returned to Bristol and rebuilt as LL, though those on which bodybuilding had already begun were completed at the shorter length.

The KS-type double-deckers began to reach operators in August of that year, the earliest examples being in the 80th sanction, which also included 'plain' K-types. A

further combination not uncommon for a time on LL and KS models was the building of 8ft-wide ECW bodywork on the 7ft 6in chassis, and even after 8ft versions had become usual, there were operators which ordered 7ft 6in LL or KS vehicles to meet their specific needs.

The 8ft-wide chassis options were slightly later in appearing, deliveries of complete examples, both single- and double-deck, beginning in December 1950. The 8ft KS chassis was designated KSW, which also began to appear in the 80th sanction, and the corresponding single-decker was LWL, as already used for the vehicles exported to South Africa, examples for Tilling fleets beginning to appear in the 83rd sanction.

The system of applying a suffix using figures to signify the number of cylinders and a letter to signify the engine make continued. There was one example of a long L-type with AEC 7.7-litre engine, an LL6A, built for Maidstone & District as part of a final batch of fifteen LL-types in fulfilment of an order placed before the cut-off for 'outside' business in 1948, when a 30ft two-axle single-decker would have been illegal, but modification of the order to the new length was accepted – the remainder of the batch were LL5G models.

Deliveries of Bristol chassis to non-BTC companies against orders outstanding since before the cut-off point were tailing off just as the longer models were coming into production, the M&D order being the main exception though W. L. Silcox of Pembroke Dock took a couple of

The end of a beautiful friendship. Rotherham Corporation had been almost exclusively a user of Bristol motor bus chassis from the mid-1920s until 1949, purchasing its first examples in 1923. Although the numbers supplied were never large, there had been examples of the 2-ton, 4-ton, B, J, JO5G, L5G, K5G, K6B, L6B, and KS6B models. The cut-off of supply caused by nationalisation was delayed by orders that had been placed for extended delivery, though twelve Crossley were delivered in 1949. The example shown, No.110 (FET 810) on chassis 82.048, was one of the final double-deck batch of six KS6B models supplied in 1950 – Rotherham was the only non-Tilling operator to receive examples of the KS-series chassis. East Lancashire bodywork had been favoured since 1940, but these late examples were built by the Bridlington branch of that firm, this one being photographed in front of the famous Beverley Bar. Three L6B and nine L5G were also supplied in 1950-51, having East Lancs centre-entrance 32-seat bodies, thus conforming to a tradition in body layout which extended back to 1927 examples on B-type chassis, but the L6B buses were rebodied as double-deckers in 1952. Crossley received Rotherham's orders for double-deckers supplied in 1951 and 1952, but this make also then became unavailable and Rotherham switched to Daimler bus chassis, the latter make having been favoured for trolleybuses in the undertaking's fleet.

LL5G chassis (81.196 and 197) bodied by the operator and not placed in service until 1951-2. Among double-deckers, Rotherham Corporation's final order for twelve K-types were completed as KS6B, placed in service in 1950.

For a brief period, Bristol deliveries became quite complex until production settled down at the new dimensions. As it turned out, the KS, KSW, LL and LWL models, virtually unknown outside the Tilling fleets, with no publicity supplied to the technical press, were built in quite substantial numbers. The KS and KSW double-deckers continued in production not only until the Lodekka

entered regular production in 1954 but were still being built, admittedly in diminishing numbers, until 1957, by which date 1,352 had entered service. The LL- and LWL-type single-deckers had a shorter run of continuous production, but 480 buses with the 39-seat rear-entrance ECW body entered service in 1950-52, regular manufacture of these chassis having ended in September 1951, but a final batch of 15 were built for Wilts & Dorset in 1954. There were also 163 with ECW's full-fronted coach body which formed the Tilling group's standard new coach intake for the 1951 season.

Thus there were 2,012 of these final-generation versions of the K and L types that had served operators so well. Although unsung in terms of publicity, they were sound and likeable vehicles, with the rugged nature of earlier types wedded to more spacious bodywork and the greater refinement that had been introduced on the later examples of the shorter versions. More on the later deliveries will appear in the next volume.

W. L. Silcox & Son, of Pembroke Dock, was an independent operator which lived up to that adjective in terms of fleet policy. An 'unfrozen' K5G with Duple body had been allocated in 1942 and other Bristol vehicles were added in post-war years. In a fleet list quoted in Buses Illustrated in 1953, there were, in addition to the K5G, six L5G with Strachans 35-seat bodies dating from 1947; three K6G, two with Davies bodies and one by Barnard, of 1949; two K6G with Metro-Cammell bodies from Birmingham trolleybuses placed in service in 1952 and another with body by the operator then yet to enter service; three L5G and two LL5G, all with Silcox bodies, four completed in 1951 and the last, the other of the LL5G models, seen here, which entered service in 1952. Number 12 in the fleet, registered ODE 600, it had chassis 81.196 and the body seated 41.

ECW introduced an enlarged 30ft by 8ft version of its 1950 full-fronted body for the 1951 season, retaining the curved-waist full-fronted styling but with the radiator concealed by a decorative grille, as fashionable by then, yet thereby losing some of the 'quality' look associated with the distinctive Bristol radiator. A total of 163 were built on Bristol LWL6B or, in a few cases, LL6B chassis, mostly accommodating 35 in spacious seating and entering service that year, with a small number in 1952. They were to be found in most Tilling fleets and, looking noticeably larger than their predecessors, were given the nickname 'Queen Mary', the liner of that name still being a by-word for immense size. Crosville KW253 (MFM 684), on chassis 83.313 is seen at Bettws-y-Coed station.

A more traditional interpretation of coach styling was to be found on some LL6B coaches for Western and Southern National. Some were in Royal Blue livery and had an extended 37-seat version of the standard early post-war standard style for this operator, being built by Duple, which had also produced some late examples of the shorter version, though to similar style to the earlier ones built by Beadle. However others, painted in cream and green livery and carrying their operators' own fleetnames, though basically similar and also by Duple, were of the half-canopy style – there were ten Western National and four Southern National coaches in the batch. They were intended primarily for local excursion and touring work in the south-west of England but on summer Saturdays were apt to be used on Royal Blue duty, as in the case of Western National 1301 (LTA 739) on chassis 83.136 seen here turning into Victoria Coach Station, London, followed by a Crosville Bristol-ECW LS coach, representing the next generation of vehicles. Even within the Tilling group, more inclined to keep vehicles longer than in BET, such coaches as these LL6Bs had become regarded as old-fashioned within a few years and when the batch were withdrawn in 1964, most were sold for scrap or export.

Most of the LL-type chassis received 7ft 6in wide ECW bodies, and although such vehicles were apt to be regarded at first as a stop-gap measure before general adoption of the 8ft width, there was less pressure to increase width than length and indeed some operators found this combination suited their needs in rural areas where some roads were narrow. Lincolnshire No.785 (GFW 846) was an LL5G, 83.036, delivered in the Autumn of 1950. This operator continued to favour the Clayton destination indicator, which had been standard since the pre-war days when the concern was under BET influence and took bodywork to BET Federation design with similar destination boxes. Despite a higher output of Bristol engines, the Gardner 5LW still had a considerable following within the Tilling group, and from 1950 had been uprated with a maximum output of 94bhp in place of the previous 85bhp, still at the traditional 1,700rpm, which was helpful on a 30ft vehicle, inevitably heavier than the shorter equivalent model.

The most enduring of the versions of K and L models introduced to meet the post-1950 length regulations in production terms was the KS-series, and especially the 8ft-wide KSW. Not only did this continue until the Lodekka came into general production from 1954 but then proved still to have a following of its own, continuing to be built, admittedly in more modest numbers, until 1957. The largest user was the Bristol undertaking itself, which built up a fleet of 353 examples with highbridge ECW bodywork between 1950 and 1957. It was doubtless cheaper to build than the more complex Lodekka, and was of well-proven durability, but had its own merits where overall height was not a problem. All passengers except those seated over the rear wheel-arches faced forwards, with a good view forward, save perhaps for the seat directly behind the driver, as evident in this scene showing 8078 (OHY 941) on KSW6B chassis 90.036 about to set off for Cheltenham not long after entering service on 1st July 1952. This was the first example of the type in this fleet with platform doors, thereafter fitted to some of the Country Services examples.

The LWL, on the other hand, was seen more as a stop-gap until the next generation underfloor-engined single-deckers came into production. Indeed, the Tilling companies were unusual in putting substantial numbers of front-engined single-deck buses into service in 1951-2; the BET and Scottish groups had, in most cases, decided on the latter and were either putting them on the road or waiting until they could be delivered. With the exception of one batch of vehicles built to special order, production of L-family buses ceased in 1952; production of the chassis had ended in September 1951. Thames Valley took 21 LL6B in 1950-51 and then 30 LWL6B in 1951-52, all with standard ECW rear-entrance 39-seat bodies, including No.616 (GJB 254) on chassis 85.168, seen here at Reading station. This bus survived as a consequence first of being used as a supervisor's office during bus station rebuilding at Maidenhead, and then a period as a driver-instruction vehicle in 1966, and was preserved.

Below: The Autovac fuel lift device, drawing fuel from the main tank by means of vacuum and acting as a header tank, allowing it to flow to the engine under gravity, had been almost universal on full-sized British bus chassis in the mid-1930s. It had to be mounted quite high to ensure adequate flow to the engine when climbing a steep gradient and the forward nearside face of the dash panel on a half-cab forward-control bus was a convenient location. However, from about 1937, small mechanical fuel-lift pumps mounted on the engine became more common and the Autovac disappeared from most makes over the next few years. Bristol evidently saw no reason to change and retained the Autovac until 1950, even though it became more noticeably obtrusive with the lower bonnet level adopted at the end of 1945. Not until the new KS and LL range appeared in 1950 was it replaced by a lift pump.

Above: The lowbridge K-series bus also had a short-term future once the practicality of the Lodekka had been proved by the prototypes. In 1951, however, this was still a little way off, and the example shown, KSW5G 84.068, was supplied to Eastern National as No. 4142 and registered SHK 524. It was allocated to the Bedfordshire area, and when responsibility for this was transferred to the United Counties company in a Tilling group rationalisation with effect from 1st May 1952, it became No.878 in the latter's fleet. It is seen here in rush-hour service in Luton early in 1959, in company with Luton Corporation buses.

This view shows how the upper-deck occupants of a lowbridge bus were seated only a little way below the roof level – forward vision on the ECW body of the time was obscured by the shallow hinged ventilating windows. The lower-deck nearside seats gave a less obstructed view, and the Autovac no longer intervened. Here the occupants seem busy with newspapers, but the author used to enjoy riding in this seat in a KS-model, with the lengthy bonnet almost giving an illusion of sitting in the front passenger seat of a powerful car of that era, even if it was actually only five-sixths occupied with a 5LW engine, as in this case. Post-war Bristol K and L family buses were possibly the only types in which it was possible when thus seated to read the chassis number, shown on a substantial cast plate mounted on top of the frame, just below the nearside headlamp.

21　The Light Saloon prototypes

Interest in underfloor-engined single-deckers, with almost the whole floor area free for passenger space, had been growing for some years. Aside from the remarkable Bristol project dating back to 1920 that had not been built, there had been German and American designs put into production in the 1930s, and towards the end of that decade a joint effort between Leyland and London Transport had produced the latter's production batch of TF-class Green Line coaches in 1939.

It was the Midland Red concern's decision to standardise on own-make vehicles of this type for its single-deck needs from 1946 that really set British operators and manufacturers thinking, but urgent need for buses put the emphasis on what were basically existing models among the big producers. The initial thinking on underfloor-engined models at AEC and Leyland was related to quite heavy-duty types with 9.6- and 9.8-litre engines, partly with export potential in mind, though only prototypes had appeared up to 1950.

Within the Tilling group, some experiments in lightweight front-engined vehicles had been conducted from 1945 by J. C. Beadle Ltd, of Dartford, Kent, a bodybuilding concern among whose regular customers, often for rebodying or coach bodywork, were several of the Tilling operating subsidiaries. The first four used mechanical units from small pre-war buses, a Commer, a Leyland Cub, a Bedford and a Dennis Ace, built into integral body shells constructed in aluminium alloy and seating 33 passengers, with full-width cabs but of rear-entrance layout in conformity to Tilling practice. Further such buses, mostly seating 33 or 35, were then put into small-scale production in 1948-49. There were 24 for Lincolnshire using Leyland Cub units, then 50 widely spread through the group using new Bedford OB-type units, followed in 1949-50 by a dozen using Morris-Commercial units with an engine of Saurer design and 20 more Cubs, for Crosville.

Meanwhile, a further development was Beadle's co-operation with Sentinel in the construction of a lightweight underfloor-engined bus by Sentinel, of which a prototype example for the Southern National fleet was at the 1948 Commercial Motor Show.

The foregoing demonstrates the strength of interest in lightweight construction within the Tilling group at that time, and although the standard Bristol K and L chassis with ECW bodies were about average for their period in terms of unladen weights, by 1949-50 this was enough to set Bristol and ECW's thinking along lines not pursued

elsewhere until 1952 or later. An indication of the line of thought reached at Tilling headquarters by June 1949 is in the same letter from Stanley Kennedy to operators mentioned in regard to the Lodekka. It said that "In the case of the single-decker, the trend of design is towards a vehicle of somewhat lighter construction than at present, with the engine under the floor..." In fact, at that date the interest in reduced weight was true only within the group, plus the Beadle and Sentinel concerns from where the idea had stemmed, perhaps reflecting a little of the isolation caused by Bristol and ECW's enforced withdrawal from the open market. Yet, as it turned out, the logic of the conclusions reached by Tilling, considering only its own needs, were to be taken up by Leyland and AEC for a wider market from 1952-53.

At that date, it was expected that the length permissible would be 28ft, and it was anticipated that such a bus would have a seating capacity of 40 with a single front entrance, but Kennedy's letter said "If the 30ft by 8ft box dimensions were granted, this would allow the use of a very satisfactory 42-seater with doors at front and rear for rapid loading, or 44 with a single entrance." At the shorter length, it was explained that "an additional door behind the rear axle cannot be used without undue shortening of the wheel base."

The letter went on to say that Bristol and ECW had been collaborating to produce a 'Light Saloon' along these lines, of integral construction mainly in aluminium alloy with lightened transmission and axles. The intention was to use a Bristol engine, based on the AVW but 'flat' and with four cylinders, having a 6-litre capacity, but for the purpose of producing a prototype vehicle as quickly as possible a Gardner 4LW engine was being converted for mounting under the floor. In fact, such a Bristol four-cylinder engine never appeared – if it was to be of six-litre capacity the cylinder dimensions would have had to be increased from those of the AVW. Indeed the increase to 115mm bore from 110mm that was adopted for the BVW engine built for later Lodekka vehicles from 1958 would have been almost exactly right, giving 5.936 litres in four-cylinder form.

The unladen weight of the vehicle was to be about 5 tons, and it was remarked that "These full-sized vehicles, having units designed to give a life of upwards of 100,000 miles between overhauls, should be suitable for operating very economically as stage carriages on routes where double-deckers cannot be used..." However, provision was being made to use a six-cylinder version if required for

The 'Light Saloon', as originally conceived, was aptly named, the entire structure being in aluminium alloy. The idea of much closer co-operation between what would normally be called chassis and body makers had proved to have effective results in the Lodekka. In the case of the LS, the same principle of sitting the saloon floor directly on what was now called an underframe, and attaching the body pillars to the ends of the outriggers, was used to reduce weight. Here the underframe of the prototypes was itself aluminium and in this case set relatively high so as to allow the horizontal engine to be accommodated entirely below floor level.

This picture, understood to date from 1950, shows what proved to be the second vehicle to be completed, becoming LSX.002, though it seems probable that it was the first planned. When it was expected that the overall length would be limited to 28ft, a four-cylinder engine was planned and although the aim was that the production version would have a Bristol engine, it had been agreed that a horizontal version of a Gardner 4LW engine would be used to speed completion of a prototype. The fuel injection pump of the Gardner engine is visible in the centre of the underframe of this view.

express or luxury coach duty. The accompanying questionnaire on Tilling group operators' anticipated needs for 1951-52 included both four- and six-cylinder versions of the Light Saloon, and also the MS, plus Beadle-type 30/32-seat buses with Bedford, Morris or Gardner 4LK engines (this last-mentioned option did not materialise but is a pointer towards the later Bristol SC type). There was also mention of Bedford 26-seaters for one-man operation. In fact, Tilling group purchases of Beadle integral buses ceased after 1950, and the Bedford OB ceased production that year.

The first public indication of development of the Light Saloon was an announcement carried by *The Commercial Motor* on 24th February 1950 to the effect that Bristol and ECW planned to produce an integral-construction single-decker making extensive use of light alloys in the underframe and body with a choice of horizontal power units having four, five or six cylinders. This was, indeed, the line followed, though the form of construction was

perhaps better described as semi-integral. Clearly the experience with the Lodekka had been of value, and in one respect the Light Saloon, as it was called, was similar in that a separate body underframe was eliminated. In this case, the 'chassis' was described as an underframe because it required temporary reinforcement to allow it to be delivered to the ECW works at Lowestoft for bodying, the beam strength of the complete vehicle being achieved by the uniting of the two.

The underframe of the two prototypes built were in aluminium alloy, ECW having used similar material for its body structures since 1948, so these vehicles were very largely a light alloy product in regard to structure and panelling. The unladen weight of the first prototype, built to the 30ft by 8ft dimensions which were in force by then, was 5 tons 12 cwt in complete form, a remarkably low figure bearing in mind its specification, with a horizontal version of the Bristol AVW six-cylinder 8.15-litre engine, called the LSW, though the prototype had an experimental

The first LS prototype, LSX.001, seen after entering service with the operating department of BTCC in 1951. With its Bristol 8.1-litre engine, a horizontal version of the AVW, and an unladen weight of only 5tons 12cwt, a lively performance was available, as conveyed by this picture. It seems that the tendency to roll may have been considered a little excessive, and when the vehicle was returned to the Motor Constructional Works in July 1953 to be fitted with a Gardner 5HLW engine, it also received 8ft-wide axles in place of the 7ft 6in type originally fitted. It returned to service painted in standard bus livery in place of that shown. It was converted to single-door 44-seat layout in 1956, remaining in service until 1967.

version designated XWA, and a five-speed gearbox. With a maximum output of 100bhp at 1,700rpm, it gave good performance potential – clearly it was felt that the larger engine had a wider justification for the bigger vehicle.

The gearbox had synchromesh on second, third and the direct fourth gears, the overdrive fifth being of the constant-mesh type, it being felt that synchromesh was unnecessary for this ratio, considered to be relatively easy to engage. First and reverse were of the sliding-mesh 'crash' type, normally engaged only when the vehicle was at rest. All gears were straight-toothed but the noise level from this unit was modest and relatively low-pitched, as was typical of Bristol gearboxes of that era. The rear axle was of a simple spiral bevel type, there being no need to use any form lowering the level of the drive line on a vehicle which was bound to have a relatively high floor level to allow the engine to be beneath it. The main floor was 3ft 2in above ground level, but there was a slight ramp downwards to the platform level alongside the driver, where it was 2ft 10½in, claimed to be the same as standard single-deckers of the time. The driver's seating level was noticeably lower than that of the passengers.

The underframe was almost flat-topped, so arranged as to accommodate the engine by interrupting the run of the right-hand sidemember with part of the frame assembly offset to the right at that point. With the Bristol engine, the fuel injection pump and other auxiliaries were beneath the cylinder block and most servicing was intended to be carried out from below. In other respects, the chassis specification was generally orthodox, with conventional beam front axle, leaf springs, cam-and-roller steering and triple-servo brakes using Clayton Dewandre units.

This first LS prototype, LSX.001 was delivered from ECW back to Bristol Tramways & Carriage Co on 12th December 1950. The body, number 4978, was of two-door layout, a feature favoured on quite a number of earlier single-deckers in the BTCC fleet, and it seems that the undertaking's policy in such matters influenced the whole group to some degree for a time. Even so, the seating capacity was 42, in line with the Kennedy letter of 18 months earlier, and quite a high figure for a 30ft bus.

The second prototype, LSX.002, had a Gardner 4HLW engine, the horizontal version of the 4LW, and had a single entrance door though still seating 42. The choice of engine and the fact that the ECW body number, 4255, implies a 1949 date suggest that this might have begun as the original Light Saloon prototype, possibly at 28ft length, but then temporarily laid aside in favour of the six-cylinder version before being completed at 30ft but retaining the four-cylinder engine. It was placed in service by Eastern Counties Omnibus Co Ltd on 26th June, 1951. This vehicle was still under construction when press descriptions of the model appeared in trade journals at the end of January 1951, when it was announced that production models would have the underframe built up from pressed steel sections, welded together, the reason quoted being a shortage of suitable light alloy materials at the time.

It was also announced at the same time that there was to be an initial batch of 150 production vehicles, but manufacture of these did not begin until about 18 months later. In fact, 152 were produced in the initial LS sanction, the 89th. This was just after regular production of L-type chassis ended, deliveries of these being completed in September 1951; the first production LS underframe went to ECW in November 1951. In addition to the steel underframes, these also had 8ft-wide axles instead of the 7ft 6in type used on the prototypes. Accordingly weight was a little up, typical bus versions being around 6tons 5cwt unladen, but this was still well below the figures not far short of 8 tons applying to contemporary models such

as the Leyland Royal Tiger or AEC Regal IV. Deliveries of LS models to operators did not begin until the Summer of 1952.

Most of the production LS vehicles had Gardner engines, the coaches generally having the 6HLW while the 5HLW was the usual unit in bus versions, almost universally so among early deliveries. Neither of these engines had been those chosen for the prototypes, though a minority of production vehicles, mainly coaches, had the Bristol engine, and just five had the 4HLW, these again going to Eastern Counties.

The LS was quite a 'civilised' vehicle, though the seat spacing in the standard 45-seat bus version was rather tight and interior finish somewhat plain by comparison with the L-type in standard form. The flexible engine mounting made even the 5HLW seem reasonably quiet – indeed it was not always easy even for interested passengers to identify which Gardner engine was fitted when making brief journeys at modest speeds, though the 6HLW was livelier and more noticeably smooth-running at speed. The coach versions were comfortable vehicles, well suited to long-distance services and comparing well with those used by other companies at the time.

More details of these and later examples will appear in the next volume.

Appendix 1

Annual production of Bristol chassis from 1913 to 1951

Year	No. of chassis	Main models sold & remarks
1913	31	C-series
1914	51	C-series.
1915	4	W prototype and 3 C50 goods
1916-19	-	(Wartime aircraft production etc)
1920	100	4-ton
1921	221	4-ton
1922	3	4-ton
1923	43	4-ton & 2-ton
1924	176	4-ton & 2-ton
1925	149	4-ton & 2-ton plus A-type prototypes
1926	113	4-ton, 2-ton, A & B
1927	175	B, 4-ton, 2-ton & A
1928	121	B, 4-ton, 2-ton & A
1929	188	B, 2-ton, plus C, D & E prototypes
1930	161	B, 4-ton, 2-ton, D
1931	72	B, D, 4-ton, G, J
1932	80	B, D, G, J, 2-ton
1933	134	B, G, H, J
1934	123	B, G, H, J
1935	277	GO5G, G.JW, JO5G, J.JW, J.NW
1936	409	GO5G, G.JW, JO5G, JO6G, J.JW, J.NW
1937	413	GO5G, JO5G, JO4D, JO6A, JO6G, K5G, L5G
1938	630	K5G, L5G, L4G, L6G
1939	612	K5G, L5G, L4G, L6G
1940	209	K5G, L5G, L6G
1941	76	K5G, L5G
1942	52	K5G, L5G, L6GG
1943	2	K5G post-war prototypes
1944	76	K6A
1945	330	K6A
1946	476	K5G, K6A, K6B, K6G L5G, L6A,.L4G, LL5G
1947	798	K5G, K6A, K6B, K6G L5G, L6A, L6B, L4G, L6G, LL6G
1948	752	K5G, K6A, K6B, K6G. KW6G L5G, L6A, L6B, L4G, L6G, LWL6G
1949	1002	K5G, K6A, K6B, K6G, KW6G, Lodekka prototype L5G, L6A, L6B, L4G, L6G
1950	927	K5G, K6A. K6B, K6G, KS5G, KS6B, KSW6B, 2nd Lodekka prototype L5G, L6A, L6B, L6G, LL5G, LL6B, LL6G LS prototype
1951	493	KS5G, KS6B, KSW5G, KSW6B LL5G, LL6B, LWL5G, LWL6B, 2nd LS prototype

Note. Numbers of chassis are derived from an annual production list compiled by BTCC; numbers of vehicles entering service each year tended to vary, depending on bodybuilding delays, sometimes considerable, and other factors – in periods of low sales, chassis were apt to remain in stock.

Appendix 2

Sanctions in Post-war Period

The following table shows the pattern of sanctions in the post-war period up to 1951.

Sanction No.	Type	Quantity	Dates	Engines
61st	L	150	1946-47	A, 4G, 5G, 6G
62nd	K	150	1946-47	A, B, 5G
63rd	L	200	1946-47	A, B, 4G, 5G, 6G
64th	K	200	1947-48	A, B, 5G
65th	L	200	1947-48	A, B, 4G, 5G
66th	K, KW	200	1947-48	A, B, 5G, 6G
67th	L, LWL (export)	200	1947-48	A, B, 4G, 5G, 6G
68th	K	200	1948-49	A, B, 5G, 6G
69th	L (export)	100		
		Hyderabad	1948	5G
70th				
71st	L	200	1948-49	A, B, 5G, 6G
72nd	K	100	1948-49	A, B, 5G, 6G
73rd	L	200		
		(some 'R')	1949-50	A, B, 4G, 5G, 6G
74th	K	200	1949-50	A, B, 5G, 6G
75th				
76th	K	200	1949-50	A, B, 5G, 6G
77th	LWL (export)	75	1948	6G
78th	K	200	1949-50	A, B, 5G
79th	L	200	1949-50	A, B, 5G
80th	K, KS, KSW	200	1950-51	B, 5G, 6G
81st	L, LL	200	1950-52	B, 5G
82nd	KS, KSW	105	1950-51	B, 5G
83rd	L, LL, LWL	345	1950-51	B, 5G
84th	KS, KSW	200	1951-52	B, 5G
85th	LL, LWL	199	1951-52	B, 5G
86th	KSW	98	1951-52	B, 5G

A. & R. Granham Ltd, of Kirkintilloch, was one of Bristol's most regular customers between 1923 and 1938. Although only a modest-sized concern, examples of 4-ton, B, D, J, JO5G and L6G were added to the fleet over that period, a record all the more remarkable since Bristol was an almost unknown make in Scotland during that period. Seen here is the second of three JO5G models supplied to this fleet, chassis number JO5G.14, registered SN 6814, and having Cowieson 30-seat coach bodywork, which entered service in June 1935. It was among nine Bristol vehicles among the 26 buses and coaches taken into stock by W. Alexander & Sons Ltd when that firm acquired the business in July 1938, a special class, G, being created for them though all were sold off by 1944.

INDEX

Acknowledgements and Photocredits - Bristol Volume 1

Thanks are due to many people who have helped me with the content of this book, either since work on it began, or in building up the store of information on which it is based. Some of the latter goes back over half a century, much gained from study of the technical press, little nuggets picked up in conversations with fellow enthusiasts, as well as learning much from countless journeys in Bristol buses. Steadily I learnt more, not least from contact with the firm itself, and road testing some of its products when I was Editor of Bus & Coach in the 1960s, though that relates to the later story I plan to tell in the next volume.

More specifically in regard to writing this one, I must thank Allan Macfarlane, Mike Tozer, Allen Janes and Martin Curtis, all acknowledged Bristol experts, who provided the answers to many questions and/or searched their archives for photographs to good effect. Maurice Doggett is in a similar category, with the ECW connection as his speciality, helping in pursuing some patent queries. I am grateful to B.J. (John) Cox, who had been in the drawing office at Brislington around 1950, for some useful insights into design matters in that period.

I must also thank the Omnibus Society for permission to reproduce photographs which include some taken by Charles Klapper and S.L.Poole, the latter during the 1939-45 war period. Geoff Atkins responded to my request for pictures with a characteristic selection of vehicles in service over the years.

Geoff Lumb and David Meredith also read text or pages and I must give my usual thanks to John Senior and the good ladies at 128 Pikes Lane, Glossop for effective support. Margaret Davies performed miracles in turning my rough page layouts into the finished product, not least finding space for my captions, while Carolyn Senior kept track of the pictures, itself no mean task.

As so often is the case, writing this book has been a voyage of discovery, and I am happy to share the many fresh items of information that came to light with readers. Conversely, the responsibility for any errors or omissions must be mine.

Specific illustrations are credited as follows:-

G.H.F.Atkins	24(top),32(top),33(bottom),38,39(top and centre),48,63,66(top),67,71(top),115,137(top)
M.S.Curtis collection	19,80,121
A.Janes collection	20(top),23(top left),50,56,58,60(bottom left),61(top)
D.A.Jones	90(centre)
D.S.Giles	39(bottom),90(top),104(bottom)
J.C.Gillham	97(top)
G.Lumb collection	129(centre)
A.Macfarlane collection	24(bottom),26(bottom left),28,29(top),31(top),34(bottom),37(bottom),40,41,42(top),44,45,46, 47,49,51(top),52(top),54(bottom),55,59(top),61(bottom),64(top),73(top),107,108(top),110(bottom)
R.Marshall	89(centre),90(bottom),95(bottom),103,105(bottom),106(bottom),109(top),118(top),147(bottom),153
Omnibus Society	52(bottom),64(bottom),65,69(bottom),75(bottom),87(top),105(top),137,138,
J.F.Parke (A Townsin coll)	94
Photofive	131(bottom)
D.F.Roberts collection	140
J.A.Senior	91
Senior Transport Archive	29(centre),97(bottom right),104(upper),110(top),111(bottom),116(top),125,126(bottom),132, 139(bottom),142,146(bottom), 48(bottom)
Brush	53(bottom)
Cravens	72(top)
Duple	95(top)
ECW	36(top),37(top),54(top),57(top),68,70,71(centre and bottom),72(bottom),73(bottom), 74(bottom),75(top),78,79,81,82,84,86,87(bottom),88,89(top),92,98,99,109(bottom),
R.N.Hannay	85(top & centre),89(bottom),106(top right). 117,120,131(top),144,146(top),147(top)
Park Royal	102,122
Roe	29(bottom),31(bottom),33(top),34(top),72(centre),93
A.Townsin	74(top),96,97(bottom left),108(bottom),111(top)
A.Townsin collection	22(lower),32(bottom),35(bottom),43,51(bottom),60(top and bottom right),62,80(top),112(bottom), 100(centre & bottom),106(top left),113,114,116(bottom),118(bottom),119,124(bottom),127, 128,129(bottom),135,136,143,145,149,151
M.J.Tozer	69(top),83,126(top),130,148(top),152
M.J.Tozer collection	9,10,11,12,13,14,15,16,20(bottom),21,22(top),23(top right,bottom),25(top and bottom),26(top and bottom right), 27,30,35(top),42(bottom),53(top),57(bottom),59(bottom),66(bottom),76,77,85(bottom),97(centre), 100(top)112(top),123,124(top),129(top),133,134,141
University of Reading, Museum of English Rural Life	25 (centre)